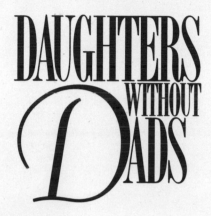

DAUGHTERS WITHOUT DADS

DAUGHTERS WITHOUT DADS

Lois Mowday Rabey

OLIVER
NELSON

THOMAS NELSON PUBLISHERS
Nashville • Atlanta • London • Vancouver

Published in Nashville, Tennessee, by Thomas Nelson, Inc., Publishers, and distributed in Canada by Word Communications, Ltd., Richmond, British Columbia.

Unless otherwise noted, the Bible version used in this publication is THE NEW KING JAMES VERSION. Copyright © 1979, 1980, 1982, 1990, Thomas Nelson, Inc., Publishers.

Scripture quotations marked NIV are taken from the HOLY BIBLE: NEW INTERNATIONAL VERSION. Copyright © 1973, 1978, 1984 by the International Bible Society. Used by permission of Zondervan Bible Publishers.

Printed in the United States of America.

Library of Congress Cataloging-in-Publication Data

Rabey, Lois Mowday.
    Daughters without dads / Lois Mowday Rabey.
        p.   cm.
    Includes bibliographical references.
    ISBN 0-7852-7813-3 (pbk.)
    1. Children of single parents.   2. Fatherless family.   3. Fathers and daughters.   4. Child rearing—Religious aspects—Christianity.
I. Title.
HQ777.4.R33   1994
306.874—dc20   94-24376
                                                                        CIP

2 3 4 5 6 — 99 98 97 96 95

TO

*the girls and women who have suffered
the loss of their fathers . . .
and to those people around them
who fill in the gaps with
love, concern, and care.*

Contents

HEALING AND HOPE

Acknowledgments

A big, warm thank you to Victor Oliver. Victor is an encouraging and inspiring friend, a man of great integrity with a wonderful sense of humor. Thank you, Vic, for being you.

This book would not have been possible without the input from the many women and girls I interviewed. I thank them all for their willingness to talk about a painful subject.

Many professionals—counselors, teachers, pastors—willingly took time out of their busy schedules to provide insights and talk with me about their observations of daughters who have suffered the loss of their fathers. My thanks go to Dan Allender, Steve Babbitt, Brent Curtis, Eldon Daniel, Pat Hartsock, Marilyn LeVan, Kent Miller, Doug Moore, Kathy Pisanic, Doug Rosenau, Fran Sciacca, and Sandy Trinca.

I want to thank the many personal friends over the years who have ministered to my daughters. You have enriched their lives and been a tremendous source of support to me.

Thank you to Lauren McCann and Rebecca Thompson for many long hours of copyediting.

During the long days at my computer, I had an invaluable "right arm." Without Karen Hopkins the rest of my world would have fallen into disrepair. I thank you, Karen, for being such a competent assistant, a good listener, and an encouraging friend.

My daughters, Lisa and Lara, have been constant sources of love and encouragement to me. I thank them for being willing for me to expose some of their own struggles over the loss of their father. And I thank them for being such bright spots during some of the dark times we have shared.

A Very Special Thank You
to
Steve

• For helping me convert disconnected ideas into a readable work.

• For seemingly endless hours of editing.

• For encouraging me to persevere when I wanted to play instead of sit in front of my computer.

• And especially for loving me and marrying me while I was in the process of writing this book. Surely God knew that only a writer could fall in love with another writer in the middle of a project.

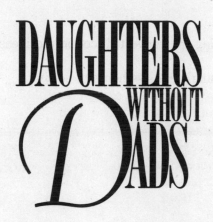

THE DILEMMA

Chapter 1

Where Have All the Fathers Gone?

*B*ump, set, spike.

To the uninitiated, these three words seem unrelated. But to me and others who know about the intricacies of volleyball, the terms *bump*, *set*, and *spike* define the difference between success and failure. To win, a team had better be able to bump (when the first player bumps the volleyball up into the air), set (when the second player sets up the shot for the next player), and spike (when the third player smashes the ball over the net) with accuracy and force.

I learned all about bumping, setting, and spiking as the mother of a star player on a girls' volleyball team from the local Christian high school. As I watched Lara, my younger daughter, and her teammates completing their warm-ups before the opening game of the season, I shared their anxiousness to carry the banner for their school.

Clusters of parents on both sides anticipated a decisive win, and for the next hour or two, the cares of the day for parents and students would be forgotten in the intense action of the game. A few mothers talked quietly of their daughters' first-game jitters. But the girls looked great—all eager and prepared. Pony tails bobbed and "high fives" were shared all around as the girls made final preparations for play. Then, the starters were announced and the game began.

Suddenly, all the parents stopped talking and became thoroughly engrossed in the game. One minute they would be cheering and applauding a wonderful play—the next minute grumbling or yelling about an alleged bad call by the poor official. What a sight to see otherwise mature, godly parents turned into screaming fanatics!

Such behavior is the norm for high-school sporting events. After all, these aren't objective observers but highly partisan parents watching their beloved offspring. Objectivity dies and parental partiality prevails. But just as surely as they have turned into a mad mob, they will reclaim their capacity to act civilly and think clearly when the game is over.

I was focused on my daughter, Lara, who is always a joy to watch, until my interest in the game was interrupted by a startling observation. My eyes moved from one girl to another—nine girls on the team altogether. Nine girls who had parents in the stands urging them on to victory. Nine normal-looking girls who were intense about their every move, hoping to contribute to a win.

Then I looked at the parents and started making mental calculations. As I counted, I realized that six of the nine girls were being raised without their fathers. Two of them had lost their fathers years before in accidental deaths. The other four were children of divorce.

I checked and rechecked the numbers in my mind. Six of the nine girls were fatherless; they were daughters without dads. And in various ways, they were suffering significant losses.

Their losses were certainly not evident. A casual observer could not look at them and tell which girls came from traditional two-parent homes and which ones did not. But the impact of their losses affected all areas of their lives.

I understood some of the meaning of those losses because I was one of the single mothers. My first husband, Jack, was killed in a hot-air balloon accident when Lara was seven years old and her sister, Lisa, was ten. Lisa and Lara are part of a growing number of daughters being raised without the loving presence of a father at home. Many of their friends are in the same boat, but as a result of divorce, not death.

My thoughts were brought back to the volleyball game as the parents around me leaped up in response to a successful spike. In a few moments, the home team went on to a decisive win. The girls ran excitedly into the locker room, reveling in the thrill of victory. I joined the other parents outside the locker room as we waited for our stars to appear. We were a happy, smiling group, and it was the beginning of another promising season.

But my spirit felt a little heavy as I stood there with the other single mothers. I knew that while life held many wonderful moments for all of us, it also held much pain and challenge for us and for our daughters without dads.

THE CHURCH IS NOT IMMUNE

My new awareness led me to research the phenomenon of daughters without dads. I interviewed one hundred girls and women who had lost their fathers or were raising daughters without their fathers. I spoke with counselors, pastors, and friends of families without a father at home, and I investigated statistics of single-parent homes. In my research I found that

- One out of every four children in the United States lives in a single-parent home.
- Eighty-nine percent of these homes are headed by women.
- Far more daughters being raised by one parent are being raised by their mothers than are being raised by their fathers.

The Christian community is not immune from this growing social trend. Churches and Christian schools have seen an increase in the single-parent homes represented in their congregations and student bodies.

My daughter attends a private, conservative Christian school. Her volleyball team is not an accurate representation of the entire student body, but it does reveal that the student population is no longer made up completely of children raised in traditional family units.

No longer can we look in our churches and other Christian institutions and expect to find only the mom-and-pop-and-two-kids Christian family. More and more wives are without husbands, meaning more and more daughters are without dads. Even if we are not among the fatherless, these people are our neighbors, colleagues, friends, and brothers and sisters in Christ. They may seem normal and well adjusted, and they may appear to have successfully coped with their loss. But underneath their calm exteriors, much pain may still remain.

When one part of the body of Christ hurts, all the other parts hurt with it. Many in the church are hurting. I hope that this book will help them understand their plight and relieve some of their pain. May it also help others reach out to those in pain by agreeing—in love—to be meaningful participants in the healing of these damaged lives.

THE DAUGHTER WITHOUT A DAD IS THE GIRL NEXT DOOR

Jill and Addie lived next door to each other in a nice but not overly wealthy subdivision. Both attended second grade at the nearby elementary school.

Jill was an only child of a single mother. Her father divorced her mother when she was two years old. He moved away and never came back again. Jill couldn't remember her father at all. And her mother didn't keep any pictures of him around, so Jill didn't even know what he looked like.

Addie, on the other hand, had a father and a mother. To Jill, that was the way things were supposed to be. Jill knew that Addie's father worked in an office. He wore a suit and a tie every day and carried a little brown suitcase that Addie's mother called a briefcase. Addie's mother didn't work. She was at home all day. If Jill got sick at school, she called Addie's mother, who would come and get her, take her to Addie's house, and care for her until Jill's after-school baby-sitter arrived.

Addie also had a teenage sister and brother. They were seldom home, but when they were, they were always doing something in their rooms—talking on the phone, listening to music, or whispering with friends who came home with them. When Addie and her siblings weren't home, they were at cheerleading practice, football practice, band rehearsal, or some other activity. That part of Addie's world was a mystery to Jill.

From Jill's perspective, Addie's house was a warm and busy place, full of people, activity, music, ringing phones, and pleasant scents floating out from the kitchen. What a contrast to Jill's house, where Jill and her mother were usually alone. And often, Jill was there by herself when her mother had to work late.

Usually the girls walked home from school together, but one very cold afternoon, Addie's mom picked them up. At Addie's house, there was a fire in the fireplace, and the girls sipped steamy hot chocolate as they lined up their dolls' out-fits for the afternoon's fashion show.

Jill's mother worked, so she was never able to pick them up. They never played at Jill's house, either. They could have, Jill supposed. The baby-sitter was there every day after school. But they always played at Addie's. Jill liked it better that way. Sometimes Addie's mother even let the girls help her bake something special for Addie's dad.

Jill liked Addie's dad. Of course, she didn't know much about dads. But he was big and kind and had a warm smile. He was always nice to Jill. He would ask her how she was and how her mom was. She always said that they were fine, and Addie's dad would smile his warm smile and pat Jill on the head.

The girls had just finished ushering their dolls through the "winter review" fashion show when they heard the garage door go up. Addie dropped her doll and ran to the kitchen door.

"Daddy!" she squealed.

"Hi, sugar," her dad replied as he scooped her up in one of his big arms.

Addie wrapped her arms around his neck and pressed her little face against his weathered one. They both smiled as he placed her on the floor next to him.

"Hi Jill," he said. "How are you?"

"Fine, thank you."

"And how is your mom?" he asked, still smiling.

"Oh, she's fine."

"That's good. Tell her we said hello."

It was time for Jill to leave. She held her jacket collar tightly around her neck as she ran home in the dark. Her fingers didn't work well in the cold as she fumbled to get the door key unpinned from the inside of her jacket. Once inside, she pinned the key back on right away.

"Before you do anything else," her mother had said time and time again, "pin the key back inside your jacket."

The baby-sitter had gone home. She left each day about fifteen minutes before Jill's mother arrived. Jill had learned to be a "big girl" for those fifteen minutes. She told her mother that it didn't bother her to be alone, but she always counted the minutes until she heard her mother's car pull in the driveway.

Unlike Addie's house, Jill's house was very quiet. The phone didn't ring much, and there was never any music playing. Jill's mother was kind and loving, and Jill loved being with her. But she was tired most of the time. Jill understood. Her mother had to work and do all the things that families with two parents do.

Before long, her mother walked in the door, and Jill felt relieved. She was glad to see her mother. Plus, they would be eating dinner soon.

But that night in bed Jill clenched her teeth and tightened her jaw to stop the tears. She didn't know why she felt like crying. Nothing had happened that day to make her cry. She hugged her pillow close to her face. She closed her eyes and pretended she was hugging Addie's dad.

I don't know what his face feels like, she thought, *but I don't think it feels like this.* The tears slid softly onto the pillow.

A WORLD OF OPPORTUNITIES AT OUR DOORSTEPS

Addie's father had a profound impact on Jill. He may not have been aware of it. Jill may not even have been aware of it. But the relationship he had with his daughter gave Jill a glimpse of what a father-daughter relationship looked like, and it showed her something of what she lacked in her life.

While we all sympathize with Jill, it's good for her (and others like her) to find out about healthy, godly relationships, even if that means she will realize what she is missing. Only then can she begin the ordeal of seeking healing from the pain of her losses and move on to interaction with others in spite of those losses.

As the number of fatherless families increases, the opportunity for Christians to meaningfully live out the Great Commission increases, too. We are commanded to love our neighbors as ourselves (Matt. 19:19) and to look after orphans and widows in their distress (James 1:27).

Daughters without dads are everywhere. They don't live in a few, isolated cases of broken homes somewhere on the other side of town. If we are aware of the needs of people we meet every day, we can more intentionally reach out in love to them.

In raising my daughters alone over the last nine years, I often felt somewhat isolated. But with the help of God and a few close friends we worked through our nontraditional situation. God gave grace to our family to believe that He was still in control of our lives, even though our circumstances seemed out of control. He gave a spiritual sense of security that allowed us to move on, even though we felt awkward.

The close friends were vital links between us and the Christian community. Had they not been there, I know that the sense of distance between our family and other families with both parents at home would have seemed much greater.

Whether divorced or widowed, women raising their daughters alone grapple with a feeling of alienation. They may be active in churches, and yet still feel cut off from the mainstream of life in the body of Christ. Initially, I was somewhat concerned that a book focusing on daughters without dads would reach only the smallest of audiences, but now I realize many women and daughters face the consequences of lives without fathers. In fact, I know at least ninety women who are raising daughters alone or who are struggling with the absence of a father in their own lives.

As I interviewed some of these women for this book, I found a yearning to better understand their own situations. And as I talked with people who knew these single mothers and daughterless dads, I sensed a desire to help and comfort these fractured families. Not only daughters and mothers suffer from the absence of a father; everyone who comes in contact with them feels the pain.

"No man is an island," said the English poet and preacher John Donne. We are involved with one another to varying degrees and at varying levels of intimacy. This book endeavors to foster love and compassion for the millions of daughters without dads.

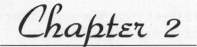

Chapter 2

Help in the Midst of Havoc

*A*re you a daughter without a dad? A girl's relationship with her father is designed to be wonderful, but many things can happen to alter or destroy that sacred bond.

Maybe your father died years ago, and you still wrestle with the way things were between you.

Your father may live in the same house with you, but he may be emotionally distant.

Your parents may be divorced, so your relationship with your father is always changing and uncertain. You may be with him on weekends and with your mother during the week. Your vacations may be spent traveling back and forth between the two of them. You may feel like a piece of emotional baggage being shuffled from parent to parent.

You may have stepparents and stepsisters and stepbrothers who complicate everything in your life—from the way you handle your Christmas shopping list to the way you define your personal identity.

Perhaps your father left decades ago, but you still have many ghosts, including unanswered questions and poorly understood emotions.

There are no easy answers or pat solutions offered here. But simply looking at some aspects of your life—your loss, your response, your current network of relationships, your relationship with God as your heavenly Father—will help you in the process of moving toward healing.

This book is based on the assumption that our most important relationship is the one we have with our heavenly Father. This doesn't rule out the importance of earthly fathers—or diminish the impact on our lives when that relationship is less than the best—but God the Father is our best source of healing and comfort. Unfortunately, many women's negative involvement with earthly fathers has affected their views of God; thus, the greatest source of healing is clouded by a dark mist of confusion and pain. We will explore ways of recovering love for our heavenly Father, even if earthly fathers have been fairly poor role models.

MANY WAYS TO HELP

But this book is also designed to help people who are around daughters without dads. No area of life escapes the fingerprint of a father on a daughter. That may be a blessing when the presence of a loving father softly touches his daughter. Or it may be a brutal blow when that loving presence is gone. And individuals who relate to a hurt daughter can guide her to a fuller, happier life.

Perhaps you are related to a daughter without a dad. You have a unique opportunity to be a meaningful participant in her healing. The challenge is to do so without expecting immediate positive change and without becoming so discouraged that you miss the joy available in your relationship.

Or maybe you're a dad that a daughter is without. Maybe you're a father who is not living at home due to separation or divorce. This book also speaks to you. You still have a very significant role to play in the life of your daughter—if you choose to accept it. Some of the men I interviewed told me what they would have done differently with their daughters after their divorces. Others shared how they have maintained good relationships despite difficult situations.

In addition, this book can benefit friends, pastors, teachers, stepparents, and stepsiblings—all of whom have their own needs in relating to daughters without dads, and all of whom could work to improve their relationship with these girls.

DAUGHTERS OF DIVORCE

Most daughters without dads are the children of divorced parents. They are not wholly without their fathers. They may never see their fathers, but they live with the reality that these men are alive somewhere on this planet, even if they don't seem to care enough to be in touch with their own flesh and blood.

Daughters of divorce who do see their fathers are constantly bouncing back and forth between two households. "Without" for one of these girls means that she is without the consistent, loving presence of her father at home. And she has a whole new way of having to be "with" him.

When my husband died, I felt that his death was worse for my children than divorce would have been. At least if we were divorced, I thought, he would have been around for the girls to visit. I have since changed my mind. The loss of a father by death is a devastating blow with lifelong effects. But the loss of a father by divorce is often more difficult to deal with because of the complexities of the situation.

Daughters of divorce suffer from an almost inevitable feeling of rejection that children whose fathers died do not. When a father is lost through divorce, the number of people the daughter has to relate to—her new network of family and friends—is increased and the actual households double. The father and the mother still have a relationship—however good or bad—that the daughter sees and evaluates.

Some people adjust to change more quickly and easily than others do. Those who continue to suffer several years after a divorce may feel that they are doomed to lives of unhappiness. They may think that their feelings are inappropriate and, therefore, deny any expressions of how they feel. Others who seem well adjusted may be hiding their true feelings, even though they may mistakenly be viewed as models of how to cope with loss.

As with all life ordeals, divorce causes tremendous stress and strain. But unexpressed worries and fears lead to deeper problems later in life. Eventually, the results of years of incorrect thinking may surface in an inability to relate in healthy ways to others.

The book *Second Chances* by Judith Wallerstein and Sandra Blakeslee examined the effects of divorce by studying children who were developmentally normal, did well in school, and enjoyed good psychological health. They interviewed family members immediately after a divorce, then followed up with additional interviews at eighteen-month, five-year, and ten-year intervals. They concluded that only one child in ten felt a sense of relief when quarreling, unhappy parents divorced. These "relieved" children were usually older children who had seen and suffered outright violence in their parents' marriages.

If parents divorce when a child is very young, the child may not have seen or understood many of the reasons for the divorce. She may remember only that daddy was once home, and then he was gone. She may not have witnessed the unhappiness, quarreling, or other less visible reasons for the parents' separation. Although it may be good that some children are spared the details of their parents' disagreements, it also hinders their understanding of why their parents couldn't stick it out and stay together.

Even when children remember quarreling, they might prefer the uneasiness of those situations to the fear created by the father's absence. At least unhappy parents are there to provide for the needs of the children.

It may not be actually any healthier for parents to stay together for the sake of the children than for them to divorce. But the studies conducted for *Second Chances* show that the majority of children did not feel any relief at the parents' divorce, no matter how bad the home scene.

I spoke with some teenagers who disagreed with the suggestion that they would be happier if their quarreling parents stayed together. For some of them, the tension is so great that the teens wish their parents would divorce. They are old enough to understand all the sarcasm and negative remarks that their parents hurl at each other. They feel that the loss of security would be preferable to the constant arguing.

Wallerstein and Blakeslee also pointed out that many children feel abandoned during their parents' divorce. In a *New York Times* book review of *Second Chances*, Carol Tavris notes, "Fewer than 10 percent recalled any adult who spoke to them sympathetically as the divorce unfolded. Many parents, wallowing in their unhappiness and bitterness toward each other, simply stop caring for their children."[1]

Opportunities to Reach Out

The pressures on any divorcing couple are immense. As a result, the situation presents an excellent opportunity for people in the Christian community to lend a hand. Many of us avoid whatever makes us uncomfortable, and divorce certainly makes us feel that way. But if we can lay aside our discomfort, we may be able to reach out to children suffering from their parents' divorce.

Children thrive on continuity in their lives. And they like to know that what matters to them matters to their parents. A parent in the middle of a painful divorce may no longer chauffeur her daughter to after-school functions. The daughter, on the other hand, desperately needs to feel involved at school and secure in her place there. If a parent can't keep up with a child's schedule, other adults may step in temporarily and provide much-needed continuity in the child's life.

Sometimes, we don't say anything because we don't know what to say. We may feel truly sympathetic toward children, but we may not even acknowledge to them that we know what they are suffering. Children may be comforted to hear adults say that they are sorry for the pain they are undergoing at the moment.

If there's anything children of divorce are certain to experience, it's the pain of alienation. According to *Second Chances*, "After 10 years, half of the children had lived through a parent's second divorce. Of the children whose mothers re-married, fully half said they did not feel welcome in the new family. A shocking 35 percent of the children had poor relationships with both parents at the 10 year mark, and 75 percent felt rejected by their fathers."[2]

Divorce is not a solution. It is a result of sin. The sin may be as blatant as a marriage partner's committing adultery or as subtle as one partner's unwillingness to relate meaningfully to the other partner.

People often think they have solved all their problems by divorcing the source of their grief. Instead, they need to understand the underlying reasons for the failure of the marriage so they can reduce the risk of making the same mistakes again. If these mistakes are repeated, the children are in jeopardy of going through the trials and tribulations of divorce once again. Parents who never assume personal responsibility for a divorce have little success in communicating well with their children, and good communication is essential for children to adjust to the new situations divorce has placed them in.

If the child doesn't feel welcome when her mother remarries, her mother and her stepfather need to determine what is contributing to the child's unhappiness. If the child is being unreasonable, the adults need to affirm and reaffirm that the child is welcome.

According to the authors of *Second Chances*, 75 percent of the children of divorce they studied felt rejected by their fathers. Therefore, fathers need to do all they can to help their children feel accepted. Spending time with the child is a big factor. Likewise, the child won't feel accepted if she believes she is not a priority with the parent.

The review of *Second Chances* in the *New York Times* states, "The most useful message in 'Second Chances' is that humans do not now, and never did, take their attachments lightly. We become deeply connected to our families, even to family members we think we detest, and we do not bear separations lightly."[3]

It is good news that attachments are meaningful to all of

us. It is bad news that a lot of families will continue to suffer from divorce. But it is certainly better to understand what is going on in relationships than to deny that anything unusual is happening at all. And what is going on is that daughters of divorce do not take lightly the dissolution of their families. They may act as if everything is fine, and they may even say they are OK. But inner pain often troubles them.

Caring people who are willing to uncover that hidden pain and administer the healing touch of love can soften the blow of separation. Divorce is a fact in the Christian community today, so the need for active love is there. Whether divorce is right or wrong is not the issue. The issue is the impact of divorce on a daughter being raised without her father at home.

With love and hope, the situation is not all gloom and doom. It is serious, life-changing, and complex. It is not, however, beyond the reach of God's restorative and healing power.

VICTIMS OF EMOTIONAL DISTANCING

Living in a home with both parents, a daughter may appear to have a father. But looks can be deceiving, for she may have lost him to emotional distancing.

An emotionally distant father is physically present but emotionally unavailable. He may love his daughter but not know how to express that love. As a result, he seems unloving or uncaring when he plays the ever-stoic, uninvolved patriarch of the household—issuing decrees and administering punishment.

This situation is difficult for concerned Christians to address because everything seems as it should. A father may be home, may appear loving, may seem to do all the right things dads do, and may do nothing considered openly abusive. But in practical terms he may be more absent than a father who is dead.

When I interviewed girls and women whose fathers were emotionally distant, I found deep—and often unresolved—

pain. Emotional distancing is a very subtle but damaging form of abuse inflicted by a father.

A friend of mine—a mother of three in her mid-forties—described her relationship with her father this way: *"My father 'missed' me. He simply never saw me for who I am. He only saw me the way he wanted—and when I didn't live up to that, he shut me out."*

This woman grew up always performing, always trying to win the approval of her father. She didn't have the freedom to learn who she really was or what she wanted for herself. She spent all her time trying to be what her father thought was the perfect daughter.

Finally, as an adult, she was able to say, "Enough is enough." She realized that she would never have her father's approval—no matter what she did—and she experienced the freedom to live as she wanted to. And she acknowledged that her father's lack of approval did not mean that she was a worthless human being.

Later, she saw that the real cause of her father's disapproval was rooted in a spiritual issue. As a teenager, she had accepted Christ, but her father wasn't a believer. As she became more vocal about her faith, his disapproval intensified. She had to reach the point of agreeing to disagree with him, much to his displeasure.

Christian Fathers Fail, Too

A father may be a Christian and still be completely unmoved by and unavailable to his daughter. He may not be able to put aside his preconceived ideas of how his daughter should be and instead see how she really is.

One forty-year-old married woman described this "missed" and "shut-out" feeling this way: *"When I was seventeen, I was especially excited about a high-school party that friends of mine were having. They had rented a fire hall, had hired a live band, and had ordered the food to be catered. My mother and I had gone shopping for a new outfit just for this event.*

"The evening of the party I came downstairs in my new outfit—eager for my father's praise. He was sitting in a chair in the living

room reading the newspaper. He looked up, never changed his rigid expression, and said, 'You may NOT go to the party in that get-up.' I had on black velvet slacks and he did not approve of slacks. I was so shocked and hurt. I began to explain that all the girls were wearing slacks. I would be laughed at if I showed up in a dress.

"He held firm and said the matter was settled. As he held his paper back up in front of him, I tried to get him to look at me around the paper. I pleaded and cried—sincerely begging him to try to understand. He kept reading the paper. Finally, I grabbed the newspaper out of his hands and got on my knees in front of him. I held his face in my hands trying to pull it down so he would have to look at me. He sat with his hands in the same position as when he stoically held the paper.

"His face could not be moved, and his eyes went back and forth as if the paper were stiff in his hands. He completely ignored me. He read a paper that wasn't there rather than see me. He never even tried to understand how I felt. He still doesn't."

That father may have felt he was being a good disciplinarian and the perfect Christian father in not letting his daughter go out in clothes that he considered inappropriate. But his approach was also inflexible and out of touch with how women had been dressing for the last four or five decades.

The result was tragic. The woman continued, *"I decided to never let him hurt me that badly again. I decided I would give up on trying to explain how I felt about anything. Sure, my father hurt me again. But I never tried so hard again to communicate to him how I felt. Our relationship became a surface one. He never really knew me at all."*

A daughter who is "missed" by her father can experience many of the same losses that daughters of death and divorce suffer. She will feel "without" a father, perhaps with more frustration, because he could be there for her if only he would.

SURVIVORS OF DEATH

"Daddy's in heaven." "Your father is gone." "He's dead." No matter how they are communicated, these words pierce the heart of anyone who has lost a loved one. Death is a final separation—at least until we're in heaven ourselves. There can be no more words, no more soft touches. We cannot ask one more question or bestow one more loving embrace.

My father is still living, so I haven't personally experienced such a loss. But I've watched my daughters receive these words and go on to live without their father for nine years now. And I've interviewed numerous women who lost their fathers to death years ago yet still feel their influence.

When "without" means loss by death, we may think the issue is closed after about a year. But death is hard to understand, and unanswered questions may prevent closure. The true story of Janet Ray, published in the February 1989 issue of *Reader's Digest*, told of an eighteen-year effort to answer such questions.

Janet Ray was a child when her pilot father was shot down during the aborted Bay of Pigs invasion of Cuba in April 1961. Because Janet was not convinced that he was actually dead, she began researching and saving newspaper articles on the Bay of Pigs. As a college student, she spent her spring vacation in the Little Havana section of Miami, talking to people about the incident and asking if they knew her father. She wrote letters and sent telegrams to Fidel Castro. He never answered.

But in April 1979, Janet received an envelope from Peter Wyden, who was writing a book on the Bay of Pigs. He had received pictures of two dead American pilots from the Cuban government. Janet was able to recognize one of them as her father. She continued to plead with officials of the Cuban government to confirm or deny if they still had her father's body. They finally admitted that her father's body had been in the Havana morgue for the past eighteen years. Janet arranged to have his body sent back to the United States and buried with military honors.[4]

Dealing with the impact of a deceased parent is sometimes ignored because those around the daughter think she has returned to an imagined state we call "normal." We may inaccurately assume that because things look as they did before the loss there is no more needed healing.

Daddy may be in heaven, gone, dead—but his daughter is still here, coping with his absence. When she is aware of and understands some of the implications of her father's life and loss, she will be better able to enjoy life and deep relationships.

A SIN WORSE THAN LIVING WITHOUT

Perhaps the greatest loss of father occurs in that breach of the father-daughter relationship when a father violates his daughter sexually. In such instances, a daughter certainly experiences her father's presence but in no way experiences his love.

Victims of sexual abuse may develop sexual problems that may be acted out in opposite ways: promiscuity or asexuality. Eating disorders may also plague women who have been sexually abused. Numerous problems may result from sexual abuse: low self-esteem, difficulty establishing and maintaining healthy relationships, trouble coping with stressful situations, inability to grow in maturity, and blocked spiritual growth.

Sexual abuse is a complicated issue, but the road to recovery for the sexually abused woman involves the reestablishment of trust in men and God. Therapy can be beneficial, but a daughter and her abusing father seldom reach a healing in their damaged, twisted relationship. Sexual abuse is such a horrifying violation of the woman that it is almost impossible to erase the damage done. Forgiveness can happen, but it is usually communicated between the involved parties and God—not between daughter and abusing father.

A RANGE OF HURTS AND
A GOD OF LOVE

So intense are the pains experienced by daughters without dads that I would hesitate to write this book were it not for one crucial fact—God loves us and cares for us. And His grace is sufficient for our needs.

I'm no believer in superspiritualized pat answers. And much of the advice given here includes the recommendation that daughters seek professional counseling to help them through their pain. However, my belief that our God is the Great Physician—for bodies and especially souls—is the foundation upon which this book is based. It is my prayer that as the stories in this book open up painful places in your heart, you will allow God's Spirit to enter those places with His healing balm of love and life.

AND NOW, BACK TO THE VOLLEYBALL GAME!

Soon after I realized that six of the nine girls on Lara's volleyball team were fatherless, I filed that thought in the back of my mind and returned my attention to the game.

The girls on Lara's team play, smile, and act just like everyone else. They don't bemoan their losses—in life or in volleyball. They accept their losses in life, and they move on to the next game of volleyball, hoping for a win.

As they come out of the locker room after each game, they are greeted by enthusiastic fans and proud parents. Three of them walk out of the gym between two proud parents—while the other six walk out with their arms around their moms.

As I left the gym with my arm around Lara, I found my mind wandering: *I wonder if anybody realizes how many daughterless dads there are. And I wonder if anybody would read a book about it.*

May your reading of the following chapters enrich your life.

Chapter 3

The Evolution of the American Family

*I*t was 1945, and World War II was over. American troops—content that the world was again safe for democracy—came home to enthusiastic, flag-waving patriots and victory parades. Those who didn't come home were honored for having paid the highest price possible in their country's pursuit of peace and freedom for all mankind.

Families were reunited. Men put their uniforms in attic trunks and resumed their roles as heads of households. Women exchanged their hardhats for aprons and happily left their jobs in American factories to return to their kitchens. Children began to know dad as a real person instead of an image in a photograph.

Norman Rockwell captured this image of the American family in his renowned illustrations for the covers of *The Saturday Evening Post*. And, of course, all American families were as picture-perfect as Rockwell depicted them. Weren't they?

Soon it was 1952, and Dwight D. Eisenhower, a popular war hero, was elected president of the United States. The "Ozzie and Harriet" show—complete with all-American sons Ricky and David—made its TV debut. And the song "I Saw Mommy Kissing Santa Claus" was at the top of the pop music charts. But it wasn't some strange Santa Claus mommy was kissing—it was actually father dressed up in a red suit receiving Christmas Eve kisses from mommy.

The American family was stable, structured, and idealistic. It was headed by a firm but loving father, supported by a submissive and hardworking mother, and kids, even though they will always be kids, found it in their hearts to respect mom and dad pretty well.

Role models were easily defined. Father was the breadwinner, mother was at home, and children didn't challenge their parents' authority. The culture of the day was based on moral positions consistent with biblical principles. A person didn't have to be a Christian to live a godly looking lifestyle; godliness—at least a tame, watered-down version of it—was synonymous with the American ideal.

Most people had faith in God, though, or at least they were affiliated with a traditional church. Church was a part of the socially accepted criteria for Joe Citizen. And God, up in His heavens, was smiling down on this beautiful land called America.

HOW THINGS HAVE CHANGED

Real life probably wasn't as picture-perfect as a Rockwell magazine cover. People struggled with relationships then, just as they do now. But the prevailing attitudes of the time encouraged the moral structure of the family. Adultery was frowned upon. Divorce was uncommon.

By the sixties, however, many of those support systems began to change. Values were being challenged. Kids were asking why things were the way they were, and adults couldn't come up with any solid answers. A gradual shift in moral standards dramatically affected the American family and the American way of life.

The following chart gives a sweeping view of two centuries of moral decline:

| Biblical Morality | 1800–early 1900s | "Certain things are right and wrong, and I know why." |

Abiblical Morality	1940–1950s	"Certain things are right and wrong, but I don't know why."
Immorality	1960–early 1970s	"Certain things are right and wrong, but I don't care."
Amorality	late 1970s–present	"There's no such thing as right and wrong."[1]

Four decades of rapid social change have brought us from the Rockwellish fifties to the wild and woolly nineties. Our country has moved from a value system that provided a measure of support for the traditional family structure to the current condition, which was described by *American Demographics* magazine as "the postmarital society."

If a modern-day Rockwell attempted to depict today's typical American family, he would have to replace the Thanksgiving turkey scene of the fifties with a composite portrait of all the current possibilities, which would include families with mom and dad working, single-parent homes, alternate-lifestyle homes, multifamily (stepfamilies) homes, single-person households, and other family patterns. And the evolution of the American family continues. Where it will stop, nobody—not even the demographers—can tell.

If our artist wanted to do some research on the American family before he began his painting, he could refer to statistics like these, which reveal the significant social trends making yesterday's traditional family an item for the history books:

- Fifteen million children in the U.S. live with one parent.[2]
- One out of four children under eighteen lives with one parent.[3]
- Eighty-nine percent of children in single-parent homes live with their mothers. Eleven percent live with their fathers.[4]
- Every day, 2,989 kids see their parents divorce.[5]
- Fifty-four percent of all adult women work.[6]

- Eighty-two percent of teenage girls expect to be working full-time at age thirty.[7]
- Two-thirds of all first marriages probably will end in separation or divorce.[8]
- Since 1980 the number of divorced men in America has increased by 42 percent.[9]

If these statistics aren't frightening enough, what is worse is realizing that each one stands for thousands—or millions—of disrupted lives. As families rupture, children—and particularly daughters—are among the hardest-hit victims.

YESTERDAY'S TV MENU

You can look at statistics. You can look at the millions of individuals who make up the statistics. But if you really want to have fun with your investigation of social trends, you'll watch television. That electronic gadget is an interesting monitor of society's trends—or at least its dreams.

Television became a member of many American families in the 1950s. Game shows, variety shows, and some sports coverage were the early choices of televised entertainment. And that's precisely what TV did—entertain. In the early days of TV, issues were not the issue. The American family gathered around the TV's "electronic hearth" to see what they had been listening to on radio.

In the fifties, the family show made its debut, and television gave the American viewing audiences an idealized look at themselves. What Americans saw in TV's mirror made them pretty happy.

Some family members might come and go, but one family member remained constant: dad. He was the well-dressed businessman who perfectly balanced his responsibilities to job, family, and neighborhood. We never really knew exactly what kind of work he did. We never saw him at work. But one thing's for sure, he wasn't a workaholic—or any kind of "aholic" for that matter.

Here's the basic fifties menu for the perfect father: he was stable, home on time every night, calm in a crisis, the dispenser of wisdom, and the king of his castle with family members willingly accepting whatever he dished out. Of course, he never dished out anything negative. He didn't have to, because life never confronted him with anything negative. He never struggled with unemployment, infidelity, emotional flare-ups, insubordination at home or at work, taxes, AIDS, drunk drivers, gang warfare, juvenile crime, inflation, foreign terrorism, acid rain, the greenhouse effect, or anything like that. In fact, TV's perfect dad never struggled with anything!

The paragon of the successful family TV show was "Father Knows Best," which always opened with the pivotal event of the perfect family's day—the arrival home of father, Jim Anderson. Mother was usually in the kitchen preparing the family dinner. The kids—two girls with a boy sandwiched between—ran in and out of the living room where father sat reading the paper before dinner. Ultimately, father's advice resolved all problems because, after all, "Father Knows Best."

Ward and June Cleaver were the scrubbed and placid parents of the "Beav." Although Beaver Cleaver was the central character on the popular show "Leave It to Beaver," mom and dad had an omnipresent influence. They were a stable family, and dad was the perfect family man and dependable breadwinner.

"Make Room for Daddy" presented dad with a little more humor than some of the other shows. But daddy was still the center around which the universe of the family rotated.

TV'S NEW AND IMPROVED (?) AMERICAN FAMILY

In the seventies, Archie Bunker blustered into American homes as the star of "All in the Family." Archie was a bigoted, male-chauvinist pig—just the kind of guy everybody loved to hate. His wife, Edith, was an empty-headed, frumpy housewife. Daughter Gloria was struggling to bring the values of the women's movement into her relationship with her husband, Michael. The happy foursome lived in Archie's big house where he daily screamed at Edith, at Gloria, and at Michael, whom he unlovingly referred to as Meathead.

But nobody liked Archie. He was television's paternal anti-hero—an image to scoff at. He was what the generation of the seventies did not want to be. Americans no longer lived within the male-image confines of Jim Anderson or Ward Cleaver, but they didn't want to be Archie Bunker, either.

TODAY'S BANQUET OF CHOICES

Then TV's man of the eighties appeared. Cliff Huxtable of "The Cosby Show," Steven Keaton of "Family Ties," and Jason Seaver of "Growing Pains" were sensitive family men who treated their wives well. Those dads looked much different from Jim Anderson and Ward Cleaver, even though they had a few similarities to the TV dads of old.

An article entitled "Television Makes Room for Daddy" summarized the new TV dad: "'The Cosby Show' premiered and the traditional TV dad was again head of the household—to a point. Sure, fathers were wise again, but they weren't infallible. They were respected, but the right to the last word was a joint venture shared with their wives. After all, Mom usually had a career of her own."

The role of fatherhood is now being written by baby boomer parents—those born after the war. They see things differently. Alan Thicke, who plays father Jason Seaver in the show "Growing Pains," commented about the new TV father, "I think what reflects the baby boom parents of the Eighties, supposedly, is the enlightened relationship of more equity between the parents and children." Lisa Schwarzbaum, author of the article, attributed some of the latest changes in the TV dad to the role of baby boom-era writers:

Did someone say boomer? In the past two years, as boomer writers, producers and programers have had babies of their own, fatherhood as an onscreen longing has peaked. Now the yikes-we're-grown-ups responsibilities of parenthood are a continuing plotline on several shows, including "thirtysomething" and "A Year in the Life," where sensitive dads like Michael Stedman and Jim Eisenberg worry whether they're spending enough quality time with their infant daughters. Taking care of baby is THE story on "Day by Day" where a stockbroker and his lawyer wife open a day-care center in their home.[10]

Overall, the modern TV dad is still a fairly decent, family-loving kind of guy. But what's happening on mom's side of the fence? How does TV portray the contemporary mom? There, the picture is not so simple, as we plainly see after sampling a few of the new female-dominated shows.

MORE-THAN-EQUAL TIME FOR MODERN WOMEN

During one recent week, sixteen prime-time shows featured women in new kinds of roles. *Newsweek* said this about the trend:

The women's movement in TV has been evolutionary, not revolutionary. June Cleaver stayed home and nurtured her nuclear family. Mary (Tyler Moore) Richards got a job, but only as a go-fer for the guys. Chrissy in "Three's Company" was most liberated in a bath towel. Alexis in "Dynasty" has power, but that makes her evil. Meanwhile, Claire Huxtable, as television's current paragon mom, can do everything but convince us she's real.

It's been said that all TV trends define their cultural eras. That's a valid assumption: only a fool would deny that an entertainment form with a nightly following of 50 million must reflect its audience's attitudes to hold their allegiance. What are the women who inhabit today's network series telling us about the post-Reagan, post-feminist nineties?

It's OK to work . . . according to one recent study, 75% of TV's female characters in 1987 worked outside the home.

It's OK to be alone . . . a record proportion of TV's female population live without husbands or children.

It's OK to mess up . . . by now even casual prime-time visitors have absorbed the message—Superwoman doesn't live there anymore.

It's OK to mouth off . . . as with most of her prime-time sisters, Murphy (Brown) uses her tongue like an Uzi, especially on any male within range. Though sexual combat is hardly new to TV, it's never been waged from the female quarter with such deadly precision.[11]

WARD AND JUNE WOULD BLUSH

TV families like the Huxtables are a logical evolution from fifties-era families like the Andersons and Cleavers. Even some of the female-dominated shows can be seen as springing from these rich television themes.

What, then, are we to make of new shows like NBC's "My Two Dads"? Clearly, the family situations presented in this show spring from the amoral confusion of the late eighties and early nineties.

The story line is this: Nichole, a darling thirteen-year-old, waltzes into the lives of two men in their thirties—claiming that one of them is her father. But no one knows which one. The mother has died and her mother has willed the daughter to the two men—either of whom could be the child's biological father, since both had sexual relationships with the mother.

The three unlikely family members share a loft apartment. Both dads date. Both dads love Nichole. And Nichole loves her two dads.

All in all, it's the kind of fairy tale situation that can occur only on TV. Nichole never seems troubled about finding the identity of her true father or even her own identity. It's just another happy, funny, less-than-real-life scenario from the folks who brought you "Ozzie and Harriet."

TELEVISION—REFLECTING OR DIRECTING LIFE?

Television has moved into a new place of prominence in our lives. Instead of being merely a mirror that reflects who we are—or want to be—TV is now a constant companion.

According to an article in *Life* magazine, "most Americans spend more time with television's families than with their own. Schoolkids in this nation of 20 million working mothers return to empty houses and watch 'Dennis the Menace,' whose mom is always home." The article also stated that TV is Americans' primary leisure-time activity, occupying an average of seven hours per person per day.[12]

A daughter without a father might watch "My Two Dads" and think that thirteen-year-old Nichole is indeed lucky to have two such great guys as fathers. They are good-looking, pleasant, funny, loving, and caring men. It's a cute show. I like it—as long as I don't think about its implications.

When I think about the premise the show is built on—that Nichole's promiscuous mother blessed young Nichole with the best of all possible family situations—I become a little uncomfortable. What does the basic plot say to young people? True to the creed of the amoral eighties, no moral issues are presented or discussed. No thought is given to Nichole's feelings. Nor is there any remorse over the loss of her mother.

Is "My Two Dads" a realistic portrayal of modern life? Are most men as concerned and caring for their offspring—even if they are not sure the child is their offspring—as are Nichole's two "dads"? And how is young Nichole going to treat sex when she begins dating in a year or two?

Am I making too much of a little thing? Can a daughter without the guidance of a moral, stable father untangle the messages she receives when she watches this show and others that present complicated relationships in such a simplistic manner? What does a daughter being raised by her mother think of her mother's role when she sees women presented in so many different lights?

As we enter the nineties, there is no traditional TV family. Instead, we see a potpourri of values and social trends. In short, anything goes.

TV'S BRAVE NEW WORLD

In Aldous Huxley's novel, *Brave New World,* people were kept happy with constant supplies of the drug Soma and were bombarded with a supply of pleasant sensations. Modern TV is much the same. Few conclusions are drawn. Much is presented. Choices are endless. And it's all fun, fast-moving, and pleasant. After all, if it were unpleasant, advertisers would take their money and run.

The latest twist is the talk shows, which are sinking lower and lower in their efforts to give the public what they think they want. Nicknamed "Freak of the Week" or "Nuts and Sluts," the new talk shows with Oprah Winfrey, Geraldo Rivera, Sally Jessy Raphael, and Phil Donahue give viewers everything except a serious treatment of issues.

As I was thumbing through an issue of *TV Guide,* I found the following sampling of what these shows covered during the week: wives and mistresses; sex and teenagers; family conflicts; children charged with death of other children; men's views of breast cancer; prostitution; senior citizens and sexuality; exhibitionism; children and divorce; child pornography; teenage evangelists; and unusual marriages. Quite a list, huh? And a number of the shows didn't have listings of what they were running for that day.

TV broadcasts the clamor of many voices. Daughters who view life without the stabilizing perspective of a loving father have one less guideline when they evaluate what they see and hear.

And we can't count on the TV networks to monitor themselves. In 1971 cigarette commercials were banned because

of the harmful effects of smoking. But now family-type entertainment is interrupted with commercials for feminine hy-
giene products and condoms. We've come a long way, baby.

It may be argued that the new commercials promote products contributing to good health. Yet an ad for condoms may
have an unhealthy moral impact on a mixed group of teenagers. At the very least, it can be embarrassing.

And network censors allow all kinds of sexual situations to
be depicted on prime-time shows. With all the seminudity
and cleavage on TV today, it's no wonder they call it the
Boob Tube.

CHRISTIANS AND TV

If TV is a mirror of what our society is all about, the
Christian church is in trouble. Things haven't been the same
since the TV evangelism scandals hit the newspapers in 1987.
And along the way, Christianity's influence on society has
been damaged.

One church leader expressed his concerns: "Denver Arch-
bishop J. Francis Stafford acknowledged he believes U.S. society is increasingly distant from the gospel. American
colleges, entertainment industry and the press are a class of
'culture forming' agents that are profoundly secularized. This
secularization affects the family, sexual attitudes, the work
ethic and minorities."[13]

When Christianity moved from the pew to our living room
sofas, it entered an arena not unlike the Colosseum of Rome.
Television is big business and involves big money. Big money
and big business necessitate powerful people playing a serious
game to meet and beat the competition. It appears that the
lions won the battle for TV.

Christians still have their broadcasts—tucked away on ca-
ble channels or local independent stations. But mainstream
TV paints Christians with a dark brushstroke. The result is
that we Christians have one more dirty filter through which
we run our ideas and our values about life.

Christian TV has an opportunity to contribute truthful

insights to a waiting and hungry audience. Frankly, we could use some prime-time shows that reflect a Christian view of the family. Unfortunately, the competition for audiences is fierce, and probably few unchurched people will watch Christian TV.

THE PRODUCT OF MASS MEDIA INPUT

Aside from God, the only constant in life is change, and the pace is quickening. One author commented, "In the middle of the 20th century, it was estimated that the pace of change was as much as 50 times greater than the average pace in previous centuries."[14]

In earlier times, families could stand as bulwarks against outside pressure, protecting their members. But for many young people today, families themselves are changing, leaving few islands of calm in a fast-moving sea of transition.

Today, too much change produces stress, and stress causes emotional and psychological problems. And for many people, strong families aren't there to share the load. Psychiatric hospitals and clinics are trying to care for the overstressed and underloved.

James Schiffman wrote in the *Wall Street Journal*,

The number of Americans between the ages of 10 and 19 discharged from psychiatric units between 1980 and 1987 ballooned 43 percent to 180,000 from 126,000 according to the National Center for Health Statistics. The figure is all the more striking because the population of that age group shrank 11 percent during that period.

Many mental-health experts say that the rise of teens in psychiatric wards isn't due to a national epidemic of crazed kids, but to a convergence of trends in the 1980s that favor incarceration over other kinds of care. Family turmoil—divorce, remarriage, frequent migration—and two career households have left many parents either too busy or too distracted to deal with adolescents.[15]

Today's young women face many choices and pressures that their predecessors didn't face. Many of the options are good ones, but they present women with confusing and complex choices to make. It may be good for women to have the choice between working and raising a family, but how individual women live out the realities of these dual roles is never simple.

In the midst of all these changes, daughters without dads lack the male perspective and support of their fathers. As a result, choosing between the many available options becomes more difficult. Stress is increased. And the more daughters hear what the world says, the greater potential for greater stress.

Society no longer offers its members a norm for behavior. Sure, laws define illegal conduct. But aside from that, it's an open market. And although Christian teachings on morality haven't changed, women's roles in the family and church are changing. Even the Christian community is feeling the tensions.

The role of father has changed, as has the picture of the perfect family. A daughter without a dad faces her world like a little girl at the foot of the Tower of Babel. There are so many voices. There is so much confusion. And a steady stream of information and opinions is continually poured into our homes more quickly than we can process it.

Processing information would still be a dilemma for a young girl, even if she had a loving father at home. But it would be filtered. She would have some added protection, guidance, love, and acceptance that a daughter without a dad does not enjoy.

She won't find the answers to life in the mirror of her TV set, but there is another source of help. She has a Father who is not confined to a TV script. He is not hampered by a world that does not acknowledge Him. He can meet her personally and change her life. That doesn't mean she will live happily ever after, but it does mean she can claim God's promises and live fully and richly.

Chapter 4

Truth and Healing

Things can look pretty grim. Families are disintegrating. And more than ever, daughters are growing up without the positive influence of their fathers.

Daughters without dads see healthy, happy families and wonder if God knows that their family is not complete. Fear that perhaps God isn't listening is denied because it produces greater fear. If God isn't listening, where is He?

FAITH AND PAIN

Why are we surprised by the presence of pain coexisting with the presence of God? It must be due to teachings on comfortable Christianity, cheap grace, and the gospel of wealth, health, and total prosperity. In my Bible, I read that pain is a constant partner of true faith.

Scripture is a canvas of conflict. Military battles are painted with bold strokes of death and destruction. Our ongoing battles with sin and temptation are found throughout the pages of God's Word, beginning with Adam and Eve's troubles in the Garden of Eden described in the book of Genesis, and continuing through the cataclysmic events in the closing chapters of the book of Revelation.

Those who believe that God is gone when pain is present misunderstand what life is supposed to be like. Nowhere does God promise that His presence will erase pain. Instead, He promises to provide grace and strength for endurance and to turn struggles into crowns of gold.

We may think that life is supposed to look like a pleasing

portrait that we can view comfortably from across a room. But we live right up on the canvas, so close to the masterpiece that we cannot distinguish what God's magnificent brush-strokes are unveiling.

We may have heard that the presence of God results in life being calm and peaceful. However, Scripture teaches that the blessings of God are experienced most fully in the context of suffering. A blessed life may be lived in faith and peace, even though it is wracked by death, divorce, and pain.

THE HUNGER FOR GOD

During times of fast-paced social change and deep personal pain, people intensify their quest for God. In our day, though, many look outside the church and the revelation of the God of the Bible.

C. S. Lewis once wrote that when man abandons belief in God, he opens the door for belief in anything. Today, many seekers after truth have abandoned Christ and the teaching of the Scriptures, but that doesn't mean they have abandoned their quest. Instead, a broad range of gods—old and new—has been invited in to fill the spiritual void.

Spiritual seekers find themselves in a vast supermarket of spiritual options. One brand of religion promises more fun and fewer constraints. Another allows shoppers to pick and choose from various traditions and creeds—blending them in a personal spiritual potpourri. Others make no promises aside from pure, sensual pleasure. In the midst of it all, God cries out, asking those with ears to hear to sense His still small voice.

Eastern religions, which have become increasingly popular in the United States since the sixties, give believers an oppor-tunity to work toward a higher state of awareness. Through the law of karma and the process of reincarnation, the individ-ual can achieve Godhead and be done with pain and uncer-tainty.

New Age religions—which are often modern repackagings of ancient creeds—permit believers to create a personal religion from scratch. They can include elements of Eastern faiths and visitations from personal spirit guides or deceased gurus, or they can ignore all external faiths in the search of personal godhood. These new religions receive acclaim because they are relatively easy to follow and well-known personalities endorse them.

Hedonism, an ever-popular contender in the field of faiths, is also making a strong comeback. In times of trial and tribulation, nothing beats the worship of self in the pursuit of pleasure. For many tired seekers, hedonism provides an enticing alternative to a life of suffering for an unseen God.

Satanism is also finding followers throughout the country. But why would anyone even be interested in the occult? In a recent cover story, *Moody Monthly* provided an answer:

> "There's no question that the media are making people more aware of the issue," says Cynthia Kisser, executive director of the Cult Awareness Network in Chicago. "The second thing is, the marketing industry is definitely pushing, among young people, products that play on this interest. We're seeing much, much more reference to Satanism in music, videos and literature. With this mystique and the thrill it seems to give people in terms of how it shocks parents, shocks the school, shocks the church, it is an exciting avenue to dabble in. It's the new thing to do."[1]

I was talking to a friend about the allure of Satanism. He suggested that people are attracted to the power Satanism offers. People caught in the midst of tremendous social transformation are looking for ways to have control over their lives—and possibly the lives of others. Satanism and the occult, through spells and other tricks, offer the seeker a taste of such control.

With all the alternatives available from seemingly pure pleasure to supernatural power, why would anyone choose the God of the Bible? Why would a God who sent His Son to a cruel death on a cross be worth the trouble? We must answer these questions if we are to find the truth and discover ways of helping the millions of daughters suffering the loss of their fathers.

GOD IS TRUTH

An afternoon spent shopping in the spiritual supermarket can be dizzying—let alone a lifetime spent there. But thankfully, there is an answer. We don't have to sample every spiritual product offered to us. God exists, and His size fits all.

God is who He says He is, and His promises are true. Other spiritual options promise a variety of temporary, pleasing solutions, but they lead to desolation and despair. God presents the cold, hard truth: I am, I always have been, and I love you!

We know that God is truth because the Word of God confirms it, testimonies of believers confirm it, the presence of the Holy Spirit in lives confirms it, evidence of the reliability of Scripture confirms it, and because God reveals Himself to people. The true path of fulfillment is the Christian life, and its destination is heaven. We will suffer along the way, but we can experience joy in that suffering.

There is a lot of pain in the Christian community. Some is the result of sin, and some is the result of entering into the sufferings of Christ. If you are a daughter without a dad, you know the language of pain. If you are close to a daughter without a dad, you know that vocabulary, also.

Sin may have been involved in the breaking up of a family. If so, repentance needs to take place. After that repentance, the family needs to move toward healing. Part of being able to heal is to understand that God is present, He is worth choosing, He is truth, and He exists side by side with trials.

Instead of being overwhelmed by guilt and fear because of our circumstances, we can count on God to weave the fabric of faith into our lives if we let Him:

My brethren, count it all joy when you fall into various trials, knowing that the testing of your faith produces patience. But let patience have its perfect work, that you may be perfect and complete, lacking nothing (James 1:2–4).

Though now for a little while, if need be, you have been grieved by various trials, that the genuineness of your faith, being much more precious than gold that perishes, though it is tested by fire, may be found to praise, honor, and glory at the revelation of Jesus Christ (1 Pet. 1:6–7).

History also supports that God is present in the midst of great conflict. The flames of evangelism have burned brightest under the oppression of persecution. From the martyred apostles to the persecuted church in atheistic countries today, God continues to infuse His people with power while they work under tremendous pressures. And God desires to bring beautiful things out of the suffering of fatherless daughters, too.

Despite our personal circumstances, our fears, and our often conflicting feelings, God is here. God is operative in a world that does not even acknowledge Him, and He is operative in the lives of believers who may be experiencing great trials.

GOD IS REAL

God exists, and He can be reached through Jesus. Jesus answered, "I am the way, the truth, and the life. No one comes to the Father except through Me" (John 14:6).

A daughter without a dad may have a hard time experiencing God the Father as her spiritual Father. Her poor relationship with her earthly father may have polluted all her images of what a father is.

She must begin where each of us begins—with a personal relationship with Jesus Christ. She needs to see that she is not perfect and never will be; that God provided a substitute for her payment of those things in her life that are not perfect—and that substitute was Jesus Christ; that Christ is the perfect man who is also God; that He paid the price for her wrongs on the cross; and that by accepting that fact and Him into her life, she is forgiven.

No matter who you are—a daughter without a dad, a single mother, a divorced dad, a friend of someone in this situation, or a bookstore browser—if you have never established your relationship with God by accepting Christ as your Savior, you need to pause here for a moment. This book is written with the assumption that truth comes through a personal relationship with Christ. All the solutions proposed here are presented in light of that relationship. The opportunity to experience God as Father is preceded by the acceptance into your heart of Jesus as your Lord and Savior. Without Him, all the suggestions will be only Band-Aids on an open wound. The only truly healing solution to any of life's problems is found in a relationship with Christ.

If you have never prayed and asked Christ to come into your life, now is a good time to do so. If you do not feel that you would be sincere in doing that, continue to read but also pursue Him for yourself personally. Talk to people who have such a relationship, and pray that God will reveal Himself to you.

If you have already accepted Christ as Lord and Savior, your place before God is secure. Perhaps your circumstances right now have caused you to doubt that security. You need not feel like it is there for it to be there.

No matter what your age, your place before God is that of a loved and accepted child. You can come to Him with all your fears and frustrations and find Him waiting with open arms. Secure before Him, you can begin to experience Him as the father you may not have at home today.

GOD IS ACTIVE

Jesus told the disciples of the coming of the Holy Spirit:

> But now I go away to Him who sent Me, and none of you asks Me, "Where are You going?" But because I have

said these things to you, sorrow has filled your heart. Nevertheless I tell you the truth. It is to your advantage that I go away; for if I do not go away, the Helper will not come to you; but if I depart, I will send Him to you. And when He has come, He will convict the world of sin, and of righteousness, and of judgment: of sin, because they do not believe in Me; of righteousness, because I go to My Father and you see Me no more; of judgment, because the ruler of this world is judged.

I still have many things to say to you, but you cannot bear them now. However, when He, the Spirit of truth, has come, He will guide you into all truth; for He will not speak on His own authority, but whatever He hears He will speak; and He will tell you things to come (John 16:5–13).

What does the work of the Holy Spirit mean for a daughter without a father, or for someone who relates to a fatherless daughter? It means the presence of God in one's life; the Holy Spirit is the power link to God. Anyone who has truly accepted Christ also has the presence of the Holy Spirit dwelling within.

Peter declared, "Repent, and let every one of you be baptized in the name of Jesus Christ for the remission of sins; and you shall receive the gift of the Holy Spirit" (Acts 2:38). Sin is present for everyone except Christ. But if the person is repentant, sin is forgiven. Then power to live in the midst of great difficulty is accomplished by the working of the Holy Spirit. Even though God may not seem to hear or be active in the circumstances of life, He is there when Christ has been accepted, and He has sent His Holy Spirit to empower the individual to live through pain.

There is a lot of controversy in the church today about the function of the Holy Spirit. But some things are beyond controversy, such as the following: each believer receives the gifts of the Holy Spirit; the Holy Spirit is present in the lives of believers, even if they do not feel His presence; every believer has the ability to be and do what God calls him or her to do by the power of the Spirit.

GOD IS OUR FATHER

God is Christ, the Holy Spirit, and God the Father. The doctrine of the Trinity is difficult to comprehend because our minds have finite capabilities. Many of the mysteries of God remain mysteries.

Volumes have been written on the attributes of God, on finding Him and knowing Him, yet we still "see in a glass darkly." He is simply too big, too wise, too kind, too just, and too perfect for us to articulate.

How, then, can a girl hope to experience God as her Father if He is so awesome? Because He *is* her Father and He will give grace to know Him if she seeks Him. It takes time and effort, but realizing that God is in her life and is in the role of Father is a beginning.

Many names in the Bible reflect God's role as our parent. All of these names are connected to the word *Jehovah,* which is derived from the verb *to be* and means that God is the ever-living One, the only living One, and the self-existent One. Here are some examples of these names: *Jehovah-Jireh,* "the Lord provides"; *Jehovah-Rophe,* "the Lord who heals you"; *Jehovah-M'Kaddesh,* "the God who makes you holy"; *Jehovah-Shalom,* "the God of peace"; *Jehovah-Rohi,* "God who is our Shepherd"; *Jehovah-Tsidkenu,* "the Lord our Righteousness"; and *Jehovah-Shammah,* "God is there."[2]

Any human parent who successfully provided all these things would be viewed as a good parent. In fact, God as our Parent provides some things that no human can provide. No earthly parents can make us holy, be our righteousness, or heal us. Our parents can provide certain things—a place to live, food, clothing, emotional security, limited protection, their presence—but no one can parent as completely as God can.

Near the conclusion of His Sermon on the Mount, Jesus

told His followers about God's promises to those who seek Him:

> Ask, and it will be given to you; seek, and you will find; knock, and it will be opened to you. For everyone who asks receives, and he who seeks finds, and to him who knocks it will be opened. Or what man is there among you who, if his son asks for bread, will give him a stone? Or if he asks for a fish, will he give him a serpent? If you then, being evil, know how to give good gifts to your children, how much more will your Father who is in heaven give good things to those who ask Him! (Matt. 7:7–11).

Perhaps your earthly father hasn't always given you good gifts. Maybe he has deserted you and your mother. Maybe he has even abused you. Whatever the case, God is the perfect Father who loves you with an infinite love.

Please reach out to your heavenly Father with open arms, asking Him to touch and comfort the hurts you have suffered from your earthly father. And never forget God's promise: everyone who asks receives.

God the Father

A little girl—or a hurting older woman—approaches an awesome God. She wants to know Him as her Father. But before she can see the "daddy" side of Him, she is overwhelmed by His majesty.

Paradoxically, those things that make Him majestic also enable Him to be the perfect, loving Father. An examination of the nature and attributes of God will help us understand who God truly is and better enable us to relate to Him in spirit and truth.

GOD'S MAJESTIC NATURE

To begin with, let's look at four of God's characteristics that give Him His majestic bearing. These qualities may make God seem almighty and unapproachable, but as we will see later, they are essential to His more loving and paternal attributes.

He Is Omnipotent

God is all-powerful, or omnipotent. He is in charge of everything. The whole Bible is an account of the sovereign authority of God. He parted the Red Sea (Exod. 14:21) and raised Christ from the dead (John 20).

When circumstances in life are out of our control, don't we tend to think all would be well if we could just have the power to do what we thought would make things right? Fortunately, we don't have that power. We would misuse it because we also don't have the knowledge of what is best for us.

God does have the power, and He knows how to use it for our best. Even the death of a father is not out of the control of the Lord. If He chose, He could prevent any death. Understanding why He allows people to die when they do is not for us to comprehend.

Sometimes we try to make ourselves feel better by listing all the positives that the death of a loved one may bring. Often when a believer dies, others are led to Christ. Or if one who is sick dies, we relieve our own pain with the thought that he is no longer suffering. These results may be true, but because God is God, He could save souls without the death of a daughter's father and He could heal all sickness.

He is powerful enough to do anything. Because He is, we don't need to be; we can rely on Him.

He Is Omniscient

God is all-knowing and all-wise. Isaiah tells us,

> Have you not known?
> Have you not heard?
> The everlasting God, the LORD,
> The Creator of the ends of the earth,
> Neither faints nor is weary.
> His understanding is unsearchable (Isa. 40:28).

The child of God can find comfort in realizing that she doesn't have to rely on her own wisdom. Making decisions when we are hurting is risky business if left to ourselves. We might make short-term decisions that would relieve pain but in the long run would prove harmful.

We may not be able to see any logical reason for God to allow a father to disappear, divorce, or die while his family is still young. If in our power, we might exercise forces over the father to do what we want him to. But God tells us that He knows what is best for us. Plus, God gives us free will to make our own choices—good ones and bad ones.

We cannot understand God's omniscience from our limited human standpoint. We have to trust Him and be willing to have some questions unanswered.

He Is Omnipresent

When a family is separated, a daughter may wish she could be two places at once. She may live with her mother and greatly miss her father. Or she may wonder what her father's daily life is like now that he lives elsewhere.

In the case of death, the desire to know about the absent parent can be strong. Heaven becomes a very personal place, and wondering what it is like is a normal mental diversion from the everyday life of planet earth.

God is omnipresent—everywhere at once. His Word gives us clues about this quality:

> "Can anyone hide himself in secret places,
>   So I shall not see him?" says the LORD;
> "Do I not fill heaven and earth?" says the LORD
>   (Jer. 23:24).

We can be assured that God Himself is with our loved ones. Whether they be in heaven or in another house across town or across the country, God cares for persons we love.

He Is Immutable

Life changes dramatically, particularly after the loss of a father, and is never the same again. Although change is an intrinsic part of life, it is not a part of God's nature:

> Of old You laid the foundation of the earth,
> And the heavens are the work of Your hands.
> They will perish, but You will endure;
> Yes, they will all grow old like a garment;
> Like a cloak You will change them,
> And they will be changed.
> But You are the same,
> And Your years will have no end (Ps. 102:25–27).

We can rely on God to always be there. Our lives may become tangled messes, but He is not thwarted by our circumstances. He is powerful, wise, ever-present, and unchanging. He is an island of certainty in a life of ever-changing patterns.

GOD'S FATHERLY NATURE

The awesome characteristics of God, the Creator and Master of the universe, evoke in us feelings of reverence. These aspects of God made Moses kneel and humble himself in God's presence.

But a daughter approaching her heavenly Father also needs to experience the love and acceptance of One so powerful. And we find such attributes in God, for our heavenly Father is not only the Creator and Father of the whole world, He is the individual, personal Father to each of His children. And He wants us to know—and experience—His fatherly dimensions: "For you did not receive the spirit of bondage again to fear, but you received the Spirit of adoption by whom we cry our, 'Abba, Father'" (Rom. 8:15).

The following look at God's fatherly aspects will help us approach Him as our divine Father.

He Is Loving

God's love is infinite; therefore, it's beyond description. But the greatest expression of that love is recorded in this familiar verse: "For God so loved the world that He gave His only begotten Son, that whoever believes in Him should not perish but have everlasting life" (John 3:16).

This verse is so familiar that we can miss its profound meaning. God as the Father loved us as His children enough to sacrifice His Son in our place. Can we even imagine what it would be like to have a child of ours killed—at our request—in order to save another person?

When we are uncertain about how to approach God as our Father, we need to see Him as One who has already done immeasurably more than any other person could begin to do for us. That kind of love makes Him completely approachable and accessible.

He Is Forgiving

Parents are often the policemen in the family. They set the rules; they enforce the rules; and they dish out the punishment when the rules have been broken.

Ideally, parents are loving guardians who show their affection for their children as they dispense justice. However, if a parent is unforgiving, a sense of discouragement can cause a child to have little faith in ever being "good enough" again.

The good news is that none of us are good enough. We all make mistakes. We all continue to make mistakes. And God, as our Father, continues to forgive us: "If we say that we have no sin, we deceive ourselves, and the truth is not in us. If we confess our sins, He is faithful and just to forgive us our sins and to cleanse us from all unrighteousness" (1 John 1:8–9).

With God, we don't even have to cover up our mistakes. He encourages us to be totally honest with Him and promises His forgiveness.

HE IS AVAILABLE

We don't have to make an appointment with God. He is not delayed at the office or out of town on business. He's not our Father only during weekends and someone else's Father during the week. We are His business. We matter to Him and may approach Him at any time, any place.

Paul asserts, "In him and through faith in him we may approach God with freedom and confidence" (Eph. 3:12 NIV). Like beloved little children, we can interrupt Him while He is doing important things, and it is no interruption at all. Even if we wander away from Him, He is there whenever we return.

HE IS UNDERSTANDING

Often, we don't understand feelings after death or divorce. But God does.

A friend of mine who went through a difficult divorce used to explain her relationship with the Lord during that time in this way: *"I could not pray. I could not even cry. I was so upset and burned out that all I could do was put myself in front of the Lord. I would simply sit in a chair and tell the Lord that I had come to sit with Him. I was quiet. I didn't read the Bible—I just sat in His presence. I heard no great revelations from Him, but I felt that He understood."*

God does understand us—our fears, our hurts, and even our reservations about opening all of these personal issues up to His examination: "For we do not have a High Priest who cannot sympathize with our weaknesses, but was in all points tempted as we are, yet without sin. Let us therefore come boldly to the throne of grace, that we may obtain mercy and find grace to help in time of need" (Heb. 4:15–16).

God made us, so He understands our feelings and pains. He wants us to bring our sorrows to Him.

THE HEAVENLY FATHER AND THE EARTHLY FATHER

The daughter who has lost her father will be affected in how she relates to God. If her biological father was cruel to her, God may seem like some big, bad heavenly ogre. If her father was distant, God may seem like some kind of galactic— and impersonal—force.

There are a few primary ways fatherless daughters view their fathers and God. By examining these, we can clarify how women relate to God and open new lines of communication between the heavenly Father and His children.

"Daddy Was Wonderful and Loved God"

The daughter whose father knew the Lord enjoys a healthy legacy that can enhance her ability to relate to God as her heavenly Father. If she can remember her father and if he lived his walk with Christ in front of her, she has a positive role model of what God is like. If she cannot remember her father, she will undoubtedly hear about him and his godliness.

Of all the scenarios of loss of a father, this one probably provides the best soil to grow bonds of love between the daughter and God. One of the dangers, though, in remembering a good and godly father is that the earthly father becomes bigger than the heavenly Father. When her father is in heaven, the daughter may think first in terms of its being where her father is and then in terms of its being the Lord's domain. It is true that both of them are there, but the memory of a wonderful father should not take preeminence over dedication to the Lord.

"Daddy Didn't Know Christ"

When a believing daughter loses a father to death and he didn't know the Lord, she may have trouble reconciling her beliefs with her experience. Her belief may be that her father, without Christ, is now suffering eternal torment in hell. But she may be unable to imagine her own father there.

We are not to judge. Sometimes it is blatantly apparent that a person does not know Christ. We can only let go of the need to know where he is after death and hope that—in the absence of any evidence of godly living—his heart changed in the last moments of life.

I have suffered through the death of a relative who apparently didn't know the Lord. It is a perplexing time. Love for the deceased person is mixed with fears of what his final thoughts were. It is tempting to say that surely God will admit that person into heaven no matter what the earthly relationship, or lack of relationship, with Christ was like. But that is not consistent with Scripture.

There is only one way to get to heaven—by accepting Christ as Savior. That need not be done walking down the aisle of a church. It can be done on a deathbed in the quiet of the heart with no known witnesses.

All we can do is present Christ to those we love and in

prayer present them to Christ. If they reject Him, at least they have heard about Him. If they accept Him in the silent moments before death, we will see them again when we get to heaven. It is not our responsibility to determine where they go.

"Daddy Knows Christ . . . but Daddy Left"

Christian parents must communicate to their children their continued faith in God and commitment to His principles even though the marriage covenant is being broken. In this book, we are not looking at the theology or morality of divorce—merely at its impact on daughters. But divorcing parents will be forced to look at the morality of the issue and how they will explain it to their children. God hates divorce but allows it in certain cases. Each individual must seek an understanding of these issues before God.

Children are not responsible for the actions of their parents. They are eventually—as they get older and more mature— responsible for their attitudes toward their parents. Forgiveness of a parent over a divorce is a part of the healing process for the child.

A separated father has an opportunity to present his relationship with the Lord to his daughter in a context that may influence her the rest of her life. If such a father seems unconcerned about the Lord, the daughter may conclude that her father has turned from the Lord, but she is not to judge.

If her father denies any responsibility for his part in the divorce, the daughter may deny responsibilities in her own life. If, on the other hand, her father accepts his responsibility and continues to relate to the Lord, she can learn that God can be heard even above the noise of difficulty.

Regardless of her father's behavior, a daughter needs to be encouraged to forgive him. His actions may not warrant forgiveness, but her relationship with the Lord requires it of her.

"Daddy Doesn't Know Christ"

If a father is at home or is divorced and he doesn't know Christ, family relationships may be very rocky. At best, the father accepts the daughter's faith and allows her freedom in it. At worst, he is openly hostile to the gospel. His hostility can cause his daughter to feel trapped in the middle: she is committed to the Lord but is the daughter of a nonbeliever.

The dilemma can be agonizing. It is biblical to "honor" her parents. But she is not to align herself with someone opposed to Christ. She should view her heavenly Father as the ultimate authority. If her father protests against something she feels is biblical, she has no choice but to do what the Lord wants of her.

It is not a daughter's responsibility to save her father, even though she has opportunities to share the gospel with him. Likewise, a believing wife can share the gospel with her husband, but he is never compelled to accept Christ. In any case, the father should be honored and respected as much as possible.

A daughter may be the only one in the family who knows the Lord. If her parents allow her, she should find a fellowship where she can grow. If her parents won't allow her to go to a fellowship, she should obey their wishes. She might try to develop a friendship with another Christian girl at school and talk with her about spiritual matters. If her parents even restrict her friendships with Christians, she again needs to obey them. Her only recourse may be to pray that God will direct her to sources of growth.

LEARNING TO LOVE GOD THE FATHER

A daughter's experiences with a less-than-perfect father may hamper her attempts to have a solid, loving relationship with God the Father. Here are some typical problems daughters without dads may encounter, along with some ideas about how they can be overcome.

Overcoming Disappointment

The loss of a father is a painful reality. When a girl sees her friends having their needs and desires met by their fathers, surely a sense of disappointment brings sadness into her life. If she is in a community of believers, she will undoubtedly be told to think of God as her Father.

But how, she wonders, does someone do that?

Before she can experience God as her Father, she needs to acknowledge the disappointment she feels about her father. There is a shadow of disloyalty in admitting that a parent is a disappointment. Most children take the blame for the broken relationship. Even in the case of death, children can feel somehow responsible for the parent's leaving. Following a divorce, this sense of responsibility is almost always present. And with an emotionally distant father, the children usually develop a codependent lifestyle of trying to keep him happy.

Acknowledging disappointment is not disloyal. A person who is disappointing can be loved and forgiven. But it is necessary to accept the imperfectness of the earthly father before living in the love of God as our Father.

Our earthly fathers and our heavenly Father are not in competition. And even children who have wonderful earthly fathers need to realize that only God is the measure of a perfect father.

Developing Spiritual Discernment

God assumed human form in the person of Jesus Christ. But Jesus is physically gone from our presence. The Holy Spirit is not a visible entity. And God the Father remains in heaven.

We relate to others with our senses and with our minds and hearts. How, then, can we really think of God as our Father if we cannot see, touch, or hear Him? What place does He occupy in our minds and hearts?

As children of God, we need to learn to replace our earthly senses with spiritual discernment. To develop in our relationship with God, we need to change the way we know, understand, and relate.

Redefining How We Relate

Often little girls have imaginary friends who are very real to them. They can "see" their friends because their eyes do not focus on scientifically observable objects that they experience and touch with their physical senses. Instead, imagination gives the friends form and substance. And they "see" their friends with their hearts.

But as little girls grow up and leave imaginary friends behind, they also seem to leave behind the "eyes" and "ears" they used to relate to their "friends."

God is real. In fact, He is the basis of all reality. However, like a child's imaginary friend, He is invisible. To relate to Him, we need to recall back into our realm of reality the existence of the unseen. Like children, we need to open ourselves to the world of faith and trust in what is not easily and logically defined. As Jesus told His followers: "Assuredly, I say to you, unless you are converted and become as little children, you will by no means enter the kingdom of heaven" (Matt. 18:3). And later, the author of Hebrews agreed: "Now faith is the substance of things hoped for, the evidence of things not seen" (Heb. 11:1).

Receiving a New Heart

When a person enters into a relationship with Christ, He gives her a new heart. A heart without Christ cannot see God. A heart without Christ, deceived by Satan, can worship an unseen god that is false. But a person with the one true God in her heart has a new capacity to see the unseen accurately, to hear the unspoken correctly, to touch God, to think as He wants her to, and to feel Him with her new heart.

Acquiring a New Way of Seeing

Relating to God in practical ways requires the seemingly impractical view of life that is lived from a spiritual perspective. The world is contrary to the things of God. What is wise to the world is foolishness to God.

A daughter without a dad needs to think in terms of what

God has to say about her, not what the world may say. The world may say that she needs to do everything in her power to protect herself: she must rely only on herself, learn to be defensive, and be cunning and even deceitful.

God has another way. He says that she is to rely on Him, that He will protect her, and that He is her defense. Again, new definitions may be required: *protect* may not mean that no physical harm ever comes to her. But *protect* will mean that she is ultimately safe from true harm to her soul because she trusts in God.

Translating life into God's terms is a challenging assignment these days. Our culture has little use for a God who remains unseen, thus confounding our scientific, materialistic biases. And if she follows God as Jesus did—by laying down her life for others, being willing to go the extra mile, and not returning hatred with more hatred—people will think she has suffered some serious mental short-circuiting.

But seeing things from God's perspective begins with the heart and moves through the mind and into behavior. And that behavior may be different from what the world recommends. It may mean being kind to an unloving father or being able to rejoice at a father's being in heaven in the midst of great pain or trusting God even though life is hard.

"BUT CAN I TAKE GOD TO THE SCHOOL PLAY?"

It's fine to discuss these new ways to view life, but what happens in a girl's daily life? How does she go to God for a hug? Can she hear God's advice about the guy at school she thinks is cute? Is God applauding when she sings a solo in the school play?

God's being a girl's Father does *not* mean that she will avoid pain as a result of the loss of her earthly father. She will. A life without pain is not promised. What God promises is better: an abundant life in spite of pain.

The pain will not always be intense. It will not be there

every day. But pain will exist in varying degrees all of her life. That is something to be understood, not feared. Accepting that pain is a part of life can be freeing. No longer does a daughter have to feel guilty about her pain. She doesn't have to worry that her faith is too small. And she will feel different from other kids. She will continue to feel that she is lacking something that many of the other kids have. She will sense that she is missing something that no girl should be forced to miss. And in many ways she is right. She is suffering an injustice.

But the feeling of being different doesn't have to be bad. Other girls may have fathers at the school play, but a daughter without a dad can still experience fulfillment. She can miss her earthly father's presence at the same time that she accepts God's presence.

A daughter without a dad will have to spend time with the Lord praying, meditating, and seeking His will. She will need to maintain spiritual disciplines with a new attitude of hunger in her heart. Her heart needs to ask God to reveal Himself as her Father.

I am over forty and have to fight to make this thought a reality. I was a single parent for nine years. I am an only child, and my father doesn't yet know the Lord. I have to mentally put my father aside and listen to my heavenly Father. Often, what I hear from my earthly father conflicts with what God tells me. Yet, what I hear from God—through His Word, through thoughts that come to me in prayer, through the counsel of His people, and through the evidences of His leading in my life and the spiritual discernment He gives me—is sufficient to guide and comfort me.

Even with many years of pulling from all these resources, I have to make a conscious effort to keep a secure reality of God as my Father. My commitment to knowing more about God and my requests to Him to show me how He is my Father manifest themselves in the reality of His presence in my life.

My daughters have been without their father since they were seven and ten years old, and they have had to face the same challenge. My older daughter is a very practical young woman. It seems harder for her to rely on God than it does for my younger daughter. She is capable and independent and has learned how to survive without a father in a responsible way. She continually struggles to discipline her mind and open her heart and allow God to participate in her life as her Father.

God is our Father. He is with her at her basketball games. He is with me as I make decisions that need fatherly counsel. Practically speaking, we don't always feel that He is here. But that doesn't change the fact that He is.

God goes to school plays and sporting events and proms. He is there in the middle of the night when loneliness seems to suffocate and in the middle of the day when pressures of life make frantic demands.

He makes a difference in a life. He sees, hears, touches, and feels the pain, and He stays.

LOSING MORE THAN JUST A FATHER

Chapter 6

Looking at Losses

"The president is dead."

The serenity of our campus and our afternoon classes was interrupted by a news flash heard around the world: John F. Kennedy had been assassinated. We felt sorrow and confusion at our loss. We also felt an uneasy sense of fear that somehow our nation was suddenly weak and our defenses were down. What did we have to be afraid of? Attack from an enemy? Seizure by forces from within? No one knew. We knew only that we had a vague feeling that democracy and the American way of life had been threatened.

TV newsmen groped for the right words to describe what

had happened. Radio announcers repeated the same message again and again. The fabric of civic life had been irreparably torn. There was no "return to regular programming," and the problem was not with our TV sets. Everything was one big, blaring transmission of bad news.

None of the students at my school went to late afternoon classes or out on dates. Instead, we tended to want the company of others as we tried to come to grips with the intensely personal and deeply communal loss.

When President Kennedy was killed, the whole nation felt a vague emptiness and sorrow. But every day, millions of people suffer loss—the loss of a job, the loss of a friendship, the loss of the willpower to stay with a plan of self-improvement. Although these losses are personal and not national, we are a nation of sufferers striving to cope with and come out on top of the painful situations we endure.

The purpose of this section is to promote understanding of various kinds of loss and to develop strategies for living through them.

THREE KINDS OF LOSS

Losses can be broken down into three basic groups. First, there are losses that are part of the natural order of things; they replace one thing with another that is better or newer or more appropriate. A young child will lose baby teeth in order to make a place for permanent teeth. A tree will lose its leaves in the fall as part of a process that will produce new leaves in the spring.

These natural losses are an accepted part of life. Certainly, no child enjoys losing his teeth. But who could survive life equipped only with baby teeth? We don't know if trees feel pain when they drop their colored leaves, but new leaves come in time—and meanwhile we are treated to a beautiful show. Natural changes bring their share of grief and joy, but these transitions are supposed to happen. Soon what was lost is replaced.

Second, some losses are controllable. When we lose a tennis

match, we can analyze why we lost, work on improving our game, and play again in an attempt to win this time around. A child may lose a chance for a gold star on a spelling test because he makes too many mistakes, so he works harder and gets a gold star on his next test. We may lose the privilege of wearing favorite outfits, but if we watch what we eat, we may be able to regain that lost right.

As with natural losses, controllable losses are a necessary part of the big picture of life. We may all be equal in God's sight, but that doesn't mean we all play tennis or spell equally well. Controllable losses can provide the impetus we need to get out on the tennis court and practice harder, or they may be the signal that our calling is to play video games in the living room. Whatever the outcome, controllable losses are helpful.

And finally, there are tragic losses. Into this category falls the loss of a president or the loss of a loved one. If you've experienced one of these losses—and we all have at various times—your body tells you immediately that this situation isn't merely a part of the natural flow of things. These losses bring tears to your eyes, knots to your stomach, and pain and tension to all parts of your life.

These losses seem to have no redeeming purpose. We have no control over them. These losses are the *absence of something that is supposed to be present*. And these are the losses I am addressing here.

LOSING A PRESIDENT—OR A FATHER

When President Kennedy was assassinated, the people of the United States suffered a tragic loss. They were robbed of something that was supposed to be present. The president was somehow always supposed to be there. He was supposed to be secure and protected. He was surrounded by a formidable network of Secret Service men who were trained to die, if necessary, that he should live. And if the end of the world was near, he could be reached by that imposing red phone.

Another tragic national loss occurred on January 28, 1986,

when the space shuttle *Challenger* exploded just seventy-four seconds after takeoff. Thousands of people at Cape Canaveral and millions watching on TV saw something that was supposed to be a flawless exhibition of American scientific and aeronautical know-how turn into an experience of horror. As with the Kennedy tragedy, the reporters struggled to control their emotions as they played and replayed the footage showing a small flame grow and turn into a swirling ball of fire.

Over and over we watched as the lives of seven astronauts were blown sky-high. Adding a personal note to this national tragedy was the loss of young Christa McAuliffe, a teacher who was the first civilian astronaut. It was the American Dream turned into a macabre nightmare.

Though many of us suffered during those national tragedies, none suffered like the families and loved ones of those who died. All losses are threatening, but the closer they are to home, the greater the threat.

The loss of a father—whether by death, divorce, or emotional distancing—is tragic. Losing a father destroys what was—or should have been—an intimate bond. The impact of this loss is significant and lasting.

And that's why we need to take a closer look at losses. All of us were created with certain needs, along with the supports to help meet those needs. When those supports are not there, we begin the frantic search for new means of survival. When a daughter lacks the support of a caring relationship with a loving father, she loses a lot.

SHEPHERDLESS SHEEP

The Bible is full of stories about losses. Although Scripture provides no detailed look at the impact of the loss of a father, it does paint a parallel picture in the relationship of sheep to a shepherd.

Sheep are vulnerable to attacks from wild animals and are unable to adequately protect themselves. That's why they need a shepherd. In many ways, daughters are the same. They are growing—but still weak—and are designed to receive their fathers' protection.

The model of a perfect shepherd is found in the familiar melody of Psalm 23:

> The LORD is my shepherd;
> I shall not want. . . .
> Yea, though I walk through the valley
>   of the shadow of death,
> I will fear no evil. . . .

Throughout God's Word we read that the people of God are the sheep and Christ is our Shepherd. He provides us with the solution to our needs, a safe place to rest, leadership, restoration, guidance, protection, the comfort of His presence, acceptance, goodness, love, and a promise of being with Him forever.

This theme is echoed in Isaiah 40:11, where we see how a shepherd cares for his flock:

> He will feed His flock like a shepherd;
> He will gather the lambs with His arm,
> And carry them in His bosom,
> And gently lead those who are with young.

We also see God's compassion for sheep who have no shepherd: "When He saw the multitudes, He was moved with compassion for them, because they were weary and scattered, like sheep having no shepherd" (Matt. 9:36).

Perhaps the most graphic picture of the relationship between sheep and their shepherd is found in Ezekiel 34:2–6, which addresses the leaders of the people of Israel. But this passage can also apply to anyone who has responsibility for others and cares only for himself:

> Thus says the Lord GOD to the shepherds: "Woe to the shepherds of Israel who feed themselves! Should not the shepherds feed the flocks? . . . The weak you have not

strengthened, nor have you healed those who were sick, nor bound up the broken, ... nor sought what was lost; but with force and cruelty you have ruled them. So they were scattered because there was no shepherd; and they became food for all the beasts of the field when they were scattered. My sheep wandered through all the mountains, and on every high hill; yes, My flock was scattered over the whole face of the earth, and no one was seeking or searching for them."

If sheep were people, they'd be pretty unhappy about the prospect of being turned into sheepburgers for ravenous wild animals. Fear and confusion would replace the calm they felt when protected by the shepherd. They would be forced to develop ways to survive without the shepherd, or they would die as victims of stronger forces.

SCATTERED DAUGHTERS

God cares about sheep, but He cares about children more. Children were meant to grow up with the support of a mother and a father. A child without a father loses much the same thing that the sheep lose without a shepherd. A daughter, wandering unprotected through life, faces some unique challenges and frustrations that result directly from the loss of her father.

Increasing numbers of little girls and young women in the Christian community feel somewhat disconnected because they don't have a father in the shepherd role operative in their lives. And many adult women have never had an adequate father-daughter relationship. Although many adult women would like to believe that not having a father is far in their past, or would prefer to put their problems of fatherlessness behind them, they are now beginning to see the effects of their loss in their daily lives.

Like sheep scattered on a hillside, these girls and women may appear safe, secure, and happy. But they are vulnerable to attack.

FINDING HAPPINESS IN THE LESS-THAN-NUCLEAR FAMILY

Before we proceed further, I must repeat that the goal of this book is not to recover some lost image of the perfect Christian family.

Many people in the church have been taught that the ideal Christian home has a mother, a father, children, and a structure with the father at its head. In some churches, this nuclear family is portrayed as the only kind of family God can honor and use.

That's fine. Many people believe such a family is the healthiest—not only for the parents but also for the children. But such a family requires a caring, responsible man filling the position of father. And the truth of the matter is that in too many American families, the father is absent.

In this book we are concentrating on finding solutions to the family situations in which people find themselves, not hoping wistfully for conditions of some bygone era. Our task is to translate God's ideals for our families to the contemporary context of increasing numbers of fatherless homes. Our challenge is to discover what the Lord would have us do with what exists. Although many families may be less than ideal, we know that Christ provides all we need to be all He wants us to be and to experience the abundance of life He has for us.

No tragedy is beyond the reach of God's restorative love. Daughters without dads are in many ways like sheep without a shepherd, but the good news is that the Shepherd of Psalm 23 is their Shepherd. He provides comfort and protection, and He brings other people into their lives to help meet their needs.

Once an understanding of loss is accomplished, daughters are able to look at the network of people in their lives and more meaningfully relate to and love them. The impact of these losses can be lessened, and God can do His healing work of restoration and reconciliation.

Chapter 7

Daddy's Little Girl

The song "Daddy's Little Girl," first released in 1949, portrays the ideal father-daughter relationship. It was popular at a time when the traditional Norman Rockwell–style family structure was the norm. Its evocation of images and its refrain of little girls being sugar and spice and everything nice still tug at women's hearts near the end of the twentieth century.

As I interviewed dozens and dozens of women for this book, I asked some of them to describe a time in their childhood when they felt like "Daddy's little girl." Most could remember a time. All of them cried at the memory.

I remember the story of one married woman in her forties whose father died when she was six years old: *"I had a little pretend steering wheel in the car next to the driver's seat. Daddy would take me with him to the [Air Force] base. As we drove in he would salute the guard on duty, smile, and say as he nodded toward me, 'This is my copilot.'"*

Or the woman in her mid-thirties, now married with two children, whose father died when she was twenty-one years old: *"I was in awe of him. What Daddy did for me was to make me feel so special. He let me know I was his precious little girl."*

My notebooks are full of comments like these from thankful women who enjoyed a loving and intimate relationship with their fathers. Sadly, I also heard my share of stories about the situations caused by the absence of such paternal love.

A little girl who has her father's love knows what it's like to be unconditionally and completely adored by a man. She knows the feeling of safety that love creates.

A SAFE HARBOR

There is security in a father's love. A girl can be silly, giggly, pouty, tearful, unreasonable, and more—and still feel precious. Having been "Daddy's little girl" can be a warm and wonderful harbor early in life. If that harbor was calm and protected, its memory brings tears and a smile to the one privileged to anchor there.

If, however, the father was absent or unfaithful or that harbor was invaded by intruders from without—storms caused by financial insecurities or arguments—the harbor turns into a watery grave. Thinking of those days brings tears of a different kind to a woman.

A LITTLE GIRL'S HEART

Social scientists and philosophers agree on one thing: it's universally inexcusable to make universal remarks. But my experience in talking to women about their fathers leads me to believe in this universal: there is a "little girl" in every female.

Not all women have the same experience with their "little girl" within. But regardless of the type of relationship with her father, what happened to a woman in that relationship affects her the rest of her life.

You can't see a bad daughter-father relationship written on a woman's face. Instead the fruits of the absence of a healthy relationship are borne in her heart.

One woman had tears in her eyes as she recalled a ritual she and her father acted out: *"I remember as a little girl being carried on my father's shoulders every Saturday night as he walked down to the corner newsstand to get the early edition of the Sunday paper. I could let go with my hands and bounce happily high above the ground. I knew he wouldn't let me fall. I knew in my heart that I was safe with him."*

Little girls start out trusting their fathers—unless they are given reasons not to. They trust their mothers, too, but with a little less gleeful abandon than they display with their fathers. As a little toddler running throws herself into her father's open arms, he sweeps her up with a bear hug of approval. She has an attitude of adoration. And that sentiment is generously returned.

A DADDY'S HEART

When the love between a father and a daughter is reciprocal, it's wonderful to behold. Just as a little girl adores, so she is adored. Even the toughest man can be seen to melt in the hands of his tiny daughter.

I became certain of this fact after watching my two daughters with their father, Jack. Lara and Lisa were about five and eight years old when the four of us packed up and went to Disney World. Along with us were Chuck and Patti, a married couple who did not have any children of their own but thoroughly enjoyed our girls.

We were in one of the gift shops at the Magic Kingdom, and Lara wanted a stuffed Minnie Mouse doll. Jack, who loved our daughters and was used to their ways, would have described Lara's request as "asking," but to Chuck it was definitely "begging." Jack kindly told Lara that she couldn't have the stuffed animal because she had already acquired quite a collection of Mouse paraphernalia from our excursion. Chuck heartily approved of Jack's firmness in not giving in to Lara's little girlish pleadings.

The next day as we got ready to leave for home, we stopped back in the gift shop to get some postcards and other last-minute things. Lara began asking (or begging, depending on your perspective) again for the Minnie Mouse doll. This time Jack gave in. A few minutes later, she bounced out of the gift shop with Minnie Mouse tucked securely under her arm.

Lara couldn't wait to show her trophy to Chuck. He smiled weakly at her and looked sternly at Jack.

"Jack, you shouldn't have done that," said Chuck. "It's only negative reinforcement for her behavior."

I had to turn away to hide my smile. Chuck was so serious,

so well meaning and totally clueless as to the effect of a little girl on her father.

Chuck had his chance to be firm a few years later with his own little girl, Lauren. My daughters and I were visiting them when Lauren was about four years old. It became evident in a matter of minutes that Lauren had her daddy wrapped neatly around her little finger.

I smiled at the sight. Chuck asked what was so funny, and as I reminded him of his words of wisdom to Jack, he nodded in agreement that no one knows the true and accurate state of a father's heart until he is a father himself. Then, and only then, do men see how their hearts can be shaped and molded in the hands of a loving little girl.

BROKEN HEARTS

Not all women enjoy a loving relationship with their fathers. For them, the image of "Daddy's little girl" is just a dream or a line from a song.

When daddy isn't there or isn't there the way he is supposed to be, hearts can break. I talked with literally dozens of women who had lived a long time with broken hearts. What they said was quite different from the ones whose fathers had been lovingly present.

There was the single woman, now in her forties and very active in church programs. Her father was home, but emotionally distant: *"I asked Daddy to just hold me. He said he couldn't—he just couldn't. I decided to NEVER ask again."*

Or the never-married woman who has had a series of poor relationships with men. Her parents divorced when she was four years old: *"My father never touched me—no hugs, no kisses, nothing—not even physical discipline."*

Then there was the woman whose father was emotionally distant. She married two men who were as removed as her father: *"I never felt loved as a child. I felt 'sent away' by my father."*

I asked a six-year-old girl to describe her father. The girl's parents are now divorced and her father recently remarried.

She said, *"Daddy is nice. He sees me sometimes. He's busy. He loves me, but he doesn't know how to show it."*

A married woman whose parents divorced when she was a teenager told me, *"I tried to keep myself from growing up. I thought if I stayed a child I could get my daddy back."*

Not all women have the opportunity to know what it's like to be "Daddy's little girl." I talked to a woman whose father died over forty years ago. The memories of his absence still haunt her: *"He died when I was little. So I never experienced the love of a father."*

Not only daughters who lose their fathers to death or divorce feel the sting of a father's absence. A married woman in her thirties with two children struggles to figure out what kind of parental role she wants to fulfill for her own children. Her confusion results, more than a little, from her difficulties with a father who was emotionally distant: *"My little girl in me is still screaming out—meet my needs! I should want to comfort my own children, but I have a conflict with the little girl in me who is needing attention."*

PATTERNS FOR THE FUTURE

Little girls' experiences stay with them as they grow into women and mothers. When a warm daughter-father relationship is the context in which a little girl lives and grows, she will not have to deal with the absence of this relationship in her later life.

In her book, *The Men in Our Lives,* Elizabeth Fishel explores the impact of the father-daughter relationship from birth through adulthood. Fishel has significant things to say about the years from age three to age five—the years coinciding with the "Daddy's little girl" age.

"The daughter makes a blueprint of attitudes that affect later choices in love, later decisions about work," writes Fishel. "In the untangling lie clues to the daughter's future. Will the daughter of the absent father try to resolve her unrequited love by seeking a man in her father's image? Or will she hold herself aloof from men, making sure she is not abandoned the way her mother was?''[1]

The women I interviewed had varied responses to life without a father. We will look at some of the healthier responses in the next section. But the common denominator was the pain of a heart broken by the loss of a loving and adoring father. Some of those hearts have greatly healed; some have not.

What begins in the heart of a little girl grows and continues to live in the heart of the adult woman. "Daddy's little girl" may grow up physically but may still be childlike and questioning as her emotional and psychological development is affected by her loss. A woman's search for a healthy identity may be interrupted by the fallout from daddy's departure.

A SPECIAL IDENTITY WITH FATHER

When a girl is young and her father is around, she learns that she has a sense of similarity or "sameness" with mommy and a sense of uniqueness or "specialness" with daddy. Girls don't understand what makes things different with their fathers until they are a little older, but they know that their relationship is truly special.

While mommy braids her hair, irons her ruffles, and helps her dress up, daddy is the intended audience of all this womanly preparation. If successful, the efforts to make the daughter lovely result in resounding curtain calls from the fatherly audience of one.

Daughters have their identities tied up with their fathers as long as things remain positive. Girls usually stop calling their mothers "Mommy" around the age of eight or nine. But many grown women still call their fathers "Daddy."

Self-esteem is a fragile thing, particularly in young children. If a little girl's self-esteem is closely tied to her relationship with her father and that relationship is interrupted by death, divorce, or desertion, the development of a healthy self-regard may also be interrupted or complicated.

In the book *Passionate Attachments*, Signe Hammer says,

"To be Daddy's Girl would mean I was somebody; my place in the world would be assured. To be rejected by Daddy would mean I was nobody and nothing: Zero. Wiped out."[2]

Daddy, for the little girl, is the final authority in approving or disapproving who she is. Many women admitted to me that they had enjoyed a fair amount of affirmation from various people. But if their fathers displayed disapproval, it was as if all the other approval didn't even count. They needed the final OK from daddy.

When fathers leave, young girls feel rejected. This is not very often the case when the loss is due to death, but it is almost always the case in divorce and emotional distancing. The "little girl" goes from being precious, adored, and applauded to being so unimportant that daddy didn't stay home to be with her.

With her father in her life, her identity was relatively secure. His departure means that her identity and her security are up for grabs. A whole host of new ingredients influences how she thinks about herself and how she relates to others. These influences will be examined in more detail later on, but it's clear that they challenge girls—and women—as they establish their unique identities.

Sometimes when a father leaves, the "little girl" leaves, too. In cases of divorce or desertion, daughters may become angry with their fathers, and that anger can spill out in myriad ways—from distrust and hatred of all men to gross sexual immorality to anger toward God.

When my husband died, my daughters had none of these destructive feelings. Instead, my older daughter, who was ten years old at the time, became an adult overnight. Her healthy "little girl," which had grown through ten years of closeness with Jack, was replaced by a new personality.

She became more responsible for household tasks. She could do the wash and prepare meals; she even had my father teach her to drive in case there was an emergency and I couldn't drive. She served as my constant and trusted helper. She seemed to be able to handle almost anything that came along.

But underneath the calm exterior of control, the "little girl" still lives. She still hurts and needs to be nurtured. She still needs to be weak and vulnerable. She still needs the feelings of trust, safety, and security that she enjoyed with her father. Just because her safe harbor was taken away doesn't mean those feelings disappear. And in fact, the effects of the loss of her father and the loss of the "little girl" in her are playing a significant role in her life now.

Loss may produce the appearance of "little girl" gone, but she's there. It often takes patience and time to touch and heal that part of a hurt girl or woman. It also takes love to see through the got-it-all-together facade many women hide behind and perceive that pain and a sense of loss are deep within. (In the next section we'll see how to help in the process of healing these women who conceal hurt "little girls.")

Appearances can be deceiving. The most professional-looking and self-assured exterior may conceal a deep wound. True feelings may be stuffed, denied, ignored. Or they may be handled inappropriately in unhealthy relationships with others, particularly men. Only through subterranean explorations of her pain and sense of loss can real health develop.

SHEPHERDLESS SHEEP EXPERIENCE FEAR AND CONFUSION

Like sheep without a shepherd, daughters who lose their fathers may feel unprotected. Fear may move in and camp in their hearts. Fear of the unknown—and how can a little girl who loses her father know what is ahead?—breeds confusion. And confusion causes even more fear. What is there to fear? Who will take care of me when daddy isn't here?

I said earlier that some people are uncomfortable with universal statements. Bearing that in mind, I offer another one: all of the women I interviewed said the thing they feared most after the loss of their fathers was the loss of their mothers. That may seem like an obvious response. But a father is one of those givens in life that many assume will never be removed. When loss occurs, through death, divorce, or desertion, a daughter loses the ability to say, "That will never happen to me."

A daughter who loses her father to death no longer feels secure that death won't interrupt her life or relationships. A daughter who loses her father to desertion or divorce fears that she may not ever have a happy marriage.

The loss of the father—and the concurrent loss of the needed protection and security he can bring—is a real threat to a daughter's well-being. It can rob her of any meaningful degree of freedom to enjoy life as God intended.

THE APPLE OF THE FATHER'S EYE

The little girl without her father is like the lost sheep that has a good shepherd. God—the Good Shepherd—leaves the other sheep, goes out to look for her, and carries her back, wrapping His arms around her and carrying her close to His heart.

She may be wounded by her loss, afraid, and confused. She may not even feel safe—at least not in the way she felt safe before her security was taken from her. But that doesn't diminish the security she has with her heavenly Father. Through a relationship with Christ and the indwelling of the Holy Spirit, she has access to God the Father with such intimacy as to call Him Abba: "For you did not receive the spirit of bondage again to fear, but you received the Spirit of adoption by whom we cry out, 'Abba, Father'" (Rom. 8:15). A girl or a woman can cry out, "Abba! Daddy!" God is her Daddy. She is His little girl.

Pain is not removed. Life is not suddenly problem-free. God's love doesn't guarantee that a father figure will be there to wipe away a young girl's tear or to hug an older daughter who has run back to her father for protection from an abusive husband.

But the little girl has a safe harbor to rest in. She has a hand to hold hers and arms to protect her. Because they are not flesh and blood like her earthly father's, she has to learn how to see and feel them. She has to experience them with her heart. As she learns more of who God is and how much she is loved—and as her faith grows—the "little girl" in her will be free to grow up. Soon, she can leave her childhood, full of unrealized needs and unrecoverable joys, behind her. She may have experienced painful loss, but she can know the reality of being the apple of His eye—the totally loved, completely accepted child of God.

Chapter 8

Social Security

*J*oAnn is a forty-year-old divorced mother of two. Her twenty years of marriage gave her plenty of experience in managing a family, preparing nourishing meals, counseling her children, and nursing back to health everyone in her house who became ill.

But her two decades of domestic service didn't prepare her for divorce and the drastic change in her standard of living that accompanied her new life as a single mother. Nothing prepared her for the long days with little pay. Nothing could have.

For JoAnn, the workday begins at 3:00 A.M., when she crawls out of bed to tackle her first job—delivering newspapers. When that job is over around 6:00 A.M., she returns home to get her kids ready for school and herself ready for her second job—working as a full-time secretary in an insurance office.

Then, at 5:00 P.M., she gets home in time to fix dinner, help her kids with homework, and see them off to bed. Then, it's off to bed herself, before the alarm rings again at three o'clock the next morning.

MEET THE NEW BREADWINNER

After my husband died, I had to learn a new life. I had to fill many of the roles that he and I had previously shared. I had to handle all the details and decisions of running the house. I had to make sure the kids had rides to school, to their sports practices, and to their friends' houses. And I had to learn to balance a checkbook.

Before my husband died, I never managed our checkbook. He handled all the finances—sitting up late one night a month to systematically do whatever he did to keep our fiscal house in order. I watched him as he sat amidst stacks of papers and bills, and I was mystified by what he did with all of it.

In many ways, I'm still mystified. I can balance a checkbook now, but I don't do well with it under any circumstances. The monthly exercise of bill paying became a consistently stressful event. My daughters learned to walk wide circles around me when the checkbook was out. They were sympathetic about my struggle but could be of little practical help.

Unfortunately, balancing a checkbook is the least of the concerns of a woman running a family on her own. Many more women have trouble finding enough money to put into their bank accounts.

The scenario of mothers managing families is becoming an increasingly common one in this country—causing great concern among teachers, counselors, and policy makers. Some of the issues confronting single-parent families—meaning women who are raising children alone as a result of divorce, widowhood, or abandonment—were explored in the February 1989 issue of *McCall's* magazine:

Ninety percent of single-parent homes are headed by women. Sixty percent of our country's children are likely to spend part of their childhood or adolescence in a family with just one parent.

Congressman George Miller (Democrat of California, chairman of the House Select Committee on Children, Youth and Families) stated, "Not only are the numbers of single-parent families increasing, but they are the most economically vulnerable families in America. Since 1974, their incomes have declined further than the incomes of any other type of family."

"So it's not some distant them; it's us," says Congresswoman Pat Schroeder (Democrat of Colorado). "There are an incredible number of women who are one man away from poverty and they don't know it."

"What happens in most divorces," says Nicholas Zill, Ph.D., executive director of the national research organization Child Trends, "is that the child goes to live with the mother, and then within a few years the father stops paying child support, stops maintaining contact with the family and perhaps sets up another household."

Today only slightly more than half of all single mothers are receiving the child support they are entitled to. And even when ordered to pay, two thirds of American fathers spend less every month on their children than they do on their cars.[1]

Included in the above article was the harrowing story of two families trying desperately to make ends meet. The two families moved in together—two mothers and their children sharing a house.

Stories like this one—as well as JoAnn's story that began this chapter—are far from rare. And while these cases may seem to be good raw material for TV shows like "Kate and Allie," the real-life drama is not quite so humorous.

Sure, it may help with finances for two families to double up. But no television show has explored the confused feelings of women and children when they lose the father, sell their house, and are forced into new relationships with others struggling for survival.

SLICING THE BREAD TOO THIN

Many courageous women are making valiant efforts to keep their families' heads above water, but they are facing some incredible odds. Three main factors contribute to the low standard of living among families where mom is the breadwinner:

1. Single mothers have lower earning capacities than do almost any other group. As mothers, they have invested much of their time and energy in child care. And for the past thirty years, women have earned approximately 60 percent as much as men.

2. Many mothers don't receive child support—either legally prescribed child support payments or informal payments—from their children's fathers. Many women are caring for all the children born in their marriages with no support from the fathers. National statistics show that only about 60 percent of eligible children living with their mothers receive any child support money at all.

3. Some also point to government benefits for mother-only families, arguing that the meager benefits provided by public assistance programs fail to meet the substantial needs of these families.[2]

Movies like *Working Girl* and magazines like *Working Woman* seem to suggest that vast numbers of women are investing their lives in careers and professions instead of raising families. But many women still choose marriage and children before furthering their education.

Many other women graduated from college, but then had families instead of making a career their top priority. When they suddenly need to become wage earners, they encounter problems getting high-paying jobs because they have been out of the job market so long.

MISUNDERSTANDING IN
THE CHURCH

If things weren't already hard enough on single mothers, many additional trials await them in the Christian church. Because my husband died, I was viewed as some kind of heroic widow in our church. But I feel sorry for women who lose their husbands due to divorce or desertion. Many of them are treated like pariahs, and the love and mercy of Christ are not extended to them as they should be.

Some Christians criticize women for entering the workplace, especially if they have young children. But those who disapprove may not be aware of the tremendous financial pressures bearing down on many women.

When women find themselves single again, the church needs to respond with love. We will talk more about this in the last section of this book.

LOSING DAD AND PART OF MOM, TOO

When daughters lose a dad, they often lose a part of mom, too. Not only does the mother have to deal with emotional loss and the grieving over the lost father, but she now carries a double burden. She has all of the tasks she had before—cooking, cleaning, nurturing, and driving—as well as the responsibility of being the breadwinner.

Most children can think of one word to describe their newly single mothers: *tired*. When mom has to do everything she previously did—plus what dad did—she is tired. She is often irritable. Stress often becomes a common element in the home.

Mom is different, too, in that her time is filled with much more than meeting the needs of her family. Little girls may have to learn to braid their own hair and do their own math homework, things mom had time to help with before.

Schools feel the change in mothers' schedules, too, because fewer mothers are able to assist in the classroom. Less than ten years ago many elementary schools assumed that every mom would take a turn coming into the classroom to help. Now few mothers are able to do that because they work outside the home.

PICKING UP THE SLACK

Daughters, in particular, feel the brunt of this change. If mom is too tired to cook, boys seem to be content with peanut butter and jelly sandwiches. Girls, however, try to fill the overburdened spot in the home.

Almost all the young women (ages eighteen to twenty-five years) I interviewed said they had learned to do domestic chores very soon after their father was gone. They simply picked up the slack where they could. When many daughters see their mothers in need, they experience a greater desire to help—and even nurture—them.

This doesn't happen in all cases, but it is certainly common. And some degree of this desire to help mom is natural and healthy. The problem occurs when the child and the parent exchange emotional roles, with the daughter becoming a mother figure to the mother, who retreats into childhood.

Care must be taken so that the roles don't become too misaligned. A daughter's deeper needs can be ignored when she is efficiently helping a parent. But a parent can become inordinately reliant on a child during this period of adjustment.

GOLD-PLATED PEER PRESSURE

Ask any kid, and she'll tell you: there's no pressure like peer pressure. It exists for children and parents, and it exists whether a father is at home or not.

For the newly single mother who is already struggling with a new world of chores and responsibilities, peer pressure can be a real killer. When children fail to realize the degree to which their standard of living is changing, the stage is set for fierce new pressures on mom.

Even families who make a conscious effort to fight the lure of rampant materialism face the continual struggle of keeping up with the Joneses and the Joneses' kids. If a junior- or senior-high-school student is in sports, parents have to shell out an average of fifty dollars for a pair of athletic shoes. If a child is involved in music, conscientious parents who want the child to practice and perform on an adequate instrument can pay out hundreds and hundreds of dollars.

Then there's the high-school prom—an event that seems to have been designed to drain a parent's cash reserves. Young men bemoan what it costs to rent a tux these days, but for young girls the expenses climb every year. And there is no way a young girl can very socially survive wearing a gown more than once or twice.

"I'LL NEVER DEPEND ON A MAN FOR MONEY!"

Conducting the interviews for this book, I talked to dozens of young women who were raised—at least in part—without their fathers. Each one wants a career. What is intriguing is their motivation: they want to be financially secure because their experience has taught them to believe that no one else will be there to provide for them.

I talked with one college junior who had done a research paper on the topic "Women and Careers." She had interviewed girls who were in college, most of whom were from divorced homes, and found that all of them were seeking careers. They viewed marriage and children as luxuries that might happen later. Most of them expressed hesitancy about marriage, stemming from a concern about what they considered to be an alarmingly high divorce rate.[3]

Girls who grow up without their fathers providing for them develop one of two widely varying images of who their mother is and of what they want to be. In that image, mom is a struggling low-level worker who can hardly make it in life, or she is a self-sufficient survivor who has overcome all obstacles to arrive at success.

Given these two options, it's clear which one the daughter will choose. The daughter's new concept of the ideal woman is a combination of entrepreneurial skills, aerobically toned body, savvy business sense, and—maybe—a mother (when her career is well established, of course). What pressure—and what a change from the image of the previous generation!

My older daughter falls in line with these desires. She

wants to have her own business, and marry, and have children. She has a strong domestic bent. But she *hates* it when some of her boyfriend's friends tease her by calling her June Cleaver. She would much prefer comparison to the heroine played by Melanie Griffith in *Working Girl,* or one of the female attorneys on "L.A. Law."

When dad doesn't, couldn't, or didn't provide, and mom simply can't, it's no big surprise that daughters without dads are leaning strongly toward financial and vocational self-reliance.

MAKING PLANS, NOT DREAMING DREAMS

Daughters without dads are also taking a hard, new look at men and reexamining their ideas about the ideal spouse. Along the way they are replacing the dreamy wistfulness of the past with more practical considerations.

I am sure that little girls still dream dreams of futures filled with love and happiness. But many seem to have given up on the deeply romantic notions of a long-lasting, passionate marriage or the presence of a gallant White Knight. Many modern women focus on masculine personality and character instead of being bowled over by outward appearances or charisma.

But what has been lost in the process? Has a life without the protection of a loving father robbed some young women of the sense of safety that can be experienced when someone stronger shields them from life's blows? Has the fear of desertion made women unable to trust a man for healthy, masculine care? Have the bad examples of many absent fathers and the abuses of male chauvinism damaged the image of loving and caring men? Is a whole new generation of women growing up with no concept of what it is like to be loved deeply and sincerely by a man? Have the battles fought during the sexual revolution rendered both sides mortally wounded and unable for any further engagement?

If so, I am sad for these women.

A father is the first man to be privileged to offer the gifts of love and protection to his daughter. If he then walks out of her life, she may stop dreaming of another man in later years and simply plan how she will protect herself from harm.

DRESSED FOR PROTECTION

In the good old days when White Knights were real and rode around on horseback, one thing was clear to see—the armor they wore for protection. It was clumsy and uncomfortable and made movement awkward. But knights of all colors wore their armor because it could save their lives.

Defensive wear has changed over the centuries. The only remnant of the full suit of armor that carried over into modern warfare was the helmet. Metal suits were replaced with lightweight bulletproof vests made of synthetics. So, an element of protection remained.

In many ways, daughters without dads are like the knights of old. Having lost a very natural form of protection when they lost their fathers, many women guard themselves with armor. In attempting to protect themselves from wounds of the memory, piercing pain, and threats unknown, they may pick up some clumsy, heavy armor.

They may put on layers of self-protection to cover damaged emotions. These layers can take the form of pretending all is well, sarcasm, humor, or anything that can be used to keep their real personality and their very real pain concealed.

Many women devise elaborate schemes to protect themselves from more hurt. Many shield themselves from any relationship with men. Others take the opposite approach and engage in a series of unhealthy relationships.

One of the saddest results of this kind of protection is that the growing girl or mature woman may be completely misunderstood. She may be perceived as aloof, cold, self-sufficient, aggressive, or unapproachable when in reality these facades conceal a wounded "little girl" trying to survive.

Whatever approach women take to deal with the pain caused by an absent father, only their heavenly Father can truly erase and heal that pain. And in the section on relationships, we will look at ways girls can learn to get through pain to experience life.

SLEEPING WITH ONE EYE OPEN

I once heard a speaker from a Communist country describing the constant fear of arrest and torture in which his family lived. Every night, the whole family would go to bed wondering if the door to their tiny apartment would be broken down and soldiers would storm in and haul them off to a fate too horrible to imagine. He remembered growing up with a feeling of never quite being totally asleep.

The slightest noise would startle everyone in the household. Lying in bed imagining the possible end of their lives each and every night robbed the entire family of any real rest. The darkness intensified the threat because the police always came at night.

Daughters without dads can live in the same kind of fear. The symbol of protection for their houses and their lives has deserted them. And now they face the insecurities of living alone and helpless on a daily basis.

I experienced some of this fear after the death of my first husband, Jack. When Jack was alive, I slept deeply and peacefully. If he was away on business overnight, I would always have a fitful night's sleep. No one ever broke into the house, so I actually was secure all the time. But that didn't change how I felt.

When he died, I was afraid that the fear at night would continue, but it didn't. At the same time I seem to have lost the ability to sleep soundly. Instead I sleep with one eye open. Some nights I lie in bed and play out scenarios of what I would do if anyone broke in or if there were a fire.

One evening a few years ago, I noticed that the sensors on our household alarm system were not working correctly. I called the people at the alarm system company and they said that the system needed to be looked at, but they could not come out until the next day. To prevent the system from signaling accidentally, I turned it off.

As I went to bed that evening, I was unusually apprehensive. Then, in the middle of the night, I woke with a start. I didn't know what caused me to wake up, but I sat up in bed and listened intently. In a matter of seconds, the beeping noise of the alarm went off. A few seconds later, it happened again. Someone must have been walking through the infrared beams downstairs.

I could hardly breathe. I didn't want to set the actual alarm off, because I didn't want the intruder to know I was aware of him. I also didn't know if the alarm would really work and call through to the police. I sat motionless for what seemed like forever. The beeping continued sporadically.

I very quietly called 911 and gasped that I thought someone was in my house. The dispatcher said she would send someone right out. I hung up and crept into the room of Lisa, my older daughter. My younger daughter, Lara, was in her usual sound sleep in her room.

Calm in the midst of trauma, Lisa got up and whispered comforting words as we both went back into my room. The beep was still audible every once in a while. Uncertain what to do, we finally decided to call a neighbor.

I picked up the receiver, and the phone was dead. Lisa and I looked at each other in utter fright. It appeared that someone had cut the line. We held onto each other, afraid to move.

When the police came, they rang the doorbell, and I dashed down the stairs. After searching, they were certain no one had broken in. The phone line was fine. They left. The beeping stopped. Lisa and I stayed together in my room and waited for morning.

The next day, the alarm service man fixed the system. He said that the batteries were low and were beeping to alert us that they needed to be replaced. He had no explanation for why the beeping stopped after the police left or why the phone had gone dead and then began to work properly.

My house was safe, and my sleep was not interrupted by

any of the imagined catastrophes that flooded my imagination. But even though the reality of security was present, the feeling of security was gone. During the nine years between Jack's death and my remarriage, I could never completely squelch that nagging sense of apprehension.

Most girls who live without their fathers feel some degree of that loss of security most of the time. They may have comfort with their mothers or other people, but that first, strong image of secure safety is gone.

Chapter 9

Swimming in Strange Waters

$\mathcal{R}$ay, a good friend of mine, used to delight in telling me about his eleven-month-old son, Grayson. Each morning, after Grayson cried from his crib, Ray would go into Grayson's room, bounce the young child, and lift him enthusiastically in the air. Both father and son enjoyed this early morning ritual, and both would laugh heartily.

Next, Ray would carefully place Grayson on the rail of the crib, holding him tightly with both hands under Grayson's arms. As Grayson steadied himself, Ray would very cautiously let go and hold his hands outstretched a few inches in front of the poised toddler. He would smile and coax Grayson to leap into his arms. Squealing with delight, the trusting child would fling himself into his father's arms.

Grayson was confident that he would be safely caught. Apparently, the young child never worried about landing on his face on the floor. He had total faith that his father would be there and would catch him. And that's the way fathers should be.

A MAN IS SOMEONE TO TRUST

Ideally, a father should be like Grayson's dad—the first male person that a child learns to completely trust. In a healthy, normal situation, a child can count on that.

A little girl's first experience with maleness is with her father. The interaction will affect her attitudes about men. If she can trust him as Grayson trusted Ray, she will have a positive early reference point in relating to men for the rest of her life.

If, on the other hand, a little girl finds she cannot trust her father, she may begin on shaky footing in her relationships with men.

If her parents are divorced, the whole issue of who daddy is gets complicated. If her father isn't there consistently, routines like that enjoyed by Grayson are interrupted. Even if a daughter had a wonderful relationship with her father, and it continues in some way after a divorce, the relationship is strained and unnatural. The role model has already changed from a man who is present to one who is absent.

More complicated still is the father who is physically there but emotionally distant. He might be able to be trusted sometimes, but he can withdraw without notice. Imagine the picture of Grayson with a father who sometimes answers Grayson's morning calls and sometimes does not. Sometimes he comes in and they play the jumping game. Sometimes he comes in and quietly takes Grayson out of bed and puts him down. And sometimes he doesn't come in at all. The male role model for any child who experienced this kind of paternal interaction would be twisted and complex, and it wouldn't be long before the child would distrust what his father would do.

Worse yet is the father who is emotionally, physically, or sexually abusive. Such a father can destroy a young girl's self-esteem and image of males.

If a girl's father is dead, she may not have a negative or frightening image of what a man is, but she may not know what it is like to trust a man. She will have to learn a process of relating that comes more naturally to a little girl with a trusting, loving father.

MEN = MY DADDY

Daughters aren't born with a preprogrammed mental image of what a loving father looks like. Instead, they learn men are what their fathers are, and through fathers, they learn what men are like. As daughters grow, they learn words and feelings that describe their fathers.

Of course, a little girl doesn't realize that all men are not like her father. That important distinction comes much later. But in her earliest years a girl considers daddy "nice," "kind," or "big"—or perhaps even "mean," "angry," or "scary." A girl whose father has died simply thinks, *My Daddy is . . . gone.*

In the early years, daddy is simply who he is, and a little girl learns to live with that. She may see that she is welcome in his lap when he comes home from work or that he likes to be left alone. She learns in what areas she can trust him and in what areas she cannot. Maybe she can call him in the morning to come in and wake her with a hug and kiss. Maybe he doesn't live in the same house with her and mommy anymore.

If a father isn't a consistent, loving presence in a daughter's life, a lasting impression is formed in her mind as she continues to revise her image of what men are. Even if she has other male role models in her life, she is most closely tied to her father. His projected image to her will influence how she views all males and how she views herself in regard to them.

OTHER FATHERS AND OTHER MEN

I remember the never-married woman in her thirties whose father and mother divorced when she was about five years old. Her sense of loss for her absent father was compensated by an overly idealistic view of other men.

She told me, *"I thought that anyone who had a father at home had a perfect father."* She went on to say that the most painful times in her childhood were when she was around her friends who had seemingly happy relationships with their fathers. As she watched bits and pieces of these relationships, she concluded that they were perfect. The feeling made her all the more sad that she didn't have that with her own father.

As this young woman entered her teens, she expected to

share some of this bliss in her relationships with boys. But her experiences were less than she hoped for, and her conclusion was that good things happened only to other people. She didn't realize that no relationship is perfect.

Now, as an adult, she knows that her beliefs were wrong. But her ability to change her expectations is greatly limited. As soon as she hits a snag in a relationship with a man, she is certain that the relationship is much less than what it ought to be and that she has—once again—been dealt a bad hand. It seems to her that good men come along for other women, but never for her. The absence of a healthy male role model early in life still creates problems for her in relating to any man.

THE SEARCH FOR THE PERFECT FATHER

Unfortunately, many girls define a model father as whatever they do not have. Like the woman mentioned above, they see only that what they lack seems to be given to others. They may observe their friends' fathers and envy what their friends have. Those fathers may become the ideal.

Even the ideal father is less than perfect. Instead of a daughter without a dad looking at other girls' fathers as the source of perfect fatherhood, she needs to look to God as her Father. Other girls' fathers are unavailable to her the way that they are available to their own daughters. And in their imperfection, they are probably not as wonderful as she may imagine. God is the perfect Father, and He is as readily available to the daughter without a dad as He is to the daughter with a human father.

Translating the image of God the Father into human terms is difficult. A man living up to that image is as rare and as wonderful as a woman living up to the image of the wife in Proverbs 31. But the standard set forth is not meant to imply that perfection can be reached. Because we are also finite in our ability to be perfect children, we experience that relationship imperfectly as well most of the time.

We must realize that no earthly man can fulfill the model given us by God the Father, and we must acknowledge that human fathers will fail us in many ways. But certain qualities of relationship between daughter and father should be present. Love, trust, acceptance, care, protection, and guidance should be present, even if imperfectly.

Many women define a model father by listing what he is *not*. He is not to be one who abuses, who shuts out, who neglects his responsibility to provide and care for, who ignores, or who hurts with unkind words and deeds.

An irony I have noticed is that daughters whose fathers have died often have better relationships with men than daughters whose fathers are alive. Part of that is because a deceased father does not hurt or disappoint his daughters. And even if he was less than perfect when alive, such memories may often perish with him.

When a girl or young woman loses her faith in the ideal of a model father, that ideal is often replaced by the model of an irresponsible father. Then she has two things to overcome: first, redefining the image of a healthy male along with the new model of a male-female relationship; and second, discovering how to heal the wounds of the possibly abusive male-female relationship she experienced with her father.

"BOYS ARE SOOOOO WEIRD!"

If girls aren't born with a preprogrammed image of the ideal father, they are born with even less information to help them figure out boys. Most often, girls think all little boys are a very strange breed.

That's normal enough. But little girls growing up without fathers have to unravel the mystery of boys without the benefit of a male perspective.

And not just any male perspective will do, either. Only a father can give a view of boys that takes into account that his daughter is very special. A divorced father living apart from a daughter can be really helpful here, but he still misses much of his daughter's sexual development and intense questioning by not living at home.

Many women I interviewed said that the hardest thing about being without their fathers was that their fathers just weren't there for significant incidents. By the time dad got there on a weekend, the confusing and troubling incident at school on Tuesday was old news.

One woman in her forties whose father died when she was a toddler compared learning about boys to learning to swim, with some major differences: *"It was like learning to swim in a pool with Mom as the instructor. The only other people in the pool were other little girls and their mothers. After learning to swim, Mom took me out to a big pool she called an ocean.*

"I was a good swimmer, so she let me go in some deep water. She was close by, and I felt pretty confident. But then the strangest thing happened. I was swimming just under the surface of the water and this other 'being' swam up next to me. It didn't have hands or feet but had a tail that swished around and moved through the water. It circled around me as if it wanted to play. But I didn't know what to do with it. It didn't look like I did, it didn't talk like I did, and I didn't know what it wanted.

"Mom explained that it was a 'fish.' It could swim in the ocean, too, and it was not anything that would hurt me. But I thought, How do you talk to a fish, or play with a fish, or just hang around a fish?"

For girls who have no consistent father figure around to interpret the "weirdness" of little boys, little boys might seem as strange as some unusual form of marine life.

Mothers can offer some insights, but they have a serious disadvantage. They don't think like little boys, and they never did. They can only guess about what is going on in those wonderful little boy minds.

I had no way to reasonably explain to my two daughters why little boys who liked them would hit them instead of saying something nice. I could tell them that that was the way it was, but I couldn't help them understand. I still can't.

Lisa and Lara and I have had many a laugh around the

kitchen table trying to understand the male creature. I have often thought that their father could have relayed useful information, whereas I could only shake my head and wonder with them at the strangeness of males.

Sometimes when boys hurt my daughters—or when men hurt me—we could only cry as we reflected upon the whys and wherefores of the matter. I remember staying up late one night with my older daughter after a boyfriend had really hurt her feelings. She was trying to decide if she should still go to the prom with him. As a godly mother, I had a loving and mature response to the situation. "Dump that jerk," I said, mustering all my maternal wisdom and insight. "Call up your friend John in New York and ask him to go to the prom with you."

She was so hurt that she considered my proposal. Thankfully, we made no decision that night.

The next morning in church I was sitting with a married couple who are good friends of our family. I told the wife, in a tearful but controlled way, what had happened. After the service she looked at me and started crying herself.

She said she could not imagine knowing what to say to her own daughters in a similar situation without the perspective of their father. We had a good cry, and I decided to let my daughter decide how to handle the prom. She wound up going with the young man who had hurt her. Meanwhile, I prayed for forgiveness of my anger toward him. They stopped seeing each other after the prom, so I didn't have to waste any more energy trying to figure out what motivated his inscrutable behavior.

When a daughter grows up without a father in the home, even the most normal male endeavors may seem strange. Since my girls became teenagers, we have had a lot of young people in our home. I am always amazed at the way boys— even big boys who otherwise act very grown up—love to wrestle around on the floor. They look to me as if they are going to kill each other. I get anxious and utter embarrassing warnings like, "Oh! Be careful." Meanwhile, they continue to throw each other across the living room.

It is tempting for single mothers to try to cut out all masculine influences and live in an all-feminine world. For such mothers, it might be easier to not allow boys to wrestle in the house, to talk judgmentally about boys when they hurt their daughters, or to categorize all men as "jerks" when there's no logical explanation for why they do what they do.

But such isolationism can be damaging to girls' development into caring young women who will be able to have healthy relationships with men. It is not really necessary for mothers to understand boys to teach their daughters to relate well to them. Principles of godly and loving behavior also apply to the mystifying behavior of boys.

"MY DAD DATES"

Teenagers who grow up in traditional families—with a mother and a father married and at home together—don't have models for dating. If they are fortunate, they have a model for a godly relationship between a man and a woman in the context of marriage.

But when a daughter's parents are divorced, she gets an up-close look at how her mother and/or father handle the dating game.

If the daughter lives with her mother, she has a bird's-eye view of how mom handles relationships with men. We will look at this situation more in the section on relationships between mothers and daughters, but believe me, it's an intriguing picture.

We will also consider how dating can affect the relationship between fathers and daughters, but for now it's important to realize that the way a father treats the women he dates—not just the way he treated his wife during their marriage—will say something to the daughter about how she is to let men treat her.

One divorced father told me that his daughter's relationship with boys had been largely determined by the way he had treated women he dated. His daughter would overhear him tell a woman he would call her, and then he would deliberately not call. His daughter saw him date several women at once, but she heard him tell each of them that she was *the* special woman in his life. His daughter would hear her father argue with these women and make promises to them that he never kept. His daughter, in turn, allowed boys to mistreat her. He said he lost his credibility with her in advising her to not allow boys to treat her badly because she saw him act the same way.

In short, parents can't expect a daughter to listen to their advice on dating if they do not live it out in front of her.

MODELS FOR MARRIAGE

Daughters without dads also develop unique ways of evaluating potential marriage candidates. For many girls, the most sensible place to start taking notes on the subject is their parents' marriage. Daughters weren't there for the process of choosing, but they sure are there for the living out of the results of that choice. And for many girls, this is a powerful training experience.

If the daughter gives her mom a passing grade for her choice of a husband, she may try to choose her husband in the same way. If the results were bad, she may make just the opposite choice. And both could be very poor ways to choose a husband.

In the case of death, often the daughter has an idealistic, and unrealistic, view of her father. Her mother may unintentionally perpetuate that image. Nothing seems wrong while in the process of keeping this positive image alive. It relieves pain, and it creates warm memories of the past.

The damage, however, comes when the daughter tries to follow her mother's example in choosing a spouse. Her evaluation of her father may have become so idealized over time that no *real* man could even meet her lofty demands. The higher the daughter's image of her father, the more unlikely it will be that any man can measure up.

If her parents are divorced, a girl may conclude that her mother made a bad choice in picking her husband. She may not be able to see that her father and mother were different at the time of their marriage than they were at the time of their divorce. She may determine to choose someone just the opposite of her perception of her father.

Without having the opportunity to see how a healthy marriage is lived out, daughters without dads may base their choices on trying to find the security they lack while trying to protect those vulnerable and painful things they do have.

Most of the women I interviewed fell into one of two categories: either they had unrealistic expectations of a man, or they lived with poor self-images, which were reflected in the kind of men they thought they would inevitably marry.

"God Wanted to Punish Kids, So He Put Them in Families"

Children in blended families—that is, children from two previous marriages joined in one new family—often have difficulties adjusting to their new parents and siblings. That was definitely the case of the daughter who told her mother, "God wanted to punish kids, so He put them in families."

This daughter did not dislike the man her mother had married the second time. But she could clearly remember the bad times when her father and mother were married, and she didn't want to relive them. The pain of a broken home can make marriage look pretty bleak.

A friend whose parents are divorced recalls the many times when she heard her mother and father having terrible screaming battles. She and her brother would hide in a closet and fearfully wait for each skirmish to end. When her mother decided to remarry, my friend was apprehensive about being in that situation again. Her only model of marriage was a fractured, distressful image. She certainly didn't want to live on a battlefield again.

Daughters whose parents had an unhealthy relationship can't accurately picture a good marriage. Most of them say they want a good marriage, but they don't know how anyone can have that, and they wouldn't know how to tell it if they saw one up close.

"I Want to Marry, but I'm Scared"

Many girls I interviewed were from divorced homes, and they repeatedly echoed one theme: "I want to marry, but I'm scared." Their predominant feeling about marriage was fear that they would have the same kind of marriage that their parents had.

Some adults I interviewed felt that their poor childhood experiences had led them to enter marriage with negative self-fulfilling prophecies.

One woman whose marriage had violently broken apart said, *"I always expected my husband to leave. My father left. And my husband left. I knew he would. Men leave."*

This fear prevents some women from marrying at all. If they have nothing to lose, they reason, there's no way they can lose it. If they don't marry, they can't have bad marriages.

The lack of a godly role model of marriage can produce protective behavior that robs women of fulfilling partnerships that *can* be different from the unhealthy and destructive relationships they may have seen at home. Or, they can enter marriages with so much fear that they miss how to have good relationships.

THE SEARCH FOR UTOPIA

The other side of the fear-and-negative thinking coin is utopian thinking—the belief that marriage can save one from bad memories, emotional scars, and self-examination, and that this marriage in particular will be the answer to the pain of life.

This thinking resembles that of the fatherless little girl who assumes that anyone with a father has a perfect one. A child who has grown up without a father and has not seen how marriage works may conclude that a good marriage means a perfect one. Like the girl with unrealistic expectations of a husband, she may have unrealistic expectations of the marriage relationship itself.

Then when the inevitable tough times come, she is disappointed. She wonders what happened. Her frustration mounts as she asks herself, *Why is this marriage not working out as I expected?* She has no frame of reference to fall back on in evaluating what is normal and what is not.

THE MYSTERY OF MEN

Girls who have had no godly model for marriage certainly have the opportunity to have good marriages themselves. But they have a few discoveries to make about everyday things that daughters raised in traditional homes take for granted.

One woman I interviewed lost her father when she was very young. She had two sisters and no brothers. She married a wonderful man, and she enjoys a fulfilling relationship. She talked of her first year of marriage with amusement: *"Men were a real mystery to me. I had no idea what it would be like to actually live in the same house with one. On our honeymoon, I found that men and women keep different things in the bathroom. It seemed so strange to me to see shaving gear. It just never occurred to me."*

This woman's experience was not negative—just different. She had never seen shaving gear in the bathroom.

After my husband died, I became acutely aware of some of these differences. For example, men don't smell like women do. It's not just the difference between after-shave and perfume. And it's not just the smell of sweat. There is a different scent about men that I never really noticed until it was gone.

I also noticed that men have deep, calm voices. After spending prolonged periods of time in a house full of females, I found that when I was around men, they sounded distinctly male.

How many more normal male traits would seem strange to a girl who has not been around her father and never been married? This lack of experience in living around men may necessitate a period of adjustment—and a sense of humor.

Daughters without dads may also have trouble evaluating how a prospective mate may fulfill the role of father. How will this man act as a father? And how will the fact that her children have two parents, instead of one, affect the way she is a mother?

The daughter is used to seeing her mother serve as both parents. What will marriage be like when the roles of mother and father are divided between the woman and the man? This mysterious person she now lives with will be fulfilling a role she hasn't seen lived out as it was intended.

FATHERS AND THE IMAGE OF GOD

God should inform all of our decisions. Ideally, we should base all our actions on a sound knowledge of the nature of God and what He wants for us.

When we define what fathers are, we should start with God and model a godly father after Him. But in reality, we tend to do just the opposite. We look at our earthly fathers and assume that God is like them. This is understandable, but in many cases it's unfortunate.

The older we are when we come to know the Lord, the more baggage and negative father imagery we have to get rid of. If a girl's only experience with a father figure has been the one of her distanced father, it will be hard for her to imagine God as loving and caring.

I spoke with one woman whose father died when she was little. She described God to me in this way:

"God could not be like my real father, because my real father was not there. I had no frame of reference when I thought about God. I thought of Him as a 'Holy Other.' There was just not enough skin on God."

This same woman talked of how she felt her relationship with God was frozen. Her father had died when she was six. She only knew how to relate to a father up to that age. How does a forty-year-old woman relate to a father? And how does an older woman learn to love God the Father after having experienced the painful loss of her own father?

Without a model for a loving father, a lot of translating has to be done to think properly about God as Father. We'll look at this also in the section on relationships.

REDEFINING FEMININITY

History shows us that the definition of the perfect woman is ever-changing. The perfect woman used to be Suzy Homemaker who devoted all of her time and attention to her loving husband and children.

Then the perfect woman was the business executive. Dressed for success and determined not to let sexual bias in the workplace stop her from achieving her ambitions, she charged into male-dominated boardrooms to exercise her will.

Next, it seemed that the perfect woman was a combination of the homemaker and the business executive. The magazine covers read, "A Family AND a Career: You Can Have It ALL!"

So, who is today's perfect woman? What we are told about the feminine ideal is, at best, confusing. Women have more options today about how they will live than they ever have before. There is no single socially defined norm. That may be good news in the freedom it brings. But it may also be bad news because of the uncertainty and tension it causes in many women's minds as they struggle to achieve some poorly defined goals.

Some of the college-age women I interviewed expressed this dilemma. They all want to have careers. Most of them also want to marry and have children. They feel freedom to do both—even if there is still conflict in the church on this issue—but realize the enormity of the challenge before them if they are to be successful in both areas. Along with the complexities of living several roles at once is the risk of losing who they really are as women.

Women are at war with themselves. In addition, as soon as they step out into society, they are torn between the conflicting roles of femininity others place on them. Hope Stedman, the character in the TV show "thirtysomething," exhibits these internal and external conflicts in episode after episode.

A woman can now be considered totally feminine while holding down a high-powered executive job. She can carry a briefcase and supervise men at work. She cannot, however, cry at a top-level meeting and still be viewed as completely competent. Is it all right for a woman to cry? Or is it acceptable only in certain situations? Is crying a sign of weakness or strength? Competence or dizziness?

It's a real mixed bag. And daughters without dads—lacking their intended protector, provider, and source of security— are forced to define femininity in isolation from one of the sources God intended in the shaping of feminine character.

MARY AND THE MODERN DILEMMA

For me, many of the trials and tribulations of daughters without dads were summarized in my conversations with Mary, who had struggled with the loss of her father as well as what it means to be a woman in today's world.

Mary's father divorced her mother when Mary was thirteen years old. She was the oldest in a family of three children and had to take on many of the household chores when her mother went to work. She gave up some school activities to be home for her younger brother and sister. She became like a parent to them because her mother was gone a lot.

One day at school, her brother got in a fight with a bigger boy and went to Mary for comfort. Mary took matters into her own hands and found the offending bully. She made it clear that she would cause the bully some problems if her brother were bothered again.

Mary developed a reputation of being a tough cookie. She had no father to defend her brother. She didn't go home and tell her mother what happened because Mary considered it settled. It was settled. But the result was that Mary, at a young age, began to be viewed as less than feminine.

Mary knew how she was perceived. She would cry alone

in bed at night about it. She hated the way boys teased her about how tough she was. But she never told them she cried. In many ways Mary was a very feminine young woman, but her femininity was never revealed to her friends at school. She didn't know how to express that side of herself and fill the role of protector to her younger siblings at the same time.

Eventually Mary achieved success in a demanding career as a patent lawyer. Many would applaud her as an example of a troubled person achieving triumph over adversity. But she continues to struggle with her self-identity as a woman. She yearns to be soft, loving, and vulnerable, but has no relationships to provide such outlets. She also denies these yearnings as incompatible with her image of someone who "gets the job done."

YOUR BOX IS TOO SMALL

Years ago the Christian scholar J. B. Phillips wrote a book entitled *Your God Is Too Small*. The book described the various incomplete images of God that some of us carry around in our heads, like "the kind old man in the sky." Phillips urged his readers to open their minds and allow themselves to come into contact with the real and living God who confounds some of our confining concepts of who He is.

In a similar vein, we can see that part of the reason for the confusion today about what is feminine and what is not is that we keep putting people into neat little boxes. We label everything, and then we draw conclusions based on those labels.

If a woman never cries, we call her tough and insensitive. If she cries at a business meeting, we call her weak and incompetent. If she wears man-tailored suits, she may project an image of unapproachable professionalism. But if she wears frilly dresses, we may call her flirty as we wonder how she could wear such inappropriate clothing.

It's not only women in the workplace who face such criticism. The woman who sees her calling as a modern-day Suzy Homemaker is ridiculed and belittled, and many ask themselves if the woman has even a portion of a brain. She may be a champion gourmet cook and have a spotless house, but some may call her "domestic," not feminine.

FATHERS AND SELF-ESTEEM

What's all this have to do with being fatherless? Simply put, fathers can be a solid source of self-esteem for growing and developing women.

Fathers who show love and acceptance for their daughters can help women define their personal identity. A girl who lives for eighteen years with an accepting father has a chance to be herself—which is a large part of being feminine—regardless of what the loud and conflicting voices around her are saying. She may have learned that it is OK to cry and be comforted and still know that she is competent. Her father's input may have given her the confidence to be what she wants to be regardless of the image conveyed.

Likewise, the absence of her father may have left her uncertain of who she is, placing her in a harsh arena to learn to survive as a woman.

THE CHURCH CATCHES UP

If there is confusion in the world, there is more in the Christian community. Even though the Christian ideal for the role of women has not changed too much, the reality of many women's lives has changed drastically.

There is a high percentage of working women—single, married, with children—in even the most conservative churches. Some of them may be in that situation by choice and some by necessity. But they are there—adrift in an institution that often tends to define femininity in terms befitting Suzy Homemaker—and they do not exemplify the ideal.

Does that mean they are not feminine? Or does the Bible allow for a broader view of femininity than that proclaimed from pulpits across our land? If the woman in Proverbs 31 showed up in your church next Sunday, would she be booted out because she is too industrious, too hardworking, and too contemporary?

This issue has caused many women to become frustrated. One woman told me she overheard some of her Christian brothers discussing her lack of femininity. The men complained that she was always "opening her own doors." She said, "Nobody gives me anything. I either open my own doors, or I get hit in the face with them as they slam shut."

PROBLEMS ON PARENTS' NIGHT

The single mother's attempts to get involved at her children's school can be upsetting.

My daughter, Lisa, graduated from a conservative Christian high school where her sister, Lara, is now a senior. Usually, when a parent wants to discuss something with school administrators (who, interestingly enough, are all male), the father goes to do the talking. But if our family wants to discuss something, I'm the one who goes.

Fortunately for me, the administrators at my daughters' school are gracious and receptive to me, although this is not universally true. These men allow me to express myself, yet I'm aware that some in the school view me as being overly aggressive. I'm aware that I'm perceived in this way, but I see my choice as either to speak on behalf of my daughters the same way their father would if he were here or to keep quiet and accept whatever comes our way.

My daughters have watched me be an active participant in several trying areas for over nine years now. It has affected the way they relate to friends and teachers alike. Like me, my daughters can seem very strong willed and even unapproachable at times. But we can't deny who we are, even though we risk being viewed incorrectly.

Sure, we're aggressive when we need to be. In the case of my daughters, they can be very aggressive on the basketball or volleyball court. This doesn't diminish our femininity, but it does challenge our confidence in how that is played out.

STANDING AS WOMEN BEFORE GOD

A woman who has grown up without the positive reinforcement of a loving father can realize that a large part of her femininity is defined in who she is before her heavenly Father. No matter what other people think or say, a woman can be completely who she is before God. He accepts her crying or screaming, mild or aggressive. She is always completely feminine with Him because that is how she was created.

Some things about women are distinctly female, such as their biological uniquenesses. Some reactions more commonly associated with women are not necessarily feminine at all, such as crying. But who a woman is as a created female being is always completely accepted before God. God may have allowed her to be in a role that appears less feminine than another role, but that does not make her less feminine.

So, what is femininity? Femininity is an attitude rather than a list of characteristics. It is accepting me as me and not being defensive about who I am. Sometimes I am aggressive. Sometimes I am weak. Sometimes I confront, and sometimes I back down and cry.

It is also accepting men for who they are. I don't think it is as important to define who they are with distinctive labels as it is to accept them—and accept them as different from women. A lot of books discuss the differences between men and women in terms of temperaments, personality, willpower, or genes. Such books are helpful in their way, but the true meaning of who we are doesn't depend on some formula. It depends on who we are as we stand before God. After we realize God has accepted us, then we can accept ourselves and others in a noncritical way.

The overall attitude that best reflects femininity to me is one of softness. Softness is not weakness or apathy. It is the manifestation of a meek and gentle spirit that flavors all of life touched by a woman who possesses it. It is the result of a godly confidence in who she is based on her relationship with God. She is not threatened by what people think or by the role she is called to live. She has a calm assurance that she is accepted by her Creator and therefore has little to prove elsewhere. God is the Author of this soft spirit, and He can create it—or re-create it—in any woman who is willing to stand before Him and ask for it.

Chapter 10

Links in a Broken Chain

*T*he highlight of any elementary school child's day is recess. For a few moments the cares of institutionalized learning are put aside for the joy of running free. The playground comes alive as children are allowed to be children.

Every playground that's worth anything has a swing set. Little girls learn early how to pump their legs to reach maximum heights. Pigtails flying, they lean back and take off.

Swing sets are basically very simple. There's the large angular metal frame. And there is the seat. And then there are the links of chain holding the whole thing together. As long as the child holds on and the swing stays on the frame, all is well. But what happens if just one link in the chain is damaged and breaks? As the chain separates, the swing comes unhooked from the frame and the once-trusting child is hurled to the ground. The result can be anything from a bit of a scare to a terrible accident.

The next time that child is on the playground in front of the swing set, her attitude will probably not be one of eager abandonment. And the once-loved swing set will be seen as an object of suspicion—not as a source of fun.

This change of heart toward the swing set is something like what life is like for the child who has lost her father. She had a source of stability that allowed for carefree abandon, but now that stability is gone and perhaps irreparably broken.

And like the child who has been hurled to the ground by the broken swing set with the broken link, she is more cautious. She has learned that her situation with her father is no longer completely safe. She learns to be careful.

She begins thinking about things that other children take for granted. And to the degree that she concerns herself with those things she is deprived of some of the whimsy of childhood. Her self-consciousness about her relationship with her departed father—like the youngster's memories of the fall from the swing—taints life a little and makes totally carefree moments a thing of the past.

OTHER LINKS IN THE CHAIN

Only one link of the chain had to fail for the whole swing to fail and the girl to fall. Likewise, a daughter who has lost her father becomes quickly aware that other links in the family chain—particularly her mother—hurt, too.

All the girls I interviewed for this book had the same response to the events following their father's disappearance: they felt responsible for their mothers. Most of them felt concern for their divorced fathers, but they didn't actually feel responsible for them in the same way they did for their mothers.

A young girl is hurt deeply when she sees her mother—her model of strength and nurture—crying. Although it may be healthy for a daughter to see her mother cry, it is still painful and often results in the daughter's taking on the responsibility for her mother's happiness.

I have seen this reaction in my own children over and over again. We have had many sweet moments just holding each other and crying. But afterward it seems that a tremendous sense of concern for me permeates their lives.

My daughters have never made plans with friends without asking if I had something to do. If I would be alone, they would ask me to tag along with them, or they would try to have people come to our house. They always know where I am and what time I am due home. If I am even a few minutes late, they worry.

Some of this caring is positive and contributes to young girls' growth into loving women. Too much of it, however, robs them of normal childhood abandon. Children have to realize that they are not responsible for a parent's happiness. They need to have the freedom to make mistakes and upset their mothers. They need to see that though things may not be smooth, their mothers will survive.

CARING FOR AN ABSENT FATHER

In general, daughters don't feel as responsible for their fathers as they do their mothers, but they surely don't want to upset them. One young girl who now lives with her mother and her mother's new husband told me how she has to be careful what she calls her father and stepfather to prevent hurting either of them: *"When I am around my real father, I have to be careful to call my stepfather by his name and not 'Dad.' When I am around my stepfather, I have to be careful to call him 'Dad' even though that is also what I call my real father. When they are both together, I have a chance of upsetting both of them."*

Another girl told me that her father now showers her with gifts. She accepts them gratefully but can't say much about them. Talking about them only makes her mother feel badly about not being able to afford equally lavish gifts. Sometimes the girl wishes her father wouldn't give such generous gifts, but she doesn't feel comfortable enough to tell him that for fear she would upset him.

Many girls feel responsible for keeping the peace between their parents. This is especially true if the father still lives at home but is emotionally distant. A daughter feels it her duty to be so good that her father won't get mad about anything.

Daughters in divorced homes often feel that they are walking on eggshells. One of the primary goals of girls I interviewed was to avoid upsetting anyone.

CARING FOR THE WEAKER LINKS

The oldest daughter in a single-parent home usually views herself as the caretaker of the other children, even if there is an older brother. She looks after the younger children, and she may even think about how she will care for them if her mother dies.

About five years after my first husband died, my daughters talked to a psychologist about death. He asked them what they would do if something bad happened to me. Lara, my younger daughter, was eleven at the time. She replied that she didn't know and the idea scared her terribly. Lisa, my older daughter, was fourteen. She calmly said that she would take care of her sister and her grandparents. She had already thought through what her role would be if that happened.

Children who feel responsible for the care of their parents and siblings experience great stress. The normal carefree times of childhood seem to disappear, and nearly every activity is viewed in light of responsibilities for other people. Before children are even old enough to care for themselves, they feel the burden of caring for others.

I interviewed one woman in her thirties who lost her father when she was a teenager. She described how she felt about her mother in these haunting words: *"She is the heartache of my soul."*

This woman's mother never remarried and never really adjusted to her husband's death. She lives with her memories and has a sad, lonely life. Her daughter sees no real solution to her mother's pain and simply grieves for her.

Many mothers recover and go on with life in a fulfilling way. Those who don't, however, are a source of sorrow for their families.

MOM UNDER THE GUN

The mother raising a daughter on her own no longer has the luxury of saying, "Go ask your father." When mother and father share child-raising duties, one parent often sends a child to the other parent to avoid dealing with an issue. When there is only one parent in the home, she has to handle all the issues all the time.

For me and many other single mothers, this unending sense of responsibility is the most difficult aspect of life without a husband and father. Sleeping or waking, at home or away, the buck stops with mom. And mom feels the pressure of being under the gun.

My responsibility for my daughters is all-consuming. I'm never far from a phone so they can always reach me. I wake in the middle of the night and run the long unending checklist that is a continual fixture in my mind. Whether the need of the moment is new shoes for school, shots for the dogs, soda pop for friends from school, or a new garden hose for the backyard—the responsibility is mine and mine alone.

I remember shortly after my husband's death, a girlfriend and I went away for a weekend so I could get a break from some of the details of my domestic responsibilities. But I didn't really feel removed from my many duties. I felt that I had to be available to my daughters, and this sense of responsibility prevented me from truly enjoying my brief time away.

Many nights I have sat alone in my bedroom and thought through weighty problems all alone, whereas when my husband was still with me we would have discussed them and reached a mutual decision. It is an intense, exhausting feeling to talk to only yourself and try to see all sides of a particular problem. I used to long for just a word with Jack—just five minutes to ask him if I were handling things the way he wanted. I would have given a lot to have his counsel and encouragement. As the years have passed, I've learned to decide on my own without the help of input from any outside source except the Lord.

My girls have seen me wrestle with these issues. They know not to bother me when I am in the middle of one of these great debates with myself. They give me a hug and go on with whatever they are doing. Sometimes when they hug me, I cry in utter frustration over wanting to do what is best and not knowing what that is. In those moments, I try to communicate to them that I am OK but that some things remain difficult even years after their father's death. I also try to let them know how comforting it is to me for them to hug me. They don't have to solve problems or make me feel better. Just to be there and care is enough.

Even in divorce, many more decisions have to be made by the parent the children live with simply because that parent is there on a daily basis. A problem may arise during a daughter's school day. She comes home and needs advice. Perhaps her mother can't decide on a proper course of action. Her mother tries to call the girl's father, but he is not home. When he does get home, he is unable, or unwilling, to help. He tells his ex-wife to work it out with their daughter.

I have heard many divorced women (and men) say their ex-spouses are completely different people from the people they married. Once-caring parents can become distant and unwilling to be truly helpful in the rearing of the children. After a divorce, it may not be possible to make joint decisions because of the damage done in the divorce.

The nonstop responsibilities can make life hectic for mothers. But mothers and daughters need to realize that over time a healthier perspective will return and life will go on. Not without pain. Not without other moments of heaviness. But with the assurance that all can survive with some of their happiness intact.

THE LONELINESS OF THE SINGLE MOTHER

Daughters without dads seem to miss their fathers the most in the recurring events of childhood and school. At the spring concert most of the dads are in attendance. Dads are heard from the bleachers at the basketball games. Graduation, the first day at college, and buying a first car are all events that dads usually participate in.

Of course, divorced dads could get involved, but few seem to take advantage of these opportunities. And even when they do appear, they aren't with mom anymore. I have sat at the back of many a school function and seen a mom on one side of the auditorium and a dad on the other. I wondered how the daughter felt with such physical distance evidencing the family split.

When dad isn't around or when mom has been widowed, a loneliness often overtakes the single mother's life, and it's a feeling shared by the daughter. All of the daughters without dads I interviewed mentioned how they look out in the audience or up in the stands and see couples sitting together and their mom sitting alone. When the event is over, people leave in groups—parents in couples, children in car loads—but the single mom goes out to her car and drives off alone.

This picture can be a painful one for the daughter who is leaving with her friends. Her good time may have a hint of sorrow as she thinks of her mom going home by herself. Sometimes, the mother can be a bit jealous of her daughter's carefree times of fun. Hopefully, the mother and the daughter can work it out so that the daughter still has her fun times with friends and the mother has her needs met, too. We'll talk more later about how mothers and daughters can work together.

LOST CHILDHOOD

When daughters lose their fathers, they also lose a piece of their childhoods. Growing up fatherless puts tremendous pressures on mothers, but it also exerts its toll on daughters. One consequence of fatherlessness is lack of stability, experienced as the feeling that at any minute things might break down or fall apart.

Loss of stability at home may lead to problems for the children involved, reported an article in *Health:*

A study conducted at the National Institute of Mental Health based in Rockville, Maryland, said:

"Each of 90 subjects had lost a parent when he or she was between 2 and 17, and nearly 80 percent of them had experienced psychiatric problems, including depression, alcoholism and a variety of anxiety disorders.

"Stability at home at the time of the death seemed to be the most powerful indicator of the child's mental outlook. . . . If the surviving parent was supportive, then the child had a strong chance of overcoming separation anxieties and insecurity in future personal relationships.

"Those who were the worst off had a surviving parent who somehow expected them to resume the responsibilities of the lost mate."[1]

Children living in the midst of instability learn to protect themselves. A certain amount of this is better than no protection at all. But becoming overprotective will cause them to miss much of life's fullness because they are afraid to experience any risk at all.

A healthy childhood environment should include a level of comfort and a feeling that nearly all is well. Children should know that what they need is available and reliable. When that stability is missing, problems occur.

LOSS OF BALANCE AND "NORMALCY"

A healthy and positive home environment with a loving mother and father can provide children with a safe and secure place to learn about the challenges of life in a balanced way. Life in such a home will have its share of tension, as mother and father express their varying views on a wide range of subjects. But hopefully, children can learn how to achieve balance and complementarity in their lives by observing the ongoing resolution of conflict.

In a home without a dad, some of that balance may be absent. Also, children continually hear at school what is "normal." If their situation is not considered normal, they may feel immense discomfort.

Girls I interviewed admitted that they do not like to talk to friends at school about a father's death or parents' divorce. The girls who had lost their fathers to death were every bit as hesitant to talk about it as the ones whose parents divorced.

I visited my older daughter a few months after she started college in her freshman year. When I asked her if she had told her suite mates that her dad wasn't living, she said no. She said she didn't know why she hadn't, but she didn't like to talk about it. All her friends had fathers at home, and she felt abnormal. She compensated by simply not talking about it.

Other girls whose fathers had died had the same reaction. The girls of divorce felt somewhat more comfortable talking with me about losing their fathers. Perhaps it has something to do with the acceptance of divorce today. Or maybe the specter of death makes anyone who hasn't experienced it at close range uncomfortable. Whatever the reason, it seemed easier for girls to talk with me about a father who is alive than one who is just a memory. None of the girls I interviewed felt comfortable talking about their fathers with peers.

MINIMIZING RISK, AVOIDING PAIN

I have always been a little apprehensive about flying. Before my husband's death in a balloon accident, I used to comfort myself with the standard bromides: "It will never happen to me"; or "The odds are that I will be safe"; or "Shucks, this airplane is safer than riding in a car."

After my husband's tragic death, those attempts at self-confidence building became hollow. The experience opened my eyes to the fact that often when we claim to be relying on God for our safety and security, we are actually casting our security on such things as odds, percentages, luck, and superstition.

But for someone who has suffered a severe loss, the ability to relieve any fear with any type of well-intended self-talk is gone. Fear must be faced head-on. What I fear has happened to me. I have lived through it, even lived through it well. But I wouldn't choose to live through a similar circumstance again. Knowing I have no choice, I have to face the fact that something painful might happen again. The plane I ride to visit my daughter at college might crash. A suspicious symptom might turn out to be a warning of cancer. And—of course—the person I love very much might die.

Grace and faith contribute to overcoming this fear, but for the child who has lost a parent, there may be years of fear as similar situations arise. Each girl I interviewed whose father had died feared for the life of her mother. Each one said that her greatest fear was the loss of her mother.

The girls whose parents divorced feared that they would make the same mistakes their parents made. They feared marriage because they feared divorce. What had already happened to them loomed in front of them as potential hurt in the future.

GOOD-BYE, HOME SWEET HOME

Although the U.S. divorce rate is close to 50 percent, many people still act as if the normal home consists of one father, one mother, some kids, plenty of apple pie, and tons of happiness. A recent *New York Times* article reveals that television shows have come to grips with the brave new world of families, even if the rest of us haven't:

> Laurie, who grew up in a home where you followed the bouncing pots and pans, watches every family show. Cosby is her favorite: "I never miss it. It's like watching 'Fantasy Island' for me. The wise and funny father; the understanding, cheerful working mother. The only major tragedy was when Theo got his ears pierced."
>
> Jane, who had seven stepfathers, loves "Dallas" because it makes her feel normal. Jane says, "The amazing thing is that everything that's happened on that show—adultery, betrayal, disappearance—has happened in my family."[2]

Laurie watched a show that was the opposite of her home situation. Her chance to experience "normal" was the half hour a week she lived vicariously through that fantasy. For Jane, "normal" meant watching a program that matched her life.

Both girls sought some way to identify with life around them. People need to feel acceptance, some sense that they are blending into society instead of standing on the outside looking in. A girl without a father loses much of what makes her feel like a normal American girl. She feels that her life is at variance with the accepted norm. Her childhood is different from that of her peers—or at least she thinks it is. And kids don't like to feel different.

APPLE PIE, MOM AND DAD, AND GOD

Ask most Christians what they think the ideal home is like and they'll probably repeat the recipe of father, mother, kids, and apple pie. But while the Christian church in the United States continues to present this picture of the ideal Christian home, reality is heading in another direction.

Furthermore, the ideal man is usually presented as a mature, godly, responsible father and spiritual leader. The ideal woman is usually presented as married, domestic, and submissive. What is the effect on children whose parents fail to fit that model? Are they to conclude that their parents aren't godly? How are they to view their place in the church? If they aren't part of what is normal in the church, what are they?

In the section on networks of relationships, we'll look at some answers to these disturbing questions. For now, let's be sensitive to the fact that daughters without the presence of loving, godly fathers have many questions raised in their minds by the everyday rhetoric of the Christian church.

Chapter 11

Missing Memories

*N*ancy was in college when her father died suddenly. After mourning his loss, her next thought was about her upcoming wedding. How could she have a wedding without her father? Who would walk her down the aisle?

Her father had talked about the upcoming wedding—about how proud he would be and how nervous, too. She had pictured the two of them participating in her ceremony. She knew exactly what it would have been like. But he was gone.

Nancy tried to make up for her father's absence by carrying remembrances of him with her throughout the ceremony. His college fraternity pin—a gift he gave her on her sixteenth birthday—was concealed in the folds of her wedding gown. And she had his photograph in her locket.

WHAT DADDY WAS LIKE

Nancy is not alone. All the girls I interviewed whose fathers had passed away responded with tears to my question, "What was your father like?"

One sixteen-year-old recalled her father in this way: *"Daddy was so big. He was strong and loving. After he died, no one ever seemed that big to me again."*

A fourteen-year-old girl whose father died when she was five years old said: *"I can't remember him really at all. Sometimes I think I do, but it is mostly from what other people have told me and from pictures. I felt guilty about that until just recently. Now, I feel OK."*

A graduating high-school student whose father died when

she was seven has disturbing memories of her father and mother: *"Daddy was gentle, kind, quiet. I can't even remember my mother before my father died. After, she was cold. I went to her the day he died to hug her. She said, 'Don't touch me.'"*

I also spoke to a single professional woman whose father died when she was in her late teens: *"Daddy always let me know I was precious to him. I remember one time he said something that hurt me. I finally went to him and told him. He cried."*

And a divorced woman whose father died when she was thirteen years old recalled her father's faithful presence: *"I remember so much. I felt like a princess with him. He always went to work late. He was not a morning person. But he was always home by 5:30 P.M. Being with us was important to him."*

All the girls had fond memories, partly because their fathers were loving and conscientious. Also, the men were Christians who had personal relationships with Jesus Christ. Thus, the daughters' fears or uncertainties about their fathers' souls were relieved.

These daughters viewed their fathers with the knowledge that they lived by principles based on a living faith in Christ and an adherence to God's revelation in Scripture. Of course, there are good fathers who aren't Christians, and they leave legacies of fond memories as well. But in the cases mentioned above, the fathers' spiritual commitment added to the daughters' sense of peace and love.

DIVORCE TANGLES MEMORIES

In the case of divorce, however, remembering daddy is more complicated. He is still alive. But remembering how he used to be may cause tensions to rise to the surface of a daughter's consciousness.

Adding to her difficulties is her observance of great changes in both parents, during and after the divorce. Certainly the biggest change is that the father used to be present, and now he is absent. The daughter may visit her father, but the very fact that he left indicates something serious in him has changed.

Janet remembered happy times before her parents divorced. On Saturdays, her father would take her and her sister on errands with him in the morning and then out to lunch. It was a special time for them. After lunch, they would go home and pick up Mom and all go out together.

After the divorce, Janet and her sister still saw their father on Saturdays. He would pick them up in the morning, and they would do errands and have lunch. After lunch, they would go back to his apartment and watch TV while he did "business" things. They wondered what their mom was doing at home alone. They wondered what their dad was thinking. He didn't talk like he used to. He wasn't mean to them—just quiet.

When they would go to bed in the guest room at their dad's apartment, they would both cry a little. Janet remembered what it used to be like—what he used to be like. She felt like a guest with her father. It never got better, and it never got worse. It was just a painful repetition of seeing him and not seeing him, of remembering how he used to be and trying as hard as she could to accept him just as he was.

THE EVOLUTION OF A MEMORY

Memories change over time. Realistic portraits of fathers give way to more idealized representations. Daughters who lost their fathers to death at an early age keep memories alive by pulling the memories along in step with their own lives. If dad was a sports enthusiast when she was six, she may remember him as the "coach of the year" when she is sixteen.

Many daughters without dads cling to larger-than-life-size representations of how fathers would act if they were around today:

"If Daddy were here, he would have told that teacher who gave me that bad grade on my spelling test what he thought of him."

Or *"If Daddy were here, he would have freaked out when I made that jump shot."*

"If Daddy were here" becomes a refrain mothers of these

daughters often hear. Perhaps the mothers use the same refrain themselves.

And whether they know it or not, other people contribute to images that may be bigger than life. It is a comfort to hear people talk about a loved one with great admiration. And death and time magnify reality.

My own daughters have an image of their father as a flawless man. He was a lovable person who lived life with a gusto that created a memorable presence. He was well loved by his friends and family.

When he was killed, there was a tremendous outpouring of love and support toward the girls and me. In the midst of that, we heard testimony after testimony of how Jack had touched the lives of many people.

They were wonderful words. I will always cherish and appreciate those expressions of respect for him. Over the years my daughters have held these thoughts close to their hearts, and the images have grown with them. Now, it is difficult for them to remember their dad as he really was versus how they think he was.

I'm glad my daughters have such positive feelings toward their father. The only danger lies in using an unrealistic memory as a measure of what any other man in the world is supposed to be. They have to remind themselves that it takes nothing away from their father to admit that he wasn't perfect.

When I make decisions, I have had to let go of needing to know what he would do if he were alive today. Jack died many years ago, when he was thirty-four years old. I don't know what he would have been like at forty-four or what he would have done when faced with what I face. I know how he related to his daughters when they were seven and ten years old. I don't know how he would have related to them in their teen years.

It can be a freeing experience to say, "I remember how he was. I can guess how he might have been today. But I don't really know. And I don't need to know." It is perfectly acceptable for a girl to think about what her father was like, as long as she occasionally acknowledges to herself that her perception of him may be inaccurate.

TRYING TO BRING BACK THE GOOD OLD DAYS

Nostalgia is a big hit these days. It seems that the most up-to-the-minute trend is dedicated to worship of the not-too-distant past. Everything from clothes to restaurants harks back to earlier days. My younger daughter has the same posters of James Dean that were popular when I was a girl. I know the lyrics to many songs on the radio today—either because the stations are playing a "classic rock" format or because new artists are producing remakes of songs from the sixties.

The times we remember and commercialize now are the times in which I was a teenager. The memories of those days are fond ones. But I have to remind myself that those wonderful days of the past are past. I can enjoy the memory but must not try to hold on to the way things used to be.

When things in the present are difficult and painful, it's natural for us to indulge the desire to revel in memories. It's a means of escape. But it can also be a way of attributing a level of attractiveness to the past that it never really had. And it isn't healthy.

Daughters who have wonderful memories of times with their fathers can easily fall into the trap of living in the past. Or they may tell themselves that the world of the past was the best world ever possible, and that such a pleasant life will never happen again except in the re-creation of their memories.

Oswald Chambers once said about death, "The Bible never allows us to waste time over the departed. It does not mean that the fact of human grief is ignored, but the worship of reminiscence is never allowed."[1] When does rekindling a pleasant memory become the "worship of reminiscence"? I believe this happens when thinking about the past is more of a focus than living in the present. When remembrance of the old prohibits enjoyment of the new, the past is exerting too powerful an influence.

DENYING THE PAST

Some of the women from divorced homes whom I interviewed could not really remember good times. The pain of divorce and the years of separation had erased the remembrance of any pleasant times from their memories.

Their memories were of fathers darting in and out of their lives. They had no reminder of consistency in their relationships with their fathers. Many of them accept their fathers as they are. They just don't remember how things used to be before their parents' divorce.

One teenager said she is always moving. Her parents divorced when she was a little girl. Both her mother and her father remarried. She and her sister go back and forth between the two houses all the time. She can't remember what it's like to live in only one house. Her situation has been so much a part of her whole life that she doesn't know how any other lifestyle works.

This loss of memory may contribute to an inaccurate picture of men, marriage, and possible relationships between men and women. The absence of happy and consistent memories may also contribute to a feeling of being abnormal. There is no frame of reference for positive and healthy relations between a man and a woman lived out over a period of years in one household.

KEEPING DADDY ALIVE

A few years ago, my daughter Lara developed a pattern that seemed unhealthy. For several nights in a row, she went to her room and looked intently through a photo album of pictures of her father.

I said nothing at first. I wanted her to feel free to express her sorrow over losing her father in whatever way she wanted. She always cried when she looked at the pictures. And she seemed to be developing a dependence on this nightly ritual of sorrow.

Finally, I asked her why she kept putting herself through so much pain. Her response surprised me. "I can't remember Daddy," she cried in real frustration. "I remember a lot, but I'm forgetting a lot, too. I'm so afraid I will forget what he looked like. I look at the pictures to try to keep a picture of him in my mind."

I hugged her, and we cried together. I could certainly understand. There were times when I couldn't remember what Jack looked like, either. If I couldn't remember at my age, how in the world could she remember someone who left her life when she was seven years old?

There is a feeling among survivors that they are somehow being disloyal if they can't remember something about a loved one who is gone. But forgetting doesn't erase what was there. Just because I can't remember something doesn't mean that it didn't happen or that it wasn't significant to me. This fact doesn't mean I am disloyal to the memory of my husband.

Daughters whose deceased fathers were believers have a tremendous advantage over those who are unsure of their fathers' eternal fate. And daughters who know the Lord will be with their believing fathers again—forever.

Lara and I talked of how she didn't have to keep a memory of her father alive because he is still alive. He isn't alive with us, but he is alive in heaven. And she will be with him again. She will know him, and he will know her.

She felt relief when she thought about this. I haven't seen her cry over the photo album since the night we talked. She sometimes cries because she misses her father, but she no longer feels pressure to remember something that is fading.

A peaceful, undisturbed part of me remembers life with my deceased husband. I don't always remember accurately, and some memories are seen as though I am looking through a glass very darkly. I know something was there, and an image remains—but I see through it. It isn't sharp and clear.

It may even fade as the mists of forgetfulness grow thicker with time. That's OK. The past is not threatened by my inability to remember it. It happened. It touched my life. And it continues to touch me. The essence of it will be mine again when I get to heaven. I don't know how that will work, but I know that it will.

THE GRIM REAPER

Although some memories are pleasant, there is one that chills the soul—and that is the specter of death. Until the Lord comes again, we pass from life to heaven through the shadow of death. The memory of death for a girl who has lost her father is a dark abyss in her past. Even with gracious experiences of the Lord at or after the time of death, there remains an element of darkness and sorrow that can raise questions for the survivors.

One woman I interviewed wondered what her father, who was killed in a plane crash, looked like when he was killed. She asked her older sister what she thought their father looked like, and her sister said, "Don't you KNOW? They identified him by his teeth. There was nothing left."

I still vividly remember one scene from the movie *Absence of Malice*, which I saw a few years after my husband was killed. The characters in the movie were having an intense conversation about a deceased friend. The dead woman had had an autopsy performed on her. One character said to the other, "Do you know what they do in an autopsy? They take huge shears and cut the person right up the middle."

I had to leave the theater. My husband had an autopsy. I wondered what that meant, but I never dared to ask anyone what it actually involved. I got my answer in that unexpected moment. I wish I hadn't heard it. It is a haunting memory that I try not to think about.

There is much written about how to help children handle death. In my experience it seems that both children and adults will remember dark images about death for years afterward. The images don't have to be damaging at all. They do need to be seen for what they are: painful memories. If they cause a person continued discomfort, they need to be looked at and dealt with.

CREATING NEW MEMORIES

The best cure for bad memories is the creation of new memories. This requires not only time, but also the commitment to live life again. For ex-wives and orphaned daughters that means living without a husband and a father in the picture. All of life seems to be divided into two time periods, before daddy left and after daddy left.

In the case of a deceased father, the memories of times before are sealed. They cannot be added to. With a divorced dad, memories are still connected to a living, breathing man, but the memories cannot be added to as before.

I recently attended a wedding of a young man whose parents are divorced. The mother has remarried, but the father has not. After the ceremony, the photographer had the family get together for a family portrait. It seemed strange to see the mother and the father together with their children—creating a new memory in a situation so different from the way things used to be. They were together for the picture, but the family was forever separated.

In death and divorce, there is an empty spot in photos— and in the gentle hearts of daughters without dads—that needs refilling. A daughter needs to accept the fact that creating memories with dad is a part of history. Then she can get on with the business of making new memories.

"I MISS DADDY"

It was about 1:00 A.M. when the silence of the night was interrupted by the telephone ringing next to my bed. I answered it apprehensively and heard my older daughter, Lisa, sobbing on the other end of the line. She is in college in California and calls me frequently, but not in the middle of the night—and not when she is sobbing uncontrollably.

I sat up abruptly and tried to think. She couldn't talk clearly. My heart was racing as I waited for her to tell me what was wrong. After what seemed like a terribly long time, she squeezed out three simple words: "I miss Daddy."

This happened eight years after her father's death. I asked her what had caused her feelings for her father to have been so stirred up. She told me she had heard the song "My Father's Chair," which poetically captures the emotional devastation of a father's early death and the child's search for the comfort in the arms of his favorite chair.

Lisa still felt the pain of her father's absence as if it were her first night without him. And what hurt her the most was that her father wasn't there to hold and comfort her. She missed him deeply, and the evocative image of the empty chair was one she could picture with emotion.

There is nothing to do to take away that kind of pain. The intensity of it passes, and we can go for long spells when we think of a loved one fondly but not painfully. Then the pain returns, then it leaves, only to return again when we least expect it. This cycle of pain and forgetting is a natural part of missing a loved one.

A FATHER'S SHADOW

Loudon Wainwright III regularly contributes to *Life* magazine. Not long ago he wrote about the continuing presence of his father in his life, even though his father died when Loudon was seventeen: "A few years ago I saw a collection of old home movies that my father had made in the mid-thirties. Since he had held the camera, he never appeared in the films, although his long, afternoon shadow occasionally fell across the scenes he shot. But his presence and the way he thought about some things and how he felt were extraordinarily evident."[2]

The remembrance of a father—and the uncanny sense of his ongoing presence in a survivor's life—is like a shadow falling across one's path. The only difference is that a shadow, unlike the person himself, cannot be felt or heard or hugged.

There is no substitute for the presence of a father who is now gone. A mother may remarry, and a daughter may have a fabulous relationship with a stepfather. But the presence of her natural father is still a loss.

We miss people because we loved them. Even though it is painful to relive tender memories or suffer again the sad sense of loss, how much sadder it would be if a father left and his absence was not felt with sorrow.

SHARING THE EVENTS OF LIFE

"I should have been at more of her school functions," said Joe, a divorced dad with one daughter in high school. Joe lives in the same town as his daughter and ex-wife, but he has very little contact with his daughter. As he put it, "I'm busy. She's busy."

But even though he has rational-sounding defenses for his absence from his daughter's life, he regrets that he wasn't there more for her. He went on to tell me that he now sees how significant it would have been to attend events important to her.

Sometimes parents think that their participation in their child's life is not needed or wanted. Many teenagers attempt to avoid tension between their parents and tell one or the other parent, "You don't need to come to my game (or the concert)." But when the parents don't come, the child feels disappointed. Who wants to perform for no audience? What audience is more meaningful than parents?

The women I interviewed who seemed to handle their situation the best were those whose mothers and fathers actively participated in their events.

WHERE'S FATHER NOW?

Amy saw her dad on weekends. During the week, she spoke to him occasionally on the phone. But Amy didn't know what he did. Sure, she knew what kind of job he had. She knew the address and phone number of his office. She even knew what car he drove, where his apartment was, and where he went to work out. But she didn't know what he did in the "in between" times.

She asked him once about his evenings. He said he read or watched TV. She could remember him doing that when he lived at home. When he had been at home, he would let her sit with him while he read. She had trouble picturing him alone. She had more trouble picturing him with another woman.

Finally, Amy stopped picturing him altogether. She accepted her time with him on the weekends. She knew a few biographical details. Beyond that, she just didn't know. And she tried to convince herself that she didn't care.

Absence creates distance in a relationship. If a daughter doesn't see her father like she used to, she sees something else. Usually she sees her life without him. What he does away from her is lost in vagueness. Who he really is may become more and more of a mystery to her. As her father becomes more mysterious, she loses a part of her past and her present.

FATHER'S IN HEAVEN

For the daughter whose father now lives in heaven, there is comfort in the midst of pain. He is absent from her but present in paradise with the Lord. It is as if he has gone on to a wonderful vacation spot that she will visit sometime in the future.

Heaven is a precious, personal place to those who have a loved one there. It is not quite so far off as when its occupants were unknown. The image of it varies for each girl, but the thought of it brings both a smile and tears. Exactly what it is like is not as significant as the knowledge that it is the place where her father lives.

A few years ago I sat by the bedside of a dying friend. He was unable to talk or respond. But as I tried to convey part of what he had meant to me, it occurred to me that he would soon be with the Lord. I felt no sorrow for him. He was ready. He loved the Lord and had served Him honorably.

While I pictured him meeting the Lord, I also imagined him meeting my husband. They had never met this side of heaven, but I felt certain that they would meet on the other side. I had a moment of envy.

It is a sweet union that the Spirit allows for those who suffer loss to share with those who are going home. This man's body had all but wasted away, but I could almost hear his soul rejoice at what was ahead. None of us look forward to death. But the other side of death is what life is all about—to arrive home.

The reality of heaven and the bittersweet emotion it evokes in no way take away from the pain and ugliness of death. Looking forward to glory doesn't take away from the difficulties of living here today. But having an experience with death can help a believer develop a healthy perspective on what is truly important and what is not. Missing someone who is in heaven can allow a person to more fully appreciate people who are present today.

Chapter 12

The Absentee Father

*W*hile many daughters are affected deeply by the loss of their fathers to divorce, death, and emotional distancing, many daughters suffer from another kind of loss. These girls have fathers, but they seldom see their fathers at school events. They don't get to spend any time with them in the evenings or during the weekends. These daughters have fathers, but the fathers have something that seems more important than caring for their daughters—a job.

A FATHER'S PRIORITIES

We have all heard sermons on the priorities of life for the Christian man: God first, family second, and work third. But the reality for many men is that work is in first place. It may be in first place out of deliberate choice, but more often, it claims top priority out of necessity. These men are bound to their jobs and depend on it for their own and their families' security. With so much dependency on their work, it's only natural that family and God struggle for second and third places, and the rest of life falls into a distant fourth and beyond.

Men who are in the pastorate or work for Christian organizations have an additional factor complicating their personal priorities: *ministry*. *Ministry*, loosely translated to mean the "work of the Lord," makes the contradiction between priorities a little more confusing. Work that is deemed "ministry" seems to carry more weight than work that somehow is "not ministry," such as working as a butcher, baker, or computer maker. Therefore, many fathers working in professional ministry think the priorities of God first, family second, and work third don't apply to them.

DAD'S TRAPPED

What is a committed Christian father to do? He has a family that is supposed to hold priority over all in his life but God. He has a job, perhaps a ministry, that is to fall in line behind the needs of the family, but it makes screaming demands on his time and energy.

Yet his work is the very vehicle providing the financial means for him to take care of his family. If he loses his job, or jeopardizes it by spending less time, his family will suffer from the lack of income.

Many men have admitted to me that they don't spend the time with their families that they think they should. But they don't know what to do about the growing demands of their jobs.

Many jobs are not static. As they say in the business world, "You're either on your way up, or you're on your way down." Many men struggle with the issue of career development. They want to increase their responsibility, their esteem—and yes, their pay. But doing so requires ever-increasing amounts of time and dedication to work.

Adding additional pressure is the necessity for travel in many occupations. Many Christian organizations, as well as secular ones, have large travel budgets and conduct much of their routine business across many miles.

Christian business leaders often give devotional messages on the importance of the family while sending men away from home for company business. Such hypocrisy seems inexcusable, but then these leaders are often just as trapped as the employees they oversee. The demands on them are usually greater than those on the men they supervise.

VICTIMS OF HYPOCRISY

A few years ago I was in the office of the school my daughter attends. The daughter of a Christian businessman was there, too. One of the office workers wished the girl a happy birthday. The girl thanked her and said something about a family celebration that night.

"Oh, are you celebrating with your family?" the office worker asked.

"Yes," responded the girl, "except for my dad."

"Is he out of town?"

"Oh, yes. He hasn't been home for my birthday in about five years," the girl said matter-of-factly.

"That's too bad."

"It really doesn't bother me. I'm used to it," the girl said with no visible emotion.

I wondered to myself what it must be like to be the daughter of such an absentee father. The situation must have bothered the young girl more than she admitted. But I can understand why she would voice no objection. Her father is a committed Christian leader in a Christian organization. She has probably been taught that what he does is for the Lord and the family should willingly sacrifice their time with him for the good of the ministry.

Many Christian women endeavor to maintain that attitude and model it for their children. Criticizing "ministry" seems so close to criticizing the Lord.

Daughters—and wives—in this situation feel trapped. And so do the men. Men who are not aggressively committed to their jobs tend to be viewed as losers. Their opportunity to advance in their work may be impaired if they aren't willing to go the extra mile—or two thousand.

Technology doesn't give fathers more time. New gadgets that promised to make life easier have only increased productivity demands. Federal Express and other companies gave us overnight delivery service, but the ability to "get it there overnight" only seemed to intensify the tension in many men's jobs. Now, with the advent of facsimile machines, men fret over getting it there within the next fifteen seconds!

Many fathers are caught in the world of work, and they have difficulty balancing its demands with those of their wives and children. The victims are everywhere: fathers who don't fully enjoy their families; mothers who feel slighted by their husbands; and daughters who feel that they have no place in a busy businessman's world.

DEALING WITH
CONFLICTING EMOTIONS

Christian daughters are taught to honor and obey their parents. And they are told to be submissive to their fathers.

But daughters also know that their fathers are given commands in the Bible—commands about how good fathers should treat their wives and daughters. When daughters see their fathers failing to live up to these biblical instructions, they feel anger, guilt, and other confusing emotions.

For daughters of fathers in ministry, the troubles can be worse. They have been taught that serving the Lord is a good and godly thing to do, and they know they live without a lot of their fathers' time and attention because of those demands on them in serving the Lord. These daughters feel guilty for feeling angry, so they suppress these feelings, only to have them surface again.

For these dadless daughters, the behavior of their fathers is teaching powerful lessons about themselves, about their importance and self-esteem, about God and God's work, and about their fathers. These daughters may sincerely feel that their fathers don't care about them. But haven't they been taught that saying words against a man of God—particularly a father—is unspiritual and selfish and maybe even rebellious?

One conclusion such daughters may reach is that God cares—but God cares most about their fathers' work, and then about families and—maybe last of all—about the needs of daughters. They may also conclude that fathers who choose the wrong priorities are really normal after all. The problem—these girls think—is with women and daughters who demand too much. Certainly such attitudes will spell themselves out in future relationships with men.

Unfortunately, many families fall victim to fathers with

misaligned priorities. And amazingly, such families are the source of men whose ministries seem to flourish while their own families languish for lack of support and attention. Surely God cannot be pleased when His servants fail to give proper attention to others in their lives who deserve their time and commitment.

WHAT CAN BE DONE?

The father's attitude makes a difference. Most of the men I know in the situation described have wonderful attitudes toward their daughters and have a sincere commitment to them.

Although these men may not be able to do much about the amount of time they are out of town, when they are home, they are really home. They attend school functions and are involved actively with their families.

Ideally, men would have the option to have more to say about the amount of time their jobs require. That won't happen, though, until leaders in individual organizations are willing to make changes that would initially cut their productivity or increase their staff. Changes of that magnitude take time to institute.

A daughter who experiences negative feelings about her father's commitment to work should be encouraged to talk about how she feels. The circumstances might not change, but she might have a better understanding of what her father faces. Her father would also have the opportunity to reinforce his support of his daughter, even though he is seldom home.

Sometimes families need the presence of the father so much that he might need to consider a job change. I know of one man who did this to be at home during his youngest child's last years in high school. It is a heart-searching decision to make, especially after years in an established position. This particular man was able to transfer within the same company. Such a decision may be very rewarding in terms of results. Yet even when results are not as anticipated, the man will have peace of mind if he is certain that the Lord wants him home more.

Loving and open communication among family members can ease some of the stress of a father's frequent absences. Children can be relieved of guilt over their feelings, and the father can more effectively communicate that he is aware of the frustration and wants to make the best of a tough situation.

NETWORK OF RELATIONSHIPS

Chapter 13

Life in a Labyrinth

The labyrinth spider is a creative and industrious creature that spins an intricate dual web system providing him with one place to live and hide out as well as another place to ensnare insects. One web is a well-ordered structure with threads of silk extending out from the center like spokes of a wheel. These spokes are then connected by concentric lines of silk that go around and around. It looks much like Washington, D.C., looks from the air. This geometrically pleasing web is the labyrinth spider's home.

But next to this attractive and efficient-looking home is another, less inviting web. The spider spins this tangled web that is a shapeless jumble of sticky threads. This is his trap for unsuspecting insects.

In a similar way, when a family structure is dissolved by death or divorce and separate households are established, the new lifestyle resembles the confusing mixture of threads created by the dual system of the labyrinth spider. The original, simple family structure is complicated by a tangled and sometimes sticky network of relationships called a "blended family." Two or more households are combined to create a blended family, as in the case of a divorced man with children who marries a divorced woman with children.

A daughter in a blended family has memories of the familiar, well-ordered family unit where she used to live. But now she has a new family, consisting of a stepfather, new brothers and sisters, and a whole new set of relatives and associates. All of the people in this network are called upon to blend together. The tangled web of relationships can make life complicated—but not impossible. In this section we'll talk about how to live and grow in this new environment.

If a daughter loses a father and her mother does not remarry, her situation is different from that of a blended family. If she is in a home where her father is emotionally distant, she also does not have the blended family network to deal with. Her family web is now smaller and more compact. We'll also look at that type of family.

BLENDED FAMILY 101

A first grade teacher gives her class an assignment in drawing. She asks the students to draw pictures of their families, including grandparents and pets.

Brenda begins by drawing a stick figure of her mother. She then draws a stick figure of a man next to her mother. This is her father. Next to her father is another figure of a woman. This is her father's new wife, Brenda's stepmother. On the other side of her mother she draws another figure of a man. This is her mother's new husband, her stepfather. Below and between the figures of her mother and father, Brenda draws a figure of a little girl. This is Brenda. She draws a smaller girl figure next to her, her sister. Next to her sister she adds a figure of a little boy—her father's new wife's son—her stepbrother. And next to the figure of herself, Brenda draws a big boy and a little girl—her mother's new husband's son and daughter—her stepbrother and stepsister.

Brenda has met other older people who are the grandparents of the stepbrothers and stepsister, but she cannot figure out where to put them on her drawing. She puts figures of her own grandparents above the figures of her parents.

Even the pets in Brenda's family have changed. Brenda's family used to have two dogs named Frick and Frack. When her father and mother divorced, her father took Frick, and her mother kept Frack at home. So now, Brenda draws a figure of a dog below the stepchildren of her father and another dog next to the figure of herself. Her stepmother has a dog, too, but Brenda is running out of room to draw Ralph.

A new animal in Brenda's blended family is a cat named Spike. Spike belongs to Brenda's stepfather's ex-wife, but comes to stay with Brenda and her mother and her mother's new husband and Brenda's sister when Brenda's stepfather's ex-wife goes out of town and needs a place to leave the cat. Brenda draws Spike on the lower right-hand corner of her paper because Spike only visits sometimes.

Sound ridiculous?! Many children live this scenario—and sometimes a more complex one—day in and day out.

WHAT'S WRONG WITH THIS PICTURE?

When a girl like Brenda looks at the drawing of her family, she may feel as if she's looking at the labyrinth spider's tangled, sticky web. What does the jumble of lines and characters make her think about herself? Who is she in the midst of such a mob?

Brenda is a daughter, a sister, a stepdaughter, a stepsister, and a grandchild. Her family network has become crowded. And she may be pressured to play many more roles than she knows how to play. She genuinely wants to please both her mother and her father. But now her mother and her father may have very conflicting desires. Her father is remarried and wants Brenda to treat his new wife like a real mother. But when Brenda acts lovingly toward her stepmother, she hurts her biological mother. If she acts cool toward her step-mother, she displeases her father.

Brenda was the older child in her family before her parents divorced. Now, her stepfather's son lives with Brenda and her mother and sister. He is older than Brenda, so she has lost the security of her senior position in the family hierarchy.

Her sense of identity is completely disturbed. She is no longer the daughter of one mother and one father with one younger sister. She is not the firstborn child in the household. She is not even the primary caretaker of her beloved dogs, since Frick and Frack have been separated and blended, too.

For Brenda and millions of girls like her, thinking about their identity in a complex network of interrelated people may seem overwhelming. With time, understanding, and loving support, a new sense of identity can provide security; in the meantime, however, adjusting to a new family web can be a trial.

SENSE OF CONTINUITY

Valerie, a divorced mother of three, told me about the impact her divorce was having on her children. They were experiencing some of the usual tribulations, but Valerie had one problem in mind: she was sorry that her children would not grow up with a sense of family history, community, and continuity.

She and her husband had divorced when the children were in elementary school. His parents lived in another state, and after the divorce, Valerie couldn't afford to send the children to see their grandparents. Eventually, they lost touch. Her children grew up never knowing much about half of their heritage.

We look back to our heritage to see where we came from. And we use the stability it gives us to look forward and imagine what we will become. In this sense, life is like a river. It flows through us from our parents and other ancestors to our children and future grandchildren. But Valerie was concerned about what happens when we are moved out of that lineage.

Girls in blended families expressed their feelings of being somehow disconnected from this stream of life. They told me that their lives felt more like a stagnant pool or wildly racing rivulet, not a strong, steady stream of continuity and stability.

MY BAGS ARE PACKED

I've traveled a lot in the last few years, and I'm always surprised at the number of young children traveling alone. With the rise in the divorce rate, so goes the rise in children going back and forth between their separated parents.

Most of the children I see appear to be seasoned travelers. They navigate complex airport terminals as if they were playing a simple game of hopscotch and seldom display fear or confusion. This is fortunate since commuting has become a part of their lives. But it is evidence of lives with heavy burdens when young children are required to shuffle from coast to coast as easily as they walk to the corner for the school bus.

Many of the girls I interviewed said they never felt really settled. Even if their fathers lived in the same town as their mothers, they were always packing and unpacking for their regular weekend visits.

One divorced father remarked that his son, after years of traveling between both parents, finally felt that he had a home when he went away to college. Although many college kids feel they have left a source of stability when they leave home, this young man had a new sense of stability by getting his own place and not having to visit back and forth all the time.

If kids are traveling, so are parents. One teenage daughter said, "Daddy is always coming or going." She described her father as always on the move. Even when she spends the weekend at his apartment, she sees him as a transient person. "He picks me up, we do stuff, he brings me home," she said, matter-of-factly. "He comes to my mom's house for only a few minutes, leaves, and then comes again the next weekend."

It isn't necessarily a father's fault that the pattern of his life is one of motion. He is caught between two households, too. It does, however, add to the sense of constant motion for the daughter as well.

MOVING IN A MAZE

The complex network of people that grows and develops around a daughter without a dad often involves lots of move-ment—and movement without clear direction. When new people enter the once-stable family home, territorial rights are challenged. And when children visit separated parents, they, too, invade territory—the home territory of the second family. It's like moving in a maze. Children are moving, but they can't really see the end of their journey and they bump into walls every now and then.

The home a daughter grows up in provides many comforts and constants, even if the home also has its share of tension. There she learns what is acceptable to people in her home and what is not. After a divorce, those things acceptable in her home may not be acceptable in the new home of the separated parent. It may mean running down some dead ends before she can learn the new rules for her new home and the people who live in it.

MISSING LEAVES ON THE FAMILY TREE

If life is a labyrinth for the daughter whose parents are divorced and remarried, it may be an island for the one whose father is dead or emotionally distanced.

Following her father's death, a daughter may find that she and her mother are up against the world. If her mother has to go to work, the sense of isolation is even greater. While the daughter of divorce may long for privacy, the fatherless girl may long for the companionship her father once provided.

The daughter of an emotionally distant father may feel like

her family has lost a major branch somewhere. The people are there who are supposed to be, but the energy is not. It may seem as if some of the leaves on her family tree are dying.

LOOKING AT FAMILY WEB PATTERNS

People who know their botany better than I do can read the age of a tree from looking at its rings. Likewise, many of the blended and upended families we see every day bear the signs of growth and struggle.

Being aware of and understanding some of the elements in the web of relationships that daughters without dads face will enhance their ability to live well. Although a spider's web looks sinister to us, it actually provides a good home for the spider. A complex network of relationships may look unwieldy, but its fabric provides an opportunity to grow in healthy and challenging ways.

Psychologist Glenn Clingempeel, who has studied stepfamilies, says that they can bring benefits to their members: "Ambiguity is a potential stress, but it also gives people new roles and new freedoms. Negotiating these roles and relationships promotes greater problem-solving ability."[1]

In the rest of this section we'll look at ways to negotiate the blended family's busy and confusing intersections.

Chapter 14

Daughters and Mothers

$\mathcal{D}$uring the nine years I was a widow, people called me "Mrs. Mowday," even though I was single. Most of the divorced mothers I know are also called "Mrs." People, especially kids, find it hard to think of someone's mother as "Miss" or "Ms."

Although the title of Mrs. may remain, the other advantages of being a wife drop quickly away. Whether his disappearance is due to death or divorce, the person that mom lived with is gone. And that person was much more than a mere boarder in the house. He was her husband, her mate, her mystically united partner. Even if parents had an awful marriage, they still had—at some time—been one.

Although a single mother's primary concern may be her children, she has some significant needs of her own as well. She has suffered a loss that requires healing. The cares and frantic activities of single motherhood may veil these pains for a long time. As a result, people around her, including her children, may assume she has successfully put to rest her needs in deference to the needs of others.

Mom may even begin to swallow her positive publicity and fall into the mistaken belief that she has been healed. But sooner or later, sleeping dragons wake and breathe anxiety into a husbandless world. Recognizing some of these unseen needs can enable her to better adjust to her new life.

I STILL FEEL MARRIED . . .

Remember when you were in elementary school and summer vacation rolled around? Those first summer days meant the beginning of sleeping late, playing all day, and relaxing after dinner instead of hurrying off to bed. It was great, but sometimes all that relaxation took some getting used to.

Before adjusting to the change, for example, you might wake from your restful sleep with a start, bolt out of bed, and panic at having overslept. Only after getting your feet into some socks might you realize that school was over for the year and summer vacation was in full swing.

It takes the same kind of adjustment to go from being married to not being married. A widowed friend told me that she would wake in the mornings soon after her husband died and momentarily think he was still there. Sometimes she would roll over in bed at night and expect to lean against his sleeping body. She was not wishing something or pretending something that was not true—she was just responding in the way she had for years.

After a divorce, a person has an even harder adjustment to make. The ex-spouse is still around, and if the couple have children, there is still contact with that ex-spouse. A divorced mom may still have to consult her children's father. What a tangled web of feelings this can create!

. . . BUT I'M SINGLE AGAIN

People who feel married have trouble adjusting to being single again. I remember the first time someone in our church asked me to go to a singles' class. I was surprised to be asked. I had never thought of being a candidate for a singles' class. I was a widow, yes, but I still felt married.

Sometimes, as time passes, life's new events begin to wash away this illusory state. The widow who wakes and thinks her husband is still there stops having that reaction after a while. She gets used to being alone. I got used to people thinking of me as a single, although I never felt that way.

While a mother is getting accustomed to being single again, her daughter also needs an extra measure of mom in the absence of dad. The single mom must juggle both her own deep needs and the new, increased needs of her child. That may require making some changes.

MOM'S OTHER FEELINGS

When I was trying to adjust to single life and attempting to meet my daughters' needs, my attorney gave me sound advice. I had been in a meeting with him and some businessmen who were helping me sort through my deceased husband's business concerns. They had advised me to make a list of all the things I had to do. As the list grew, so did my anxiety.

We broke for lunch, and my attorney pulled me aside. "Lois," he said, "you need to quit worrying about us. If you need us to clear out and give you time, say so. If you are upset with us, go ahead and get it off your chest. We aren't under the pressure you are. We can handle much more than you can."

His words were a great relief. There were times in the months that followed that I took his advice. I allowed myself to change my pace if I needed to, to put off some things that I could put off, just so I could rest or feel tired.

Many of the feelings single mothers experience remain invisible to other people. That doesn't mean they don't exist. I find that one of the best ways to handle overwhelming emotions is to give myself a break—physically and mentally. I can still be a responsible person and a good mother without being all things to all people.

Daughters and mothers need to recognize that there will be times when emotions on both sides will cause them to be irritable. That's when it's time to put things on hold, relax a little, and regroup later.

STILL A MOTHER

Motherhood is a tough role to fill. As Barbara J. Berg says in *The Crisis of the Working Mother*, "It is an ideal against which we are forever measuring and judging ourselves."[1] I think it's harder for a Christian woman because the measure for her seems to be one step above an angel, with ample portions of saint, doctor, psychologist, and coach mixed in.

While they endeavor to measure up, one characteristic of the ideal poses real problems for single mothers: the idea that the good Christian woman stays at home with her children. The evangelical prohibition against women in the workplace has softened in recent decades as the number of Christian women at home has decreased. But for many women in Christian churches across the country, it remains the same: "If you work outside the home you are forsaking your first calling. You are stepping out of line. You are violating God's law. You are a sinner."

There are exceptions, of course, but many working women carry around a big load of guilt, even if they work because of financial necessity. Just because they work doesn't mean they aren't good mothers, however. Sirgay Sanger, M.D., coauthor of *The Woman Who Works, The Parent Who Cares*, says,

> There is no contradiction between being a good mother and leaving a child in the care of another adult for part of each day. Millions of good mothers do it every day. Unrealistic goals, however, can make this look like a contradiction; a woman who sees being with her child every moment of the day as an essential prerequisite of good mothering will view not being with him as an act of betrayal.[2]

Many Christians contend it is unbiblical for women to work. They hold up their ideal with little regard for the circumstances of the single woman or the attitudes of many married women who choose to work.

Some of you who say mothers should be at home are now ready to throw this book out and complain to the publisher. But hang on. You may have good arguments in favor of mothers being at home.

The issue for the single mother is not whether it is right or wrong for her to work. Working is certainly not something immoral or ungodly. It may or may not be what is ideal for the child. But the single mom doesn't live in an ideal world. The marriage she entered into has ended—due to separation, divorce, or death. Her world has changed, and she is merely struggling to keep herself—and her children—above water.

Since she doesn't live out the picture of the Christian ideal, how can a single mother best juggle her additional responsibilities as breadwinner with her continuing responsibilities of mothering? And how can she survive the tension of living up to an ideal?

A NEW MODEL FOR CHRISTIAN MOTHERS

Without compromising biblical principles, the single mother needs a new ideal against which to measure herself. The classic picture of the ideal Christian woman is found in Proverbs 31. Surprisingly for some, it's a picture of a hard-working woman.

> Who can find a virtuous wife?
> For her worth is far above rubies.
> The heart of her husband safely trusts her;
> So he will have no lack of gain.
> She does him good and not evil
> All the days of her life.
> She seeks wool and flax,
> And willingly works with her hands.
> She is like the merchant ships,
> She brings her food from afar.
> She also rises while it is yet night,
> And provides food for her household,
> And a portion for her maidservants.
> She considers a field and buys it;
> From her profits she plants a vineyard.
> She girds herself with strength,
> And strengthens her arms.

She perceives that her merchandise is good,
And her lamp does not go out by night.
She stretches out her hands to the distaff,
And her hand holds the spindle.
She extends her hand to the poor,
Yes, she reaches out her hands to the needy.
She is not afraid of snow for her household,
For all her household is clothed with scarlet.
She makes tapestry for herself;
Her clothing is fine linen and purple.
Her husband is known in the gates,
When he sits among the elders of the land.
She makes linen garments and sells them,
And supplies sashes for the merchants.
Strength and honor are her clothing;
She shall rejoice in time to come.
She opens her mouth with wisdom,
And on her tongue is the law of kindness.
She watches over the ways of her household,
And does not eat the bread of idleness.
Her children rise up and call her blessed;
Her husband also, and he praises her:
"Many daughters have done well,
But you excel them all."
Charm is deceitful and beauty is passing,
But a woman who fears the LORD, she shall
    be praised.
Give her of the fruit of her hands,
And let her own works praise her in the
    gates.

This woman is not only a superstar; she is a *married* superstar. Does that mean that a woman who is not a wife has no opportunity to be what God desires her to be? Of course not.

MARRIED TO HER MAKER

Nor is the single mother to be pitied for the absence of a man in her life. In Isaiah 54 we read about the woman who is married to the Lord. The passage refers to the restoration of Israel and the future glory of Zion. And it clearly shows us that what we lack in human relationships we can gain in our relationship with the Lord:

> For your Maker is your husband,
> The LORD of hosts is His name;
> And your Redeemer is the Holy One of Israel;
> He is called the God of the whole earth.
> For the LORD has called you
> Like a woman forsaken and grieved in spirit,
> Like a youthful wife when you were refused
>   (Isa. 54:5–6).

The new model is that of a woman faithful to her Lord. Her measure is based not on what people may think of her but on how she relates directly to God. The Proverbs 31 woman obviously worked and was praised for her diligence and skill:

> She seeks wool and flax,
> And willingly works with her hands. . . .
> She considers a field and buys it;
> From her profits she plants a vineyard.
> She girds herself with strength,
> And strengthens her arms.
> She perceives that her merchandise is good,
> And her lamp does not go out by night
>   (Prov. 31:13, 16–18).

At the same time, she was a good mother who raised her children well: "Her children rise up and call her blessed" (Prov. 31:28).

The rub comes from many conflicting voices. The world says, "Go for it, be a woman of the nineties. Work. Be supermom. Do it all." Just look at the article titles in secular women's magazines: "Those Feisty Women . . . Why Men Fall for Them," "Six Ways to Get Yourself Noticed at Work,"

"How Office Gossip Can Get You to the Top," "Women Who Run the Country," "The Need to Succeed—Women Are Giving Ambition a Good Name." The church says, "Stay home. We'll pray you get married. Trust God."

It isn't any fun to stand between two armies of fighting warriors, both of whom are assured of the truth of their holy crusade. At present a truly comfortable middle ground is undefined. Some pillars of tradition deny reality and refuse to change. Some professed modern free thinkers throw out all traditional values. And many sincere people on both sides of the issue try to blend their views with reality.

In the midst of whizzing bullets, the ideal has to be seen by looking up. The ideal comes from a personal relationship with Christ. He does not give a simple three-step solution for each person's situation. He does give grace and wisdom for the moment. A single mother may be called to live in the tension of working and raising children, but she can have the satisfaction that she is doing what the Lord wants her to do as best she can.

MAKING YOUR CHILDREN YOUR PRIORITY

A friend was advised soon after her divorce not to get too dependent on her children. She was encouraged to date right away and have a "life of her own." But children have lives of their own, too. And they need mom.

A woman needs balance between giving to her children and taking time for herself. If she doesn't take care of herself, she will have little to give to her children. But if she focuses too much on her own needs, her children may suffer.

If children feel they aren't a priority with at least one parent, who will they feel secure with? There is no substitute for time and physical presence. If a mother has to work, the need is all the greater to prioritize time to be with her children. This may mean an empty social calendar for a while, but the long-range benefits will be worth it.

Single moms feel pressure to meet people, to remarry, to be sure they aren't being too reclusive. Opportunities abound for single adults to meet one another—both in the world and in the church. Freedom from that pressure can be experienced if a person doesn't feel guilty for not dating.

My girls have been active in sports. After my husband died, I made a commitment to be at all their games when I was in town and to make sure that I would be in town most of the time during volleyball and basketball seasons.

For years friends teased me that I would never remarry because I spent all my time in high-school gymnasiums. But since I made that decision, I had real freedom in saying no to things that conflicted with game nights. Most of my Friday and Saturday nights for the last nine years I've been with other parents in the high-school gym.

I always said that anyone I would marry would have to be willing to join me at the gym. And that's what happened. I didn't start to go out in the usual "dating" sense before my younger daughter finished high school. When my husband, Steve, and I started dating, he came with me to the games. That was quite a change for him—to spend two or three nights a week sitting on hard bleachers watching girls' basketball. But he did it—struggling valiantly to appreciate the finer points of the game. We married, and my priority for my children did not change.

Keeping priorities in line isn't as easy as it sounds. But it is freeing. When you feel God directing you in the way you are to be a single parent, go with it and enjoy your children, even if critics say you are closing yourself off from dating opportunities.

MAINTAINING A SWEET AND GENTLE SPIRIT

One of my most outspoken displays of frustration—and perhaps a little bitterness, though I hate to admit it—came as a result of an absurd incident. I got up one morning and went downstairs to let our husky inside from her morning romp. I opened the door, and Heidi came prancing into the family room. She turned around and looked up at me with great pride. She had a bird in her mouth and was chomping on it.

I screamed and pushed her back out the door. It was a sickening sight. Not knowing whether eating a whole bird is good for a dog or not, I called the veterinarian's emergency number. The lady there said I should give Heidi hydrogen peroxide to make her bring the bird back up.

I ran upstairs and woke Lisa.

"Lisa, you have to come down and help me. Heidi ate a bird, and we have to make her throw up."

Lisa looked at me like I had lost my mind, but she followed me downstairs. I held the dog's mouth open while Lisa poured the peroxide down Heidi's throat. We left Heidi outside and waited. In a few minutes, she emptied her stomach of its contents.

Then, with Lisa and me as a captive audience, Heidi began to eat the regurgitated bird parts. Sound gross? It was!

I ran for a broom and went out on the porch. Swatting Heidi with the broom, I swept the bird parts off the porch. But I did it crying and saying, "No one should have to do this. This is more than anyone should have to wake up to."

It was a pretty silly moment. But it didn't seem silly at the time. It seemed unfair. It was more than I wanted to do, but felt I had to. I spent about twenty minutes feeling sorry for myself and being angry that we even had a dog.

Now my daughters and I laugh about the bird-breakfast incident. But I wasn't laughing when it happened. I pouted and stomped around and was unpleasant for the rest of that day.

I didn't display a meek and gentle spirit. It can be hard on a soft person when circumstances are demanding. If it isn't dog trouble, single mothers have plenty of other opportunities to be tough. Be it car trouble, money trouble, man trouble, or other innumerable troubles, these women have to be tough, or they don't survive. Certain situations demand it.

Daughters without dads learn toughness, too. They see their mothers have to go it alone, and they learn how to survive where other girls may have fathers to protect them.

As mothers and daughters proceed in this way without a man in their lives, bitterness can creep in unnoticed. The effects of bitterness, however, are not so unnoticed. They produce a defensive spirit. They steal moments of joy. They build barriers against deep relationships.

A woman's circumstances may be bitter, but her response can be strong yet gentle. That doesn't mean she never loses her composure or gets angry. But after her emotional outburst subsides, she can try to handle the next uncomfortable circumstance a little better.

An old saying asserts, "We should take God more seriously and ourselves less seriously." Being able to laugh at some of life's trying tests lessens their intensity. Humor helps to maintain a sweet spirit.

Life may not be humorous, but being able to relax after a disturbing incident can help ease the tension for everyone. Mothers who display a sweet and gentle spirit, even after losing their composure, are good models for their daughters to emulate.

NOT MOTHER *AND* FATHER

Single parents often find themselves thinking in terms of being both parents to their children. "I have to be mother *and* father," is a familiar refrain.

As understandable as that is, God does not mean for me to be a father to my children. Their father provided certain things that I now have to provide, but some things are clearly beyond my ability. I'm not a man. I don't think like a man. I don't do things like a man, and I don't want to try to act like one.

The widows I interviewed spoke of trying to do things the way their husbands would have wanted. Yet there comes a time when they can only do what they can do—not what their husbands would have done.

Daughters of divorce may still have a man to relate to, but he is gone enough for the mother to think she has to be mother and father. She, too, has to recognize her limits.

MOM IS TIRED AND LONELY

A humorous sticker on our refrigerator proclaims, "I am woman. I am strong. I am tired." That sums up the feelings of many single mothers.

The single mother battles constant fatigue and loneliness. When one person is left with the responsibility previously carried by two, she will be tired. When she does have enough energy to contemplate some form of social activity, mom will also feel the void created by the other person's absence.

Carol is a forty-five-year-old widow raising two girls. They are in high school now, so Carol has some time on weekend evenings she is not used to: *"I was so lonely the other night that I took the dog out. We went for a ride, then out for a hamburger."*

Pat is a divorced mother of three girls. She works full-time in a management level job that requires her to bring work home sometimes. She has to juggle helping with her girls' homework and finishing the work she brings home from the office. Pat describes how she feels: *"I'm always tired. I work all day, take care of the kids at night—I'm exhausted. I have no time for myself, and if I did, I'd be too tired to enjoy it."*

Loneliness becomes a familiar companion for the single mother. Although she may be active at work and at home with her children, she faces life without the spouse she has grown accustomed to. The single mother has lost the intimacy shared in marriage. Even a woman in an unpleasant marriage experiences the loneliness of raising children alone.

MOM AS A PERSON—NOT A LABEL

Identifying labels are the hallmarks of our society. Golden arches direct us to the kids' favorite—and America's most highly advertised—restaurant. International symbols show us which restroom door to walk through. Elevator buttons no longer read "Up" or "Down" but feature directional arrows.

Almost all consumer items can be identified by insignias. Advertising has become the arena of the image-bearer. People no longer wear watches; they wear Rolexes or Timexes, projecting an image of wealth or practicality. Even most teenagers can identify the company that produces a certain item by recognizing its insignia. Packaging an image has become big business. Everything falls into some category where it attains its label.

Women are no exception. We've been labeled in all kinds of ways. We used to have *working women*. Now we have many varieties of working women, and a new term, *sequencing*, is coming into use. Sequencing was described in a *Good Housekeeping* article, "Women Who Work for Themselves," as "the catchy word for the life style in which a woman starts a career, leaves to bring up her children, then returns to work later."[3] Can't you just hear women of the nineties talking about sequencing instead of homemaking or having careers?

Women don't work for the label of mother. They earn it by the mere fact of being females who are parenting children. And the mother label can be modified in myriad ways. Often I hear my teenager's friends' thumbnail descriptions of their mothers: she's rad, she's spaced, she's strict, she's cool. Much of this is harmless and done in fun.

Many women work overtime trying to maintain the label of *happy mother*. But that can be exhausting and unhealthy. A single mother is already working hard to compensate for the absence of her husband and all that entails. Whether widowed or divorced, she feels a pressure to rise to the occasion and pull her family through. A woman may acquire a particular image that can trap her if she isn't careful.

For instance, being viewed as strong can cause people to always treat a woman as if she is made of steel. The treatment she receives may be harsh because she is thought to be able to take it. The result can be walls of defensiveness erected to protect against future hurt that, in turn, cause her to appear even stronger and less approachable.

Knowing who you are but allowing yourself to change can

prevent your being labeled in some restricting way. God relates to us as individuals, not as categories. We need to do the same—with ourselves and with one another.

COMMANDER MOM

In the traditional Christian home, dad is the disciplinarian. Mom may administer directives, but dad is the final authority.

When dad isn't there, even the sweetest daughter will, at times, challenge mom's authority. One of the most common and effective techniques to undermine authority thrown at mom is to bring up what dad would have done.

If dad is deceased, this is a powerful weapon. The mother wants to do as her husband would have wanted. She tries to think how he would have thought and continue his influence in the family. When a daughter says, "Daddy would have let me do that," she can make the most confident mother think twice. Eventually, it becomes clear that whatever dad would have done is irrelevant. He is gone. Mom is here. She can do only what she thinks is best. She must take into consideration what dad would have done, but act in accordance with her evaluation of the current situation.

If the parents are divorced, it may be easier to determine what dad would do. The enforcing of his decision, however, is still left primarily to mom. Children can use parents against each other in discipline issues. To defeat this maneuver, parents can agree on who is the final authority and stick to that.

Divorced or separated parents who can't agree on discipline or decision making create a tense atmosphere for their children. Children need limits, consistency, and structure. They need to understand the consequences for not staying within those established limits.

A mother may tell a teenage daughter that her weekend curfew is eleven o'clock. Then when the daughter is with her father for the weekend, he may say she can stay out until midnight. The daughter has conflicting limits. She will probably opt for the later curfew and feel justified in doing that because her father told her she could. But when she goes back and lives with her mother for the rest of the week, she and her mother may have a tough time figuring out how to handle the mother's weekday rules—after all her weekend rules are counteracted by the father.

When no agreement can be reached, the children suffer the most. Parents should do everything possible to prevent this kind of instability. If a stalemate remains, parents should not be surprised if children develop discipline or emotional problems.

MAINTAINING CONTACT

According to many social theorists, we now live in a shrinking world because advances in communications technologies have made it possible to communicate instantaneously around the world. But at the same time, communication is a fine art that is rarely cultivated in many families.

Mere talk seems to have been lost in the technological shuffle. Having long conversations at dinner is an unusual event, even in loving and stable families. Schedules often prevent families from having dinner together on a regular basis. And when they do, the articulation of real feelings may be bland fare.

Part of the lack of communication may stem from the fact that heart-to-heart talks may be threatening, particularly when emotions are in turmoil. Many young people seem more comfortable with a video or CD; they can turn it off and walk away whenever they want. Getting into a conversation with a parent about a painful subject such as death or divorce is a different matter.

But it is necessary. Along with all their other responsibilities, single parents need to commit themselves to maintaining contact with their children. If children are not told what is going on, they may reach inaccurate conclusions. Or they may conclude accurately, but have no way to work through what they have observed.

The mother of the daughter without her father should discuss the circumstance. Psychologist Judith Lowenthal and her daughter Jessica began workshops two years ago on communication between mothers and daughters. As Dr. Lowenthal explains, "Today's teens are dealing with intense peer pressure and the issues of sex and drugs; at the same time their mothers are coping with problems of their own—work, possible marital conflict, and coming to terms with aging. Sometimes a mother and her daughter are each so caught up in her own life they fail to understand that the other is facing pressures too."

In their seminars, the Lowenthals suggest various exercises parents and children can do to keep the lines of communication open. Many families aren't used to working on their communication, but these ideas are practical and positive:

1. Remind your daughter that you love her. Concede you're not perfect, but you are doing your best to help her grow up.

2. Write letters to each other expressing your feelings about the important issues in your relationship.

3. Exchange the letters and read them without criticizing.

4. Take one problem at a time and swap roles so you can see the other's perspective. Then try to work through a compromise.

5. Offer to make some changes in your behavior and thinking.

6. Ask what changes she would be willing to make.

7. Do not relinquish your responsibilities as a parent. Being totally permissive indicates you don't care.

8. Remind your daughter of the times you felt closest to her. Ask her to do the same.

9. Tell her you are sorry for times you have hurt her. Give her a chance to express her own regret.

10. Make a pact to keep talking, especially during times when you disagree.[4]

This list may look overwhelming at first glance. If so, start by trying one or two of the suggestions. The main ingredient in keeping communication going is loving acceptance of the other person. Even if her perception of things is different from yours, you can disagree with her but accept her at the same time.

I have heard girls say that they do not express how they feel because it won't make any difference. They mean that it won't get their parents back together or bring the father back to life. That may be true. But they need to see that what they think and feel does make a difference. It makes a difference in how they relate to other people and how they handle the loss in their lives.

TAKING RESPONSIBILITY FOR MOM

Every girl I talked with whose father had died felt a degree of responsibility for her mother. The oldest girl in each family felt the greatest burden, but each daughter expressed concern for the well-being of her mother. Each one mentioned increased anxiety at the idea of her mother becoming sick or dying.

Daughters of divorce had mixed reactions. Most felt responsible to contribute to the mother's happiness, but didn't feel the added responsibility for the family if the mother was ill. They could still call on dad, go stay with him, or ask him for financial help.

In the section on losses, we looked at how this sense of added responsibility can rob a daughter of a carefree childhood. She may have moments of serendipity, but a mist of concern rolls back in.

It is easy, too, for a mother to take advantage of a particularly responsible daughter. I have had to fight this tendency. My older daughter was ten years old when her father died. She quickly learned to do everything I did around the house— cook, do laundry, clean, efficiently handle phone calls, and take care of her little sister. She was a tremendous help to me. Sometimes I put too many of our household responsibilities on her. Her capabilities and my needs robbed her of some of her youth. She is a very responsible young woman, but I regret that some of the times when she should have just been having fun she was backing me up in adult ways.

TAKING RESPONSIBILITY FOR DAUGHTER

When a mother has to work and a father isn't there, who is responsible for the daughter? Certainly a working mother is fulfilling one essential form of responsibility—that of providing finances for a place to live and food to eat. But this doesn't mean she can ignore other parts of the mother's job.

In recent years, the term *latchkey child* has been coined to describe schoolchildren who come home every day to an empty home. They carry house keys, let themselves in, and fend for themselves until their mothers get home from work— whether that means a wait of fifteen minutes or four hours.

One coach told me of a little girl who hung around the gym after school. She was too young to be in after-school sports, but she was there every day. He asked her why she didn't have a ride home. She said that her mother worked, her dad was gone, and her mom didn't want her to go home to an empty house. So she just stayed around the school building until 5:00 P.M. every day. The coach let her stay, kept an eye on her, and thought about the problem he would have if more children were doing the same thing.

Churches and schools can play an important part in helping single parents with the care of their children. We'll look at how later.

THE DANGERS OF OVERPROTECTION

Every normal parent is protective. It begins when the baby is crawling on the floor and a watchful parent prevents her from sticking her fingers into the electrical outlet. That same protectiveness continues throughout life.

Single mothers may grow even more protective than their

still-married friends. Parents who have lost a spouse—either by death or by divorce—have suffered loss. As a result they may grow even more cautious so that they—or their daughters—never experience such loss again.

My older daughter is in college now and travels back and forth by plane several times a year. She travels alone and has no fear. I, on the other hand, always experience anxiety while she is in the air. The fear is not overwhelming enough for me to forbid her to travel. But it brings back the all-too-familiar reality that accidents do happen. I accept that God is indeed sovereign and I need not be with her every minute to protect her. I also accept that my protective feelings are normal.

These feelings are normal only so long as they do not prohibit her from living a healthy life. Overprotection occurs when we will not allow our children to be in any situation where they might experience risk. And life will present them with risk at every turn. In fact, we all face risk all the time. We can only determine what we feel God wants us to do and go about doing it. Being overly protective will deny children the joys of childhood and will slow their adjustment to the loss they already experience.

SAVING TIME FOR FUN

There is nothing fun about death or divorce. There is also nothing sinful about having fun in the midst of trials. I'm not talking about disrespectful behavior, but smiling through tears can be healthy medicine.

As a family moves beyond the first stages of grief and sorrow, it is good to plan things that are fun. They may be different from activities enjoyed when dad was there. Or they may be the same and may need to be lived through with some pain before the joy returns.

A new and demanding schedule after a death or divorce may make fun times seem elusive. If you don't watch out, you'll never have time for fun. To make sure they happen, plan for them, write them on your calendar, talk about them with your children, and get excited or at least try to look forward to them with some anticipation. Work on having a little fun, and these times will provide a welcome break from the new routine.

HE'S NO LONGER MY MOM'S HUSBAND, BUT HE'S STILL MY DAD

Ann's parents divorced when she was a teenager. She maintained a good relationship with her father whom she visited regularly on weekends.

Her father remarried soon after the divorce, but her mother did not. When Ann was a young woman and became engaged to be married, she asked her father to give her away. He said he would be delighted to do so.

Ann's mother said that it would be fine for her father to give her away, but that her father's second wife was not welcome at the wedding. Ann pleaded with her mother to lay aside her anger for this one event. Her mother was unrelenting.

Ann's father felt he couldn't exclude his second wife, so he didn't give Ann away. He didn't even come to the wedding. Ann's mother refused to have his wife at the wedding at all, and Ann's father refused to come to the wedding without her. While everyone else quibbled, Ann suffered.

The divorced mothers and the divorced fathers that I interviewed agreed that it was essential to lay aside their differences and get along for the sake of the children.

One mother was the object of constant verbal abuse from her ex-husband. She told me that she decided not to speak badly about him in front of their children, no matter how tempting that would be. She had reason to speak badly of him, and she could have used the excuse that she was only defending herself. But she refused to put her children in the middle. She didn't condone their father's behavior, but she didn't bad-mouth him.

Ideally, both parents should be willing to speak and relate

kindly—or at least politely—to each other and allow their children to have a relationship with both of them.

"MOM STILL LOVES DAD"

I interviewed Marian, a college senior who grew up in a close and loving family until her father died eight years earlier. When I asked about her mother, who had remained single since her father's death, Marian's eyes filled with tears as she told me, "Mom still loves Dad."

I didn't interview the mother, so I don't know if she would have agreed with the statement or not. But it is a common attitude among children whose fathers have died. They find comfort in thinking of their mother as still "in love with" their father.

There seems to be something disloyal about anything else. I find myself feeling a little defensive as I write this. I have been widowed for nine years and would not describe myself as "still in love with" my late husband. I loved him, I love the memories we made together, and I look forward to being with him again in heaven. But being "in love with" someone seems to require that he be here. It isn't that I don't love him anymore, but he's not here for me to love.

A girl whose father has died remains loyal to him, and she watches her mother closely to see how she handles her memory of him. Women have to keep a balance between warmly remembering the man they loved and moving on in healthy ways without him.

A famous child raised without her father is Caroline Kennedy. Her early struggles to deal with his oversized memory were described by Caryl S. Avery: "Old enough when her father died to have vivid memories of him, Caroline was the keeper of the flame. As a teenager, her room was a virtual shrine to JFK, filled with his pictures."[5]

It's normal to keep precious memories alive. It isn't healthy, though, to live in the past. Daughters need to realize that their mothers are not being disloyal when they do not relate to the memory of their fathers in the same way they related to the men themselves.

WALKING THE TIGHTROPE

A woman married to an emotionally distant man walks a tenuous tightrope. She has the physical presence of a father for her daughter, but not the true support needed for healthy relationships. The withdrawn, distanced father can have profound effects on the mother-daughter relationship.

One common outcome is that mom becomes the advocate for the rejected daughter. Mom becomes the glue between father and daughter. While it may appear to help the daughter, this approach creates pressure for the mother. It also allows the father to continue his improper behavior.

This is a profile of the codependent household that, not unlike an alcoholic household, features a controlling character—in this case the distanced father. All the family members avoid confronting the father with his unsatisfactory behavior. Keeping him pacified or fruitlessly trying to please him becomes their goal.

Mother and daughter join forces to keep the boat peacefully afloat. If they don't unite, then the daughter finds that she has no advocate in mom or dad. She is likely to turn elsewhere for affirmation.

This situation would certainly be handled better if handled directly. Many groups now work with families in unhealthy relationship patterns. Seeking help is probably the best way a mother can improve her home for the sake of all the parties involved.

MOM AND OTHER MEN

Contemporary greeting cards are a tremendous source of good laughs about dating relationships: "Dating is like a snowstorm, you have to suffer through a lot of flakes." Men are the brunt of many of these jokes. Single women buy the cards and gleefully send them to other women in the same situation.

But when you boil it all down, the basic message of the cards is this: all men are jerks. For an adult woman who desires to be in a relationship with a man, the idea that men are genetically deviant may be comforting. It matters not if it is true. If a guy treats you badly or a relationship goes awry, it helps to think it's the other person's fault.

Teenage girls feel much the same way. As the dating world turns, so turn the lives of most young females. And the young girl stuck in a less-than-pleasing dating relationship tends to blame the guy who seems like some mutation of humanity. Even mom can be held accountable for the unpredictable schizophrenia of most males.

The reality is that many daughters without dads receive prejudiced and unfair information about men. It may be something as simple as a funny greeting card. Or it may be the rhetoric of a militant feminist novel or play. Whatever the source of the criticism, it certainly stems from real-life situations.

But mothers should remember that their view of men affects their daughters' attitude toward the male sex. It's OK to laugh at jokes, particularly those that poke clean fun at males' plentiful idiosyncracies. But it's unhealthy to project an image of disliking all men.

There are wonderful men in the world for girls to relate to. A daughter who has lost a father needs to see these relationships even more than a daughter with the loving presence of a father. She needs to understand that although some men are hurtful and not to be trusted, many others are kind and trustworthy.

A woman who has been hurt may be reluctant to trust men again. In the process of learning that trust, it is important for her to communicate to her daughter that if God does have it in His plan for her to marry some day, He has a man whom she will be able to love and respect.

Chapter 15

Daughters and Fathers

*W*hen a father dies, life becomes divided into two periods: before daddy died and after daddy died. In a daughter's network of relationships, the unseen tie to her deceased father greatly affects all other relationships.

She may never mention him, and it may have been years since she lost him. But he is there. He is forever in her mind and heart. Her relationship with her absent father begins the day he leaves.

A daughter's response at the time of her father's death may largely determine how she handles life in the future. How she copes "that day" may be how she copes with other painful events.

I interviewed some daughters who lost their fathers to death, asking them to comment on what they remembered about the day their fathers died and when they feel the loss the most. Here are their comments.

A seventeen-year-old, the youngest in a family of four children, was six years old when her father was killed in an accident: *"The day he died I remember eating hot dogs. About six weeks later, I asked my mom when he was coming home."*

An adult woman—the younger of two girls—was a junior in college when her father died of a heart attack: *"I was shocked. I called my sister and we cried. Now, every morning I cling to the fact that each day I am a day closer to seeing him again."*

One adult woman, the youngest of seven children, was sixteen when her father died after a long bout with cancer:

"I didn't cry when he died. He had been sick a long time. Three years later I cried when I was in nurse's training."

A seventeen-year-old girl was twelve when her father died. He had been at home during a long illness: *"He had been sick so I was a little relieved when he died. I miss him a lot. A few weeks ago, I missed him so I went to his grave and sat there and cried."*

A nineteen-year-old college student is the middle child of three daughters. She was seven years old when her father died of cancer: *"I didn't cry right away. Later I cried because Mom was upset. I was confused. I felt strange going back to school because I didn't know who knew."*

The youngest of her father's daughters, a sixteen-year-old was four when her father died: *"I remember Mom telling us he died. I was confused. I didn't know what it meant except that he wasn't coming back home again. I miss not experiencing the love of a father at an age I can remember."*

A woman in her mid-forties was nine years old when her father died. She later married and had one child. Then her husband divorced her: *"I am constantly amazed that I still have to take care of myself. Daddy left when I was nine and my husband left, too."*

Many girls who lost their fathers when they were very young remembered very little. Some of them expressed guilt over that fact. They learned to handle the loss of their fathers as they got older and realized that other people had fathers at home. It was normal for them not to have daddy there.

For those girls, their ideas of what relationships with other males were supposed to be like were largely determined by how their mothers related to men. Their personal view of men was confused. They simply didn't know what it was like to live with a man, even if they had brothers.

Girls whose fathers died when they were in their teens had very strong impressions of them. Most of them idolized their fathers and carried warm memories of their times together. There is an ongoing link to the deceased father for the girl who can remember him. She thinks about what he would want her to do, she measures men in her life against her memory of him, and she looks forward to being with him in heaven.

DIFFERENT PATTERNS OF COPING

Young girls find various ways of dealing with the loss of their fathers. In fact, their methods for coping would fill up this book if we examined all of them. However, their methods fall into two basic groups: the stuffer and the nonstuffer.

The Stuffer

You can spot a stuffer a mile away. She is always composed, in control, and on top of the situation. She "stuffs"—or she buries the emotions and feelings she is uncomfortable with.

Many uncomfortable emotions well up when a father dies. Fear, confusion, pain of loss, and disillusionment are some of the feelings that frequently wash over those who have lost a loved one to death. The child who buries her feelings is choosing an inappropriate method for coping with them.

In the midst of the activity at the time of death, she may be the one who appears to be handling things the best. She compensates for her pain by being busy, helpful, and quiet. She will probably receive praise for her behavior. She cries publicly very little, if at all. No one knows if she cries privately.

If stuffing helps her to relieve some of her pain by pushing it into the recesses of her mind, she may develop this coping style as a pattern for the rest of her life, too. It may be years before some of the pain she stuffed on the day of her father's death really gets handled, but that doesn't mean her unencountered pain won't affect her in ways that she may not see. It will.

Encouraging children to express themselves can get some of these feelings out. This may need to be done by close friends instead of mom, who has her own share of coping to deal with.

Children need to understand that whatever they feel is OK.

It's OK to be angry, unhappy, confused, or fearful. The important thing is to acknowledge those feelings. If girls feel certain emotions are wrong and deny them, all future relationships will be affected.

These girls may become women who, after years of marriage, suddenly become fed up and discontented. They may not even know why. Years of stuffing how they really felt have piled up and finally exploded. What began as a way of handling pain becomes the source of the pain itself.

The Nonstuffer

The nonstuffer may express her grief in various ways. She may cry, talk, be moody, or write out her feelings. Sometimes grief will be expressed in inappropriate behavior. A child may demand her own way, may let schoolwork slip, or may become sarcastic.

Children need structure. Even in the middle of great pain, they need to know that their behavior matters and that their grief is no excuse for acting in harmful ways. It may seem cruel to discipline a child who has suffered the loss of a parent, but it may be necessary. If done in a loving manner, it is reinforcement for the child.

Sometimes bad behavior is a way of screaming out for attention. A child may feel lost in the activity surrounding the aftermath of death. Soft discipline may give her just the added support and stability she needs. Find ways of being attentive without tolerating her unhealthy behavior.

Always encourage your child to share her feelings with you, even when you are disciplining her. The feelings themselves are not bad, although the expression of those feelings may need a little tempering. Allow—and even encourage— expression, and help your daughter to talk through whatever she feels.

STAGES OF GRIEF

The subject of grief has inspired hundreds of books and articles. An article entitled "When Children Grieve," written by columnist and family psychologist John Rosemond, describes some of the traditional stages of grieving:

> Denial and feelings of shock are common at first. Children may act incomprehensible, and escape into fantasy to cope with their pain.
>
> Anger, the second stage of grieving, arises as the reality of the loss sinks in. Children will blame someone or something, perhaps even the deceased. They need a sympathetic ear at this stage.
>
> Guilt usually follows closely on the heels of anger. For example, a child who loses a parent might blame himself or herself for something done months, even years, ago which made the parent upset. Children may even try to bargain with God, as in, "Dear God, if you'll bring Mommy back, I promise to be good and never make her mad again."
>
> Acceptance is the culmination of successful grieving. At this point, the child has come to grips with the reality as well as his or her anger and is able to begin adjusting successfully to the loss.[1]

While these stages may sound suspiciously similar to the stages a grieving adult goes through, that's what really happens. As Rosemond says, "In responding to death or significant loss, children experience the same emotions as do adults, but tend to express them in slightly different ways."

Grieving is never easy or else people wouldn't have to write books to help us do it. But it is a natural process that concerned parents should help their children understand.

Accepting a father's death will allow a daughter to go on with her life. She needs to discard the fantasy that he will come back, that he is active in the present, or that she needs his current approval.

One girl feels disloyal if she does something her father might disapprove of. Another feels obligated to do what she thinks her father would have wanted. I interviewed one young woman who was pursuing a career in medicine because her father used to talk about that field. Her father died when she was ten years old. Now in graduate school, she was for the first time beginning to question whether she really wanted to be in medicine. Along the way, she recognized that her father would not have been a stagnant individual. What he thought when she was ten could very well have changed by the time she was twenty.

It's healthy to be able to change and get on with the business of living. It's also impossible to accurately guess how someone who died years ago would respond to life today. Certain values and many good memories remain, but health means moving ahead in the way God directs for you right now.

A healthy relationship with a deceased father is one in which the daughter relates to people in her present environment. She allows herself to remember good things, to free herself from guilt from not-so-good times, to receive comfort from the reality of heaven and being reunited one day, and to simply live the best she can before the Lord.

LOSING A FATHER TO DIVORCE

A daddy is someone who loves a daughter. She knows that because he hugs her, takes her places, is kind, protects her, teaches her, and provides for her. A daddy is also someone who loves mommy—at least most of the time.

"I fell out of love with your mother," Tom said in explanation to his little daughter when she asked why he was moving out of their house.

"Why did you fall out of love?" she asked sincerely.

"I don't know, I just did," Tom replied somewhat sheepishly.

I interviewed Tom many years after his divorce, and he repeated this conversation as if he had had it yesterday. He remembered how awful he felt when he told his little girl that he and her mother were getting a divorce. He had always been able to adequately answer her questions—until then. He could feel her confusion. He was confused, too.

Over the next few years, Tom felt his secure place of leadership with his daughter slip away. As a teenager, she told him that she didn't even know him anymore. Tom admitted that he often didn't know himself. He began to wonder, "Who am I when all my handy meters of identity change and go away?"

A daughter who lives through the trauma of divorce usually sees less of her father than her mother. Her mother may change in many ways, but the mother is there and provides a much-needed supply of love, support, and continuity. The father, on the other hand, lives somewhere else. Who he is becomes less easy to see.

One girl told me that she could no longer imagine what her father did when he was not at work. He had his own apartment, but she couldn't picture him being there alone at night fixing something to eat. His life was a mystery to her, and she didn't like it.

A divorced dad who wants to have a good relationship with his daughter must communicate with her. If she wonders what happened to the man who was always there and who once loved mom, the father can help her by talking with her about how he feels.

All the fathers I interviewed agreed that it was essential for them to be kind in speaking about their ex-wives. No matter how bad the situation may have been, the daughter still has to relate to her mother. These men felt it necessary to take responsibility for their part in the breakup of the marriage and be supportive of their ex-wives in their roles as mothers.

WHAT IS A DIVORCE?

One father told me that when he talked with his young daughter, she had little comprehension of what divorce actually was. She understood that Daddy and Mommy no longer lived together. She knew that she lived during the week with Mommy and on weekends with Daddy. But she didn't grasp the concept that divorce was the actual end of marriage.

This little girl felt threatened when her mother remarried.

What would happen to her relationship with her real father with the new man on the scene?

Children need to know what divorce is, and they need to know what it is not. It is not the end of contact with the separated parent. It is not the end of a loving relationship with a father who is out of the house, even if a stepfather enters the picture. And it is not the fault of the child, even though many children think it is.

Unfortunately, divorce *is* some of these things sometimes. But when divorced parents have a commitment to help a child, they should reinforce their love and support of the child. It will be painful for a child to see that her parents' marriage has ended. It will, however, be a comfort to understand that her relationship with each parent will not end.

WHEN DO I SEE MY FATHER?

Fathers who determine to carry on a relationship with their daughters must be able to put up with and have a good answer for the continual unhappiness their daughters may express about the separated family.

One teenage girl told me, *"My life is a constant going back and forth between my father and mother."* She was not complaining. She was just stating a fact she had lived with since her parents divorced when she was about three years old.

If a daughter is already in her teens when her parents divorce, the issue of when she sees her father is a little more complicated. By that time her social schedule is well in motion. Weekends are typically filled with football games, dances, and other events shared with friends. Having to make time for an absentee father may not be the most attractive-looking option on the calendar. And the daughter really can't be blamed. She may have suffered enough pain from her parents' shattered relationship as it is, and she wants to find some positive relationships of her own.

Time is a challenge for dad, too. On weekends he does errands that he can't do in the middle of his work week. He may be forced to drag his daughter around with him, much to her displeasure and his annoyance. Such times don't have to be stressful, though.

In a traditional family, weekends are catch-up time. But that doesn't interfere with the daughter's life. Her mother and father can go about what they need to do and she can, too. She is with both of them all week so she doesn't need to be there every minute of the weekend.

Daughters of divorced parents face the opposite dilemma. Their fathers maintain an active social life on the weekends and have little quality time available for their daughters. One divorced father told me that he deeply regretted dating heavily so soon after his divorce. He dated a series of women whom his young daughter had to meet each weekend. She didn't have her dad to herself.

Another father's greatest personal loss as a result of his divorce was not being a continual part of his daughter's life. He was an extra. He saw her only for brief amounts of time. They would talk about an issue in her life one weekend and by the next time he saw her, it was over with and another issue was at hand. He seldom participated in the problem-solving process.

WHERE DO I SEE MY FATHER?

Having a job that involves a lot of travel looks glamorous unless you are the one doing the traveling. Living out of a suitcase gets old quickly. An ever-present, unsettling sense of always being in a state of preparing to go somewhere becomes a part of daily life.

Daughters who travel back and forth between their parents have somewhat the same experience. One daughter told me that she doesn't really feel permanent anywhere. She lives most of the time with her mother, but is always getting ready to visit her father.

Dad often lives in a place for other single people. Most families can't afford for dad and mom to have similar homes. Apartment complexes in many communities specialize in housing the single adult. They are convenient and meet the needs of someone living alone. But they aren't the type of home environment a visiting child may be used to. The atmosphere may cast a shadow on the child's impression of how dad now lives.

How do fathers and daughters who see each other sporadically work out their activities? Do they just hang out together? Do they always "do" things? Or does the daughter join the father in his activities?

One dad described himself as a "Disneyland Dad." He explained how he always felt he had to give his daughter a great time and win her affection. So he took her on wonderful vacations. Their shared time as father and daughter was always in the context of having a "big deal" time. He was afraid if he only spent time with her, she wouldn't want to be with him.

WHY DO I SEE MY FATHER?

Relationships between a daughter and her divorced dad may be so strained that the daughter asks why she has to see him at all. She may feel that dad deserted her, so why should she make an effort to be with him? As a girl reaches her teens, spending time at dad's on the weekends can become an intrusion into her valued social time.

Unless a father has abused his daughter, there is a good answer for why she needs to see him. It is this: "Because he is your father." Although this really doesn't smooth all a young girl's ruffled feathers, it is usually enough to enforce visitation. The real reasons for doing anything have to do with our motivation—our hearts. We'll explore attitudes of the heart in a later chapter.

TAKING THE DADS' WORDS FOR IT

I interviewed dozens of divorced men for this book, and many of them have been divorced for ten years or more. They have learned some ways to better relate to their daughters, and we can learn from their experience, too. Here are a few of their suggestions:

"I don't live in the same city with my daughters, so I schedule a weekly phone call. I talk to each one individually. I ask a lot of questions about their lives—their friends, school, how they feel. I allow time for it. And I count it as a worthwhile expense."

"I allow and encourage my daughter to express her feelings. She can say anything to me that she wants to as long as she does it with respect."

"The most important thing for children in a divorce is for the parents to get along. My ex-wife and I did not, and the girls were always in the middle."

"If I had it to do again, I would be more involved in her activities. I was not at many of her sporting events in high school. I was too busy. I wish I had done more."

"Even though I don't live with my daughters I try to give them spiritual leadership. It is difficult, but I try to communicate godly principles to them."

The overwhelming advice from fathers who have been there is to maintain contact—no matter how hard it is and no matter how brief the contact. Fathers who know say to stay in touch with your children.

Sometimes fathers have grave doubts about their self-worth and their significance in their daughters' lives. After all, they haven't been ideal fathers, and their marriages have been far from ideal. And they have been absent from their daughters' lives. Some men are so overcome with feelings of failure that they don't do anything at all. But fathers and daughters generally agree that a little positive contact is better than nothing.

FATHER IN THE NETWORK OF HIS DAUGHTER'S RELATIONSHIPS

For the daughter, the new arrangements required to maintain contact with both parents are complicated at best. And the web of relationships for separated families usually only grow more and more tangled with time. If parents remarry, children grow and marry, stepchildren enter the picture—the place of each individual in the network becomes confusing.

A man who remarries obtains a new wife. But he also may become a stepfather. If so, he must learn to become a diplomat, for he has to deal with the father of his stepdaughter. He must balance all these new responsibilities with his own daughter's feelings in regard to his being a dad to another girl. On and on the scenario goes.

Later we'll talk about how to survive so many demands and how fathers and daughters have the opportunity to enjoy rich relationships, even in the context of divorce.

Chapter 16

Daughters and Stepfamilies

*L*ife in a nuclear family looks a little like a simple math problem: $1 + 1 = 2$. Even when children arrive, the additions to the family are still fairly simple: $2 + 1 = 3$, or $2 + 2 = 4$.

Divorce or death may superficially resemble these mathematical models. After all when a father dies or leaves the home, isn't it as simple as $3 - 1 = 2$? No, it's not. The family will have to cope with many issues.

Following remarriage, things can go from simple to complex mathematics. More and more people are thrown into the formula until a whole group of people end up trying to live happily together under one roof.

TRIANGLES AND SQUARES

The eternal triangle is supposed to be perfect and orderly, with three equal sides meeting each other at nice, proper angles. But the participants in many single-mother settings— the mother, the daughter, and the man mom dates—may not fit together in such a flawless pattern.

Many things place stress on this triangle, such as the times when the daughter's father/the mother's ex-husband comes to pick up the daughter for the weekend. Want to see even more stress on the triangle? Watch what happens when dad brings along his new girlfriend. Now our triangle has become a tense pentangle consisting of the two natural parents, the people the two parents are dating, and the daughter.

And wait a minute. I'm forgetting one of the most important geometric shapes—the square. What's so important about the square? A teenage daughter thinks that any guy her mother dates is a square.

Parental dating introduces a new and upsetting element into a girl's life. When she knows that the ringing doorbell means mom's date is at the door, a whole set of uncomfortable feelings rises to the surface.

Many of a daughter's concerns are caused by insecurities. As Susan H. Horowitz, a therapist with the Family and Marriage Clinic at the University of Rochester Medical Center, told the *New York Times,* "The most important thing that children want to know is how the things their parent is doing will affect them."[1]

While the parent views the date as a simple evening out and a much-needed dose of male companionship, the daughter may view it as the ominous beginning of a frightening process of losing her mother to a man. The daughter will watch carefully to see what happens when her mother goes out. And she will wonder how this man will treat her mother—all pretty threatening thoughts. Dr. Ann Baldwin Taylor, a developmental psychologist and the director of the Children's School at Carnegie-Mellon University in Pittsburgh, said, "Little children can't imagine a parent loving more than one person."[2]

A divorced or widowed woman may reach a comfort level of being ready to have another love relationship with a man, but her daughter may be unprepared for such a move and may see her mother's interest in another man as disloyalty to her father. The daughter has trouble making room in her own heart and mind for another man, so she doesn't understand how her mother can. Dr. Taylor observed, "Psychologists note that divorced and widowed parents often treat the oldest child in a family almost as if that child were an adult. They are more likely than other children to view a parent's date as a threat to their role and influence within the family."[3]

The oldest child in a single-parent home gets a certain amount of security from feeling needed. She may have a unique role with her mother, in many ways acting as a replacement for the absent father. The daughter may feel that if her mother's date becomes her mother's new husband, she will not be needed anymore.

WELL, I GUESS MY MOM HAD TO HAVE SEX TO HAVE ME!

Another problem caused by parental dating is that a child doesn't like to think of her biological parents as sexual beings, and the presence of a new man on the scene may stir up thoughts and feelings the daughter would rather not face. A child's concerns about her parents' sexuality may increase as she enters puberty.

Sure, most kids can cope with the fact that their moms had sex at least once. But much more than that and many kids grow faint. It is even more uncomfortable to think of their own mother being sexually involved with a man who is not their father. According to Dr. Taylor, "With teenagers, the picture is more complex. Their growing awareness of their own sexuality and attractiveness colors their perception of the parents' potential partners. Some young teenagers become angry at a parent's sexual activity. Most look at what the parent does as a model for their own relationships."[4]

It is important for the dating parent to restate a personal commitment to godly standards so that children clearly understand. It is a good model for children to see a parent date and to know the parent is committed to purity in a dating relationship.

LIMITED PERMISSION TO DATE

Not all children react negatively to a parent dating, and some even welcome the presence of a man on the scene. If mom takes it slowly, time and care can help to smooth the rough waters of her daughter's concern.

But mom never has carte blanche to do as she wills. She is still committed to her daughter. The following two elements are crucial if a mother wants her romantic life to be a success with her daughter: (1) communicating to the child that she is still of primary importance to the parent, and (2) following that statement up with appropriate action.

If a single parent has a date and then finds out that an important school function conflicts with that date, she has a good opportunity to show that her child is a priority by choosing to go to the school event. A child should not be made to feel guilty for being part of an event that causes the parent to cancel something else. Instead, the parent should communicate that she willingly chooses to be at the child's event.

PROVIDING ROLE MODELS FOR YOUNGER DATERS

Parents who date have a tremendous responsibility because their children are carefully watching their every move. The truth of this came home to one single father who told me that his daughter allowed boys to treat her badly because she had observed his poor treatment of some women he dated. He was not openly abusive, but he was sarcastic and insensitive. He said he wished he had been more aware of his daughter watching him and had been more careful of her feelings.

For single Christian parents, dating behavior illustrates their commitment to the Lord. There is no double standard because a parent is older than a child. Some rules may vary, such as a daughter having a curfew and a parent having a later—or no—curfew, or a daughter having a time limit on phone calls in order to get homework done. But the moral standards of the parent should be a good model for the daughter of what a Christian does when dating.

A single mother confessed she was convicted that her inappropriate sexual behavior would later affect her young daughter. The mother admitted to me that she occasionally allowed men to stay at her apartment overnight, thinking that her daughter was too young to be adversely affected. The mother knows, however, that when her little girl is older and is faced with making up her own mind about sexual behavior, the mother's poor example won't help the daughter take the higher road.

Living out biblical principles in all areas of life is the best way to expose children to the truth of Christianity. Even in painful, complex situations adults can choose godly ways to relate and communicate positively to their children.

BECOMING A STEPDAUGHTER . . .

More and more children are being raised in stepfamilies. Most often, the children live with their biological mother and a stepfather. Here's what the statistics tell us:

- "One of every six American children under 18 years old lives in a stepfamily, according to a 1984 Census Bureau study."[5]
- "Four and a half million kids live with a mother and stepfather, and another 1 million live with a father and stepmother."[6]

Even though stepfamilies are no longer a social or statistical oddity, living in a stepfamily means making many adjustments. Most of the girls I interviewed who were in stepfamilies (some in two stepfamilies because they shared time with both remarried parents) felt alone in their situations. They were somewhat aware of the statistics, and they were certainly aware of other divorced or blended families, yet they still felt somehow singled out.

They felt particularly isolated in the Christian community, where there are many stepfamilies. Nevertheless, the message from the pulpit seems to be: "Stepfamilies are not what God wanted. You are messed up!"

Many of the children had grown fairly adept at juggling

life between the many adults populating their lives. All admitted that they had a lot of people to deal with and sometimes wished life were simpler.

... AND LIVING WITH YOUR STEPMOTHER

Who among us would have fond feelings toward the wicked stepmother in the Cinderella fairy tale? Cinderella's mother had died and her loving father remarried. He, too, then died and left Cinderella in the care of his sinister wife, who made Cinderella a servant with only mice as her friends.

We all know how the story goes: Cinderella meets the handsome prince who combs the countryside to find her again. After finding a perfect fit for his tiny glass slipper, the prince claims Cinderella as his own, and the two are reunited. They marry and live happily ever after.

The stepmother gets her due—her two obnoxious daughters are out of the running for a place at the palace. And she loses Cinderella as her servant girl.

In this case it is good news that life is no fairy tale. Oh, it might be nice for each young girl to meet her Prince Charming, but it wouldn't be so nice for all stepmothers to be like Cinderella's.

Fortunately, they are not. The relationship between daughter and stepmother is, however, a delicate one.

A daughter who loses her dad to divorce usually sees him only on weekends. Right after a divorce, she may get used to having him all to herself. A father's date may be seen as a threat to the daughter. This is especially true when a girl sees her dad only on weekends, when that is the usual time he would date.

One couple had a serious problem:

A divorced dad began dating and his daughter truly liked the woman involved. In time, he remarried and, almost immediately, the agreeable daughter turned into a tyrant. She became possessive of her father and indignant to her stepmother. The father was torn between demands made by his daughter and the feelings of his new wife. The pressure drove the couple to counseling when his new wife became pregnant. He was worried sick about the reaction of his daughter and this caused a breach between himself and his wife. Among the counselor's suggestions were: don't argue in front of the daughter; settle things privately so she can view her stepmother as worthy of respect; set clear-cut rules of what is acceptable behavior and what is not; allow the daughter to be displeased about the new baby; and face and work on solving problems instead of avoiding them.[7]

In most cases, real life is somewhere between the romantic and horrible extremes of the Cinderella story. Families shouldn't wait for miracle cures, but should get to work on their nagging relational problems.

STEPPING IN (NOT STEPPING ON) AS A STEPMOTHER

It's hard to be a part-time mom. And that is what a stepmother may feel that she is to her stepdaughter.

Maybe she should not, however, try to be mom. After all, if the natural mom is still alive, the stepmother has some stiff competition. But if the stepmother is married to dad and is not in the role of mom, what role does she play?

A couple need to carefully decide the best working relationship for all parties involved. And the role a stepmother plays will be a challenge. She may be in the role of friend, but may have occasion to be with a daughter who needs to be disciplined. She may try to administer some discipline and run up against an angry cry of protest: "But you're not even my mother!"

Before a remarriage, loving communication between father and daughter needs to take place. The road should be smoother if he assures his daughter that her place in his heart and life is not threatened, and that he will still be her father even though they will be relating to another person now.

A father should inform his daughter of the extent of the stepmother's disciplinary powers. If a father gives authority to a stepmother to correct the daughter, he needs to let the daughter know that, and he needs to back up that authority with support for his new wife. If a father is not ready to let a stepmother be involved in discipline, the couple need to decide what will happen if the daughter is unruly with the stepmother.

A stepmother should never criticize the daughter's mother. Even if the daughter complains about her mother, those negatives should not be reinforced. They should, instead, be talked over with her father who can communicate with his ex-wife about the daughter's concerns.

A woman may be in a dual role as mother. She may live with biological children of her own and also have stepchildren as a result of a second marriage. Her roles with these two sets of children will probably not be the same. She needs to think through the differences. Perhaps she is primary disciplinarian for her children but not disciplinarian at all for the stepchildren. She may feel very partial in being lenient with her children and resent the demands made on her by the addition of her new husband's children. Or she may find herself torn between trying to keep her children happy and trying to win the favor of stepchildren at the same time. It's a juggling act that takes time and patience to master.

MOM AND ANOTHER MAN

Many of the same questions of identity, role, and behavior surface when mom remarries. The new man in the house may appear to be a threat. He may have a role in discipline that is poorly received. He may have children from a previous marriage that are part of his package.

A daughter who is close to her mother usually has a rough time with mom's remarriage. She has been used to having mom to herself and may fear that mom will no longer have time for her. She also has many criticisms—real or imagined— of the new man.

If her father is dead, she may have a fantasy of mom's marrying a man like dad. More than likely, no mortal could live up to the idealized version of her father. And of course, comparison of a new husband with a dead husband puts a lot of stress on mom. She doesn't want to tear down her child's father in order to build up her new husband. But mom has trouble getting past her daughter's image of her father so she can even see anyone else.

If a daughter's parents are divorced, she now has two men to relate to. Many conflicting emotions come into play here: how she feels about her biological father, how her mother relates to her biological father, how the new man in her mom's life communicates what he thinks of her dad, and whether the two men try to put her in the middle by competing with each other for her affection. The only way the daughter can live in a healthy way with a stepfather is for the adults to lay aside their own agendas long enough to agree on what is best for the daughter.

THE STEPFATHER'S ROLE

Daughters and stepmothers don't relate in the same way that daughters and stepfathers do. The biggest difference is that in the majority of cases the daughter usually has to live in the same house with the stepfather.

If the daughter is very young when her mother remarries, she may warmly welcome a new man in the house to be a daddy. If, on the other hand, she is a teenager, she may very well resent the intrusion of a strange male. Even adult women I interviewed who were not living at home any longer had trouble thinking of their mother living in the same house with a man other than their father.

One married woman in her mid-thirties whose father had been dead a number of years told me she just didn't want to have to relate to her mother's new husband. She said her mother was always trying to get them together and convince her daughter how wonderful her new husband was. The woman felt this man was forced upon her and resented it.

There is no list of steps to take and no timetable to follow in establishing a relationship between a daughter and a stepfather. Sensitivity and patience are necessary. When the daughter is a teen or older, the best approach for the new man seems to be to become the daughter's friend and not try to fill the shoes of her father.

One college girl told me that she thought of her stepfather as the man her mother is married to, not as her father. She has a wonderful relationship with him, but she doesn't want him to play daddy. She loves him for being good to her mother, but also is grateful that he doesn't need to be father to her mother's grown children.

The most positive response from girls whose mothers had remarried was that they appreciated it when the stepfather was good to the mother. Each daughter wanted to see her mother happy, but she didn't need a new father to be happy herself.

STEPFAMILIES UNDER
THE MICROSCOPE

Recently, there has been much significant research on stepfamilies. In a *New York Times* "Parent & Child" column, Dr. John S. Visher, a psychiatrist in Palo Alto, California, and his wife, Dr. Emily B. Visher, a psychologist, discussed their experience. Each partner brought four children to the new marriage. As the husband said, "We quickly learned that it wasn't going to be 'The Brady Bunch.'"[8]

Even marriage partners as well-schooled in the psychology of the human as the Vishers were not prepared for all the changes and challenges of blending two families. Their frustrations led them to found the Stepfamily Association of America in 1979 and to write three books on stepfamilies.

According to Lawrence Kutner, author of the article about the Vishers, "The first task, researchers generally agree, is to spend more time building the marriage and less time worrying about how your children feel about what is happening. That is not to say that you ignore your children's feelings. But several recent studies show that divorced and widowed parents tend to pay little attention to their own needs as couples and focus on immediate needs and demands of their children."[9]

If children in stepfamilies think that they can get more attention by dividing and conquering, they will. A daughter who is threatened by the presence of a stepfather may work hard to hang onto the security she has had with her mother in a single-parent home. She may try to make her mother feel guilty for time spent with the new man of the house; she may be unreasonable and irritable with her new stepfather; or she may make her mother feel constantly in the middle of a cold war between stepdaughter and stepfather.

Dr. James H. Bray, a psychologist at Texas Women's University in Houston who has been studying children in stepfamilies, stated, "Our research shows that the biological parent should maintain the primary parenting role and use the stepparent to back him or her up."[10]

A mother who remarries needs to establish parenting guidelines with her new husband before he moves into the house. A man may assume that he will come in and be the chief disciplinarian of the stepchildren. It is better for the mother to maintain her role as final authority in disciplinary matters while teaching her children to respect their new stepfather. Eventually, he should be able to have a meaningful role in parenting, but he will have to be patient and earn the right to be a parent.

Aside from all these practical challenges, many in the new blended families feel a mixture of sadness and relief in their new settings. Dr. David Fassler, a child psychiatrist and author of *Changing Families: A Guide for Kids and Grownups*, suggests many arguments and flare-ups may be due to this sense of sorrow: "Behind the anger we often find a lot of sadness about the losses represented by the new marriage. Many children of divorce openly or secretly hope that their biological parents will reunite. The new marriage shatters that illusion."[11]

Remarriage after the death of a father also seems to reemphasize the finality of his death. The girls I interviewed whose fathers had died and whose mothers had not remarried communicated that they were more comfortable with their mothers' not remarrying. They somehow continued to think of their parents as being married. Remarriage would end that illusion.

A healthy form of growth and closure can take place in a remarriage. But it takes time. Happy adults looking forward to a new life together find their joy tempered a little by the adjustments their children face.

HIS KIDS, HER KIDS

Once a daughter who has lost her father to divorce adjusts to a new stepmother, she may have to get used to several new stepsiblings. It is unlikely that the two original families of these children have raised them in precisely the same way. What is acceptable behavior in one family may be unacceptable in another. When all these folks are together in one house for a weekend—or until the children reach adulthood—chaos can result.

A daughter may become intensely jealous at seeing her father relating to another girl who is now his stepdaughter. She may resent her stepmother's children being allowed by their mother to do something that her father does not allow her to do. A whole new set of rules may need to be developed so that the mix of previous discipline can be replaced with something uniform. Then, of course, the daughter goes back home to her mother who has the old set of rules in place.

Stepchildren can have wonderful relationships together. The key factor in making this happen seems to be the consistent, loving concern of all parents involved. In spite of the problems, it is not an insurmountable task.

While parents seem anxious for all parties in this new conglomeration to get along as soon as possible, the kids need breathing room. They need to be able to grow to love others, not to be in a high-pressure situation where they feel forced to.

A divorced father told me how confusing it was for his young daughter to understand who was now in her network of relationships since her mother had remarried. My friend's daughter was visiting him during her Christmas vacation. He asked her what she got for Christmas—meaning those presents she had opened at her mother's house on Christmas Day. She told him of a long list of goodies. At one point, he said, "Who gave you that?" She thought for a moment and then said, "His name is John. I think he is my stepbrother, but I'm not sure. I haven't met him yet, but he gave me a nice present."

We can't expect children to automatically embrace members of a stepparent's family without time to get to know them. Even then, we can't demand that they be happy about the arrangement. But we are the reason these children are in a new environment, and it is our responsibility to help them adjust to it.

Chapter 17

Daughters and Men

*H*ow is a thought born, and how does it grow? The formulation of thoughts is a complex process. No one item can be isolated as the exclusive influence that brings thoughts to fruition in our minds. And after arriving at some conclusions about what we think, we are constantly subject to input that challenges whatever we have concluded.

Of all the thoughts in a person's mind, few are as complex as the ideas about the opposite sex. What women think about men is a hot item these days. There are many books out on the relationships between the sexes, including this one.

It would be difficult to trace the influences that shape how daughters without dads think about men, for these girls are bombarded with the things they hear in school, what they watch on TV and in movies, what they read in books and magazines, and what they gather by talking to various people. All of these affect how they relate to men.

Daughters without dads will formulate their thoughts about men from more of a distance than those whose fathers are at home. In the midst of all the voices clamoring for attention about men and how to relate to them, these young women will have to assimilate information as if it is filtered through a veil. They simply don't have the real thing at home to watch and examine.

In addition, the fatherless daughter may be operating from her own pain and sense of loss. If her father has died, she shouldn't experience long-term problems in developing a healthy view of men. But if she has lost her father to divorce, she may have difficulty seeing men as positive factors in women's lives—particularly if the divorce or marriage was bitter.

All the information that our data-rich society pours out is only theory unless it is lived out in the context of relationships. Girls can read about men, watch TV sitcoms about nuclear families, and be very intelligently versed about death and divorce. But they learn most about men from being in relationships with them.

MEN = MY FATHER

A little girl will obviously form her early thoughts about men based on her experience with her father. Depending on that early relationship, she will shape her picture of what a man is. If daddy is kind, she may conclude that all men are kind. If he is loud and abusive, she may conclude that all men are like that.

If he is not there—perhaps he died when she was young— her thoughts may be formed by what she hears other people say about her father or by her observations of other people's fathers. One teenage girl I interviewed whose father died when she was five said that she could not separate what she really remembered about her father and what she had fabricated from looking at pictures and hearing stories about him. Her view of men was somewhat confused because, as she said, "I couldn't even remember what I actually remembered."

She talked over some of these confused memories with a counselor who suggested she sit down with her mother and some of the pictures of her dad. They would take a picture and discuss what the daughter thought the picture was about, and then her mother would tell her what it was actually about. It helped the daughter understand more about who her dad was, and it helped release her from attempting to figure out how to relate to men based on how she related to a man who was just an idealized image in a photograph.

A divorced dad, though not living at home, still has a good opportunity to positively influence his daughter's view of the male population. Although his situation is not ideal, he still can be the man closest to his daughter. Unfortunately, as girls enter their teen years, it becomes more difficult to coordinate their school activity schedules with visits to dad. The divorced father may find he has to make a concerted, but flexible, effort to have time with his daughter. For the divorced dad, one of the biggest influences on his daughter and how she thinks about men will be the way he treats his ex-wife. She may be his "ex," but she is still his daughter's mother.

An emotionally distant dad in the home presents the most confusing picture. He is physically present, but the daughter probably doesn't know much about who he really is. People who are emotionally withdrawn may see themselves as neutral, but often what they communicate to others is negative. Their lack of communication may convey disinterest, rejection, or disapproval when what they feel is a personal sense of insecurity. But to a girl receiving a surface level of interaction, it may appear that this man called dad doesn't even like her. Her subsequent evaluation of men in general may focus on her lack of worth instead of on understanding who men are.

OTHER MEN

Daughters without dads don't erase men from their minds when their fathers leave. Instead, they focus on other men in their lives who can contribute to their healthy images of men.

Lara, my sixteen-year-old daughter, has a special relationship with a few adult men. One is with a teacher who has taken a personal interest in her. A gregarious type, Fran has the ability to relate deeply to a number of kids at once. He has told me on several occasions that part of why he feels drawn to Lara is that he knows she has not had a dad for most of her life and she needs some male role models.

They eat lunch together every once in a while at school and talk. Fran is a godly and insightful man. I trust him. I trust his character, his commitment to the Lord, and his concern for Lara. And I sincerely appreciate his willingness to spend time with her.

Men who can have consistent contact with daughters without dads have marvelous opportunities to make a positive impact. I'm sure it's overwhelming to be a teacher and see hundreds of kids every day with hundreds of needs. But I know from personal experience that just one word from this respected teacher is a meaningful exchange for my daughter.

Lara sees Bob, the father of her best friend Nichole, less often. But she loves him deeply. Lara and Bob have a unique kind of healthy mutual admiration society.

When I asked Bob how he thought their relationship came about, he told me, "It was really pretty natural. She was a friend of Nichole's and was around our house. She would come up to me and hug me and call me Big Bob, which is the nickname Nichole calls me.

"Lara is a very warm and loving girl with a lot to give, and I feel fortunate to receive some of that attention. I mean, she sees me from across the gym and yells to me as she runs up to me with her arms open. Who can resist that? I think a lot of men and women see a girl in Lara's situation, and they think that they have to TRY to do something. I think it's better to just let the relationship happen—don't be artificial."

I also asked Lara why she was so drawn to Bob. She said, "He's such a teddy bear. He gives big hugs and has a great smile; I don't feel like I am ever bothering him. He never seems annoyed when I run up to him and hug him. He makes me feel like he thinks I'm fun to be around. Some of the kids—especially the boys—seem a little scared of him. But I think he's a softy."

Another element in this relationship is Lara's friendship with the entire family. Nichole is her best friend and is not at all jealous of Lara's relationship with her father. Penny, Bob's wife, is a teacher at Lara's school and has a personal friendship with her, too. Lara has a typical relationship with Nichole's younger brother, Rob. She finds him pretty funny, and he seems to accept her presence in their home as normal. No one makes a big deal about Lara's being without a father. They simply accept her and love her, and she loves them. Lara is a fairly open kid, but my older daughter, Lisa, is a little harder to get to know. She is the typical older child of a single-parent home: responsible, competent, and down-to-business. In her high-school years, the men who influenced her the most were her athletic coaches. When the basketball coach she had in the tenth and eleventh grades transferred schools at the end of her junior year, she was distraught. I might not have been able to get her to walk downstairs to get something for me, but Jon could get her to run five miles a day willingly.

Lisa had already decided that Terry, the new coach during her senior year, couldn't replace the old coach in her heart, so she didn't make relating to her very easy. But Terry persisted, and he finally won her over. She saw that she could still have great memories of her old coach and have room to relate well to the new one. Terry encouraged her, worked with her, and was a contributing factor in her going on to play basketball in college.

These men, as well as many others, influence girls with fathers at home. But the role they play with fatherless daughters helps fill a painful void.

Unfortunately, mothers have to exercise extreme caution about the men their daughters are around. We have all heard horrible accounts of sexual abuse that come from seemingly innocent situations. I have been blessed in that my children have been associated with men of tremendous integrity. I would not hesitate to leave my girls alone in the care of any of these men. They are completely trustworthy.

But that is not always the case. If a mother has any suspicions, she can carefully check out the men her daughters see and the situations in which they meet, as well as read up on the subject of sexual abuse and talk to people knowledgeable in that field of counseling and get help. I caution against flying off the handle with ill-founded suspicions and accusations, but the consequences of sexual abuse are so grave that no concerned mother should shrug them off.

If a girl has no men at all to relate to, she may base her opinions of men on the boys at school, her friends' comments about their fathers, or current cultural manifestations. In this case, her mother must talk to her and help her filter this diverse input. Mom can help her daughter sort out her thoughts and help her develop realistic impressions of men.

WHAT MEN ARE AND WHAT THEY'RE NOT

I am now married, but I was alone for nine years. At different points during that time, I held different convictions about men. These weren't just ideas or conjectures; they were convictions because I was *sure* I was right.

As soon as I had a conviction firmly in place, something would happen in my relationship with a man—or to someone I knew—and I would walk away shaking my head. Suddenly, it seemed, my convictions were not as certain as I thought they were. I thought that I had figured men out, and then an exception to my convictions would come along and prove me wrong.

At one point in those years, two single women lived with me in my house. Often, my two friends, my two daughters, and I would sit around the kitchen table and utter endless phrases of amazement at the way men act. Phrases like these were common:

"*Why* doesn't he call?"

"*What* do you think he is thinking?"

"*Where* in the world are the normal men?"

"*Why* in the world did he do that?"

Finally, I arrived at a conclusion: men are a mystery. I don't know what men are, and I don't know what they are not. I don't know why they think the way they do. I don't know why they sometimes act the way they do. And I don't think they know any of those things about women, either. Since this is my final conclusion, I expect it to stand as gospel for at least a month or two.

But I don't have to know why a man thinks the way he does in order to relate to him, accept him, or love him. There are, however, some helpful things I can know. I can learn what men close to me think. I may not necessarily understand *why* they think it, but I can learn to better understand what they think and better communicate what I think. I can be willing to listen to what seems silly to me, and I can be willing to be vulnerable in saying what I think may seem silly to them.

I can also accept that sometimes what I communicate may be received with utter confusion and dismay by men, even though it makes total sense to me. Just two nights ago, my husband, Steve, and I got into what turned out to be a pretty confusing discussion. Finally, after talking it through, I felt good about what had happened. I made some brilliant closing comment, and Steve just shook his head. "What kind of look is that?" I asked. He just smiled and said, "This is merely a 'What-ARE-women-all-about look.'"

The good news for daughters without dads who are confused about men is that all women are confused about men—and vice versa. Accepting this fact, enjoying it with a sense of humor, and trying to live with it through the grace of God can allow for deep, meaningful relationships to develop even in the midst of confusion.

DATING AND RELATING

A daughter whose father died before she reached her teens may grow into a girl without the unconditional, loving acceptance and approval of the man who should be her biggest fan. When she reaches dating age, this lack of fatherly love and support may produce in her a need to always gain and keep approval from men.

A daughter of divorced parents may still have a good relationship with her father and feel his approval. If she doesn't, her situation is much like the girl whose father is dead: she lacks that primary male acceptance from her father.

Instead of teen dating being a time of fun, it may be a time of intense uncertainty for the fatherless girl. Most teenage boys are not equipped—nor does anyone expect them to be—to give all the approval that a young girl thinks she needs.

She needs to get that approval from trusted adults around

her and, ultimately, from the Lord. Mothers need to help their daughters grow in confidence and security so they do not focus on boys for the wrong reasons.

In most Christian families, there is still a sense that a young man needs to get permission from the parents to date their daughter. That permission is usually granted by the girl's father.

When dad isn't there, that responsibility falls to mom. Some mothers are so uncomfortable with this role that they totally ignore it, leaving the teenager feeling unprotected and vulnerable. When mom does check out her daughter's boyfriends, the daughter may even protest her mother's involvement. But underneath it all she may be thankful that mom is providing the sense of security she needs.

I have had mildly investigative conversations with the boys who want to date my daughters, and they have been awkward. The young man is terrified enough of asking a girl out on a date, but on top of that he has to face this woman who is talking to him about matters usually reserved for men! Most of the fathers I have talked to don't worry about sounding kind when they have discussions with boys their daughters date. Women usually want to be perceived as somewhat softer.

I used to try to think of what my late husband might have said. After a few years, I realized something: just as I don't know what men think and why they think it, I really don't know what my late husband would have said to these young men.

Soon after I was struck by this revelation I stopped trying to be mother and father. I am only mother. When I talk to young men who date my daughters, I don't try to sound like a man. I just communicate what I expect of them in the way they treat my daughters. Soon I discovered that I didn't have to say much because my reputation preceded me. The friends of my girls know what I object to, and they are very respectful of those things.

Mothers can be authority figures and be feminine, too. They can be well thought of by their daughters' friends and respected at the same time.

THE STRUGGLES OF A SURVIVOR

Daughters in single-parent homes grow up fast. Either they learn to handle the added responsibilities of their new life, or they are beaten by them.

Much of how they learn to respond will depend on how they saw their mothers respond. Daughters of strong-willed women seem to come through their growing-up years capable of handling a lot. Daughters of mothers who seem weak may respond in one of two ways: they may see a weak, passive approach as their role model for coping with life, or they may rise above their mothers' weaknesses and become the responsible figure in the family.

Either way, a strong sense of independence and reliability may be the product. These traits in young women can intimidate young men. What has been learned as a way to get through life may become a wall of strength that some young men feel unable to confront.

Girls who have learned to be strong and survive usually receive applause for their abilities. This praise can further contribute to their increasing independence. They may become more responsible than they need to be, may demand perfection of themselves and others, and may never admit when they feel insecure or unable to handle a task.

When they marry, they may bring into the marriage their self-image of controller and master. But underneath this image is a fear of disapproval and a frantic desire to win approval through performance. For these young women, the motto is: if I don't get approval, I'll do more, or I'll do it better.

A new bride may be under tremendous pressure. Despite her sincere efforts to please her husband, her demands on herself may be so unrealistic that she can't achieve them. If she has approached life with a survivor's instincts, she may have trouble relaxing in a marriage and being herself. She hasn't had the experience of living with a man who approves of her, even when she fails.

If a husband sees this insecurity and desire to perform, he can help by encouraging his wife to allow herself room for mistakes. He can also assure her that his love for her is not based on her performance. She may need to give her new husband space to do things for her. She need not suddenly become an empty-headed bimbo, but she can learn to let go of being responsible for everything in her life.

Part of the survivors' response to criticism of their independence may be to become defensive. After all, there has been good reason for their being the way they are. They have lost some of their defenses and protection so they have developed their own. When husbands ask them to lay aside some of this protection, they may become fearful and defend themselves. Love and encouragement from a strong man can help self-reliance turn into interdependence so that two can share and enjoy the responsibilities of life.

LOOKING FOR A FATHER

The opposite of the survivor is the victim. She is the fatherless daughter who has let life's circumstances get the best of her. She has not become responsible for herself; she has floundered through life waiting for a man to come along and rescue her.

She may be this way because she copied her mother's response to her loss or because she didn't follow the role of a strong mother. At any rate, she has the potential to approach marriage looking for a father figure—or a savior.

Her lack of assertiveness and her helplessness may be qualities that draw her future husband to her. She may make him feel that he alone is the strong and caring man who can care for her weaker feminine self. The danger is that in a marriage the man is not to be her father. He cannot adequately relate to her as a husband if he is taking care of her as an adult would a child.

Men who enjoy the role of caretaker may find this scenario particularly attractive. In time, however, it gets old. One man I interviewed in this situation said that after years of marriage he realized that his emotional needs as a husband were always behind his wife's needs as a little girl. He was ready to be married to a woman, but she was still clinging to the hope of a relationship with a loving father figure.

SHE MAY BE ALL RIGHT!

I don't want to be the prophet of doom here. Consequently, I must state the obvious: many daughters without dads do not fit into either of these extreme categories.

These girls have learned to be independent in a healthy way and to be realistic about what place husbands can fill in their lives. They realize a husband will not be a father. They will still have expectations that may not be met and adjustments to make in living with a man, but they may have a good start to being part of a healthy marriage.

Most brides probably enter marriage with unrealistic expectations. Camelot is the goal of many wide-eyed brides. Even daughters raised in solid two-parent homes will have seen some pain and disharmony because that exists in all relationships. But in the mind of a woman about to start her own home is the ideal that she can do better. In many cases, she can accomplish that if she works at it.

EXPLORING EXPECTATIONS

The girls interviewed, whether they had a high regard for their father or a very poor impression of him, all had idealistic and unrealistic expectations for their own marriages. They knew some of what they desired was unrealistic, but they still hoped.

This is normal. The difference for a daughter without a dad is that she does not have a safe relationship with a father to work through what to do when reality invades Camelot. She may inaccurately evaluate what events mean.

If she expects her husband to remember their anniversary every month with flowers and he doesn't, she may conclude that he doesn't love her. The surprised husband may respond with reassuring words of love and promises to do better. He may also respond with shock that anyone would ever send flowers on a monthly basis. Now, if she had a trusted, loving father to go to, he could fill her in on a normal male perspective on the issue. And he could point out that he, her father, is a normal man who forgets things and is not Prince Charming, but he loves her anyway.

By demonstrating how human love can be true love while being imperfect, he becomes a role model for her husband. If her father can make mistakes, disappoint her, and still love her, then so can her husband. The daughter without this role model may have a tougher time understanding what is normal to expect from a loving man and what is not.

MAKING ADJUSTMENTS

Girls growing up without fathers (or brothers) have to make adjustments when they marry and live with men. They don't know what it is like to live in the presence of men, even under the very best circumstances.

They have also not had to live with typical male responses to living with females. Our family was an all-female abode for nine years. We had the usual array of lotions and potions, lace and frilly things in every room. There was not a trace of male tastes and perspectives for years. I remember some of my girls' boyfriends would get a glimpse of the girls' rooms and comment on the "fussiness." My girls received the teasing well, but it was something they weren't used to. Lots of feminine touches everywhere were normal for them.

The hallmark of the routine marriage situation seems to be the appearance of a pile of men's dirty socks and underwear in the middle of a tidy room. Girls who have not seen their mothers throw the stuff in with her own dainty laundry may have a slight adjustment on their view of caring for this new man they now live with. The husband, on the other hand, has had his mother lovingly wash and return his soiled undergarments with maternal joy.

Along with the overall environment in the home, the daughter without a dad has a new issue to deal with: submission. Depending on her upbringing, she will have theoretical or theological knowledge of how submission in a Christian home is to work. She will not, however, have any practical experience in living in a home where it is operative.

This subject is a touchy one because there is such disagreement among different Christian denominations. It is an area that would be covered in almost any Christian premarital counseling, but it will be a big adjustment for a new bride to make. She has not seen her mother be submissive, regardless of how her mother feels about the issue from a doctrinal standpoint. She has seen her mother often function in the role normally reserved for a man, where she makes final decisions, handles money matters, administers discipline to the children, acts as the final authority, and takes full responsibility for the results of all these actions.

If a Christian man about to marry a fatherless daughter can realize that she has no model for this kind of relationship, he can be more sensitive to working out the details of their relationship. With dedicated effort, the new couple can arrive at a way to agree theologically while they cooperate practically.

THE HUSBAND BECOMES A FATHER

A daughter without a dad had a mother who raised her alone. The daughter may not have seen a man function in the role of father. She will, though, have opinions of how that role is to be performed.

Her husband may have different ideas. He may find it strange to have her challenge his parenting when he feels confident about being a good father. Another frustration is that he may find himself compared to his wife's mother, not to another man. After all, the only parent she saw carry out parental responsibilities was her mother.

The couple will need to agree on their philosophy of child rearing. Working through such value-laden issues can be a laborious task. The fatherless wife may have more problems agreeing on approaches than a woman raised in a traditional family with a father.

BOYFRIENDS AND MOTHERS

The man who dates and/or marries the daughter without a father has a loss himself. He does not have her father to relate to him. He has no man who loves and has lived with this woman he now loves. Men who have functioned in close relationships may be helpful to him, but it is not the same dynamic of a man and his father-in-law.

He does have a mother-in-law, though. What a grim picture that word conjures up! I hate to think of myself in those terms. But I have a relationship with my older daughter's boyfriend, Chadd, that will probably evolve to the point that I become his mother-in-law.

Chadd and Lisa have dated almost three years, so he is really part of our family. He and I have had a good relationship during that time. But each of us has struggled with how to fit this relationship into our lives. Sometimes he has been frustrated because he thought Lisa told me more than she told him. And sometimes I have been frustrated because I have felt left out of what they are planning. All in all, it's a fairly typical scenario.

Last summer when I was feeling particularly out in left field, I decided to just sit back and not bug them. But my discontent grew to the point that one night I invited them up to my room to talk. They knew that such an invitation meant something heavy.

Before I could say anything, I started to cry. Chadd looked perplexed. Finally, I told him that I was concerned about how they were doing and wanted to talk to them, but felt like a busybody female. He assured me that they wanted my input, and he urged me to feel free to say whatever I wanted. I ended up telling him that I felt frustrated because I was certain that if Lisa's father were alive there would be much he would be talking to Chadd about. Not only that, but I felt that they would do "male" things together, which I thought would be a real plus in both of their lives.

We all cried and talked and laughed. It was a good and a healing time. One of the results was an awareness on their parts that they are missing something, too—something that I cannot provide, no matter how hard I try. It relieved me, too, to be able to admit that I could not function in the role of Lisa's father, even in an area as important as her upcoming wedding.

It seems fairly typical in all-female households that when a date becomes a serious relationship and eventually a marriage partner to a daughter in that household, he also assumes the role of man of the house. It is wonderful to have a loving and caring son-in-law. If mother-in-law starts dating, though, a new ingredient is thrown into the network—the new man on the scene may pose a threat to the son-in-law. This is further complicated by the fact that the son-in-law is the younger of the two men involved.

A daughter and her husband may feel they have been adequately "taking care" of mom. And probably they have. But mom may have some spunk left and decide she is ready to remarry. Instead of the mother and her new husband being viewed as adults, they may find themselves being treated like children. When the daughter and son-in-law understand that the new husband is not a threat to their having a continuing closeness with the daughter's mother, they can work toward mutual respect and care.

HEALING AND HOPE

Chapter 18

Heading Toward Healing

Daughters without dads live with a unique orientation. The loss they have suffered makes their lives different from the lives of daughters who have the loving presence of a father at home.

We have looked at some of the losses they experience. And we have touched on some of their relationships. All of these relationships—from the complex network of blended families to their relationships with friends of both sexes—can provide both comfort and discomfort for fatherless daughters.

These girls do not experience traditional family life as it has been defined for many years, with a standard-issue father, mother, and children. We have seen, though, that the definition of the traditional family is changing. So daughters without dads have a dual challenge. They need to learn to live well in a complex situation with certain losses, and they need to adjust to a changing society at the same time.

Eighty-nine percent of children in single-parent homes live with their mothers. Therefore, the role of mothers will continue to change. As needs of children change with their ages, the demands on their mothers will change, too.

Financial needs grow and pressure increases as teens near college age. School activities multiply in the junior high years, which means mom needs to be more available to chauffeur children to their after-school events. If she is working, this is a new pressure. And when teens reach driving age, mom has a new area of discipline to handle alone. Daughters go out with their friends, and the parent-chauffeur is no longer needed. Teenage drivers need cars to drive, so single moms who are struggling to put food on the table will have to find a way to earn enough money to help toward the purchase of their daughters' wheels. Then, after high school, the single moms and daughters face the financial burden of college.

Although 54 percent of all women in the U.S. work, women still continue to earn less than their male counterparts. Legislation is being enacted to help mothers collect delinquent child support payments, but those payments usually don't make a dent in a college tuition bill.

Eighty-two percent of today's teenage girls expect to be working full-time when they are thirty years old. What does that say about their roles as wives and mothers? There is enough pressure on women to be superwomen. If increasing numbers of women will be working, that pressure is likely to increase.

And the woman who feels comfortable and called to be at home as a full-time homemaker may find new challenges in feeling significant in that role.

We may see our society completely redefining women who work *and* have children in terms of the "two-track" career plan. Mona Charen, syndicated columnist and former White House aide in the Reagan administration, says,

> The feminists cannot seem to make up their minds. Is motherhood ideologically correct or not? When Mary Beth Whitehead, celebrated "surrogate" mother, sued the

Sterns for custody of Baby M two years ago, feminists leaped to her defense, waxing rhapsodic about the unique mother-child bond. Yet, now, when Felice Schwartz suggests in the *Harvard Business Review* that employers ought to be realistic about women in the work place and recognize that some belong on the fast track, whereas others will opt for slower promotions in return for flexible hours and generous maternity leave, the feminists are outraged.[1]

So working women may be more able to choose their own track, which will allow some women to work with less aggressiveness than some of their counterparts, but will both work and raise children. These new dual-track women do not fall neatly into existing categories of career woman or homemaker. Instead, they are a blend of both.

Such changes show the diversity of our country and its women. While most women welcome a greater range of choices, some young girls may be overcome by all the decisions awaiting them.

DECODING MIXED MESSAGES

Girls raised in Christian single-parent homes have received many mixed messages from churches, fellow believers, and the world:

- Generally, they have been told that the traditional, godly family has a father and a mother at home. But what about their fathers, who are gone?
- They are told that women should be at home and not at work. But their mother has to work to put food on the table. Is that wrong?
- Certainly, they have heard, divorce is wrong. But their parents are divorced. And when they were married, the home was a site of infidelity and violence.
- They are told to believe that God is in control. But their fathers have died. They feel two conflicting emotions, nei-

ther of which is positive: either God is not in control, or He is in control and He wanted their fathers dead.

- They are taught that parents are to be obeyed and that disobedience to parents is a sin against God. But the father, who is active in the church and has a spotless reputation, has abused them. Should they fight against this abuse, or does that mean they are fighting against God?

- They hear from the pulpit that the preferred role for a Christian woman is to be married and have a family. But frankly, they don't see much future in marriage. Either a marriage is "successful" and dead, or it is shot through with hatred and animosity before it ends in divorce.

These messages, combined with the increasing options that our society offers women—career, family, career and family— can make life appear overwhelming. How can one person understand and decode all of these conflicting reports? It's tempting for a fatherless girl to throw up her hands and sigh in disgust.

Despite the confusing state in which many young women find themselves, there is great hope for where we are headed. Like people who blossom under persecution, this generation and the next have the capacity for growth and the hunger for the grace of God to rise to the occasion.

Coping with change is tedious and trying. One single mother recently told me that her biggest struggle was just to survive. She was working full-time and raising three children with no help from her ex-husband. But she admitted that life was not all pain. She and her children had many happy moments and real joy in their lives.

Children who learn to survive through difficult times are better prepared than those who are guarded from the blows of life. No one wants to be intentionally hit, but those who do face battles learn a lot in the process.

FINDING A PATH ON LEVEL GROUND

In this section, we are going to look at the present: where daughters without dads are now. We will explore possible sources of health and growth, look at how to live with loss, and see how we can live abundantly in a complex network of ex-spouses, steprelatives, and friends. We will also consider the hope we have in the future and what practical things parents and others can do to enhance the lives of all involved.

The path on level ground doesn't always look level. Sometimes it looks pretty steep. But it is available to us. Isaiah said, "The path of the righteous is level; O upright One, you make the way of the righteous smooth" (Isa. 26:7 NIV).

The key to a level path is righteousness. And righteousness is available in only one way—through a relationship with Jesus Christ. He is our righteousness.

Daughters who have suffered from the loss of their fathers head toward healing by beginning with a relationship with the Lord. With Him, they can walk on level ground through all kinds of rough territory. Regardless of the losses or the complexity of their lives, daughters without dads can experience healing and go on with life in new and hopeful ways.

Chapter 19

Mom Has a Responsibility to Mom

*I*t's a classic scene from movies and commercials. A man, his clothes a wreck and his body covered with perspiration, is crawling across the desert on his hands and knees. He's searching for water, and he had better find some soon or else he will become a snack for the vultures hovering overhead.

Nobody needs to tell the viewer the obvious truth: that man cannot offer water to another person who is also searching for water, even if he really wants to. He cannot give what he does not have.

Likewise, a woman drained of all emotional, physical, and spiritual reserves may not be able to give her child needed support in the middle of a crisis. But she can begin to walk together with her daughter in their mutual sorrow.

Suppose our friend crawling in the desert meets another sojourner on a similar mission—searching for water. There is comfort for both if they join forces and crawl along together. Each of them no longer feels alone. The encouragement and the company of another person are tremendous comforts in times of pain.

When the tragedy of death or divorce strikes a family, all the survivors are hurt. We've focused on daughters and the impact of these tragedies on their lives. But single mothers, too, may feel incapacitated. They may feel that they have nothing to give their children to help them cope. Women may have all they can do to hold on themselves. But mothers can communicate that they are with their children in the middle of their pain. They can at least comfort their children with their presence. They can begin to crawl through their particular desert together.

GET BACKUP SUPPORT

Others within the body of Christ can step in and provide much-needed support at the time of death or divorce. A now-single parent can take advantage of that added help to regain her strength.

Many people are reluctant to accept help, however. We are so used to doing things ourselves that we may view receiving help as being lazy or irresponsible. It would be nice if God had created us so that we were entirely self-sufficient. But He didn't; and we aren't. Even when everything in our society is screaming at us to pull ourselves up by our own bootstraps, there are times when we need to allow others to minister to us in very practical ways and to accept that help with gratefulness, humility, and thanks.

Church communities are usually wonderful at providing meals in a time of crisis. And often people will ask what else they can do. Be specific about your answer to that question. If you are a newly single mother and have to look for a job, ask for help with child care while you begin your new schedule. Ask people for suggestions about work. Let others know what you are looking for.

If no one in your church offers to help, go to a leader and ask about the church's services available to assist you. Almost all churches have committees established to meet immediate, emergency needs. If you are not in a church, you might want to visit some in your area and take advantage of the spiritual support as well as some practical assistance.

That time of added help can be used to rest and gain back physical strength. We have all been in emotional battles and recognize the toll they take on us physically. It is often easier to endure physical pain than soul-racking emotional trauma.

As physical strength returns, a single parent can tackle emotional and spiritual renewal. This long and strenuous process requires tremendous endurance. The parent should strive to restore herself and help her children at the same time.

MIND THAT INJURED INFRASTRUCTURE!

New York City is falling apart. According to a recent segment on "60 Minutes," many of the steel-reinforced concrete beams supporting the city's roads and bridges are disintegrating, leaving bus-sized holes and other potential hazards all over town. The city's vast infrastructure is in desperate need of repair.

Sometimes, our lives can be the same way. While things look relatively calm on the outside, the inner support systems are strained—and possibly about to collapse—under their load of tension, disappointment, and despair.

In many cases, the process of healing has to begin by looking back. Damaged emotions from a divorce or death may only be the most recent wound of an already battered soul.

A woman who is now a single mother may have been a daughter without a dad. She may have never adequately dealt with her own loss, and now finds herself faced with helping her own daughter do the same thing. Or a divorced mother may have been abused by her father as a child and now has the added pain of seeing her daughter suffer from rejection by her father.

Professional counseling is usually needed to successfully subdue and conquer the dragons of the past. If you are uncertain about where to go for sound counsel, ask a respected pastor, get referrals from friends at church, and contact Christian counseling centers.

Unfortunately, not all of them are trustworthy. Just a few days ago, I spoke with a single mother who was seeing a

Christian counselor for guidance in dealing with her past. She had been sexually abused as a child and was trying valiantly to work through some of the consequences of that abuse. Sadly, after a few counseling sessions, she and her counselor became sexually involved.

Such incidents do not negate the positive benefits that the vast majority of people receive from talking with godly, responsible counselors. But be careful in selecting a counselor. Go to one recommended by your pastor. Don't assume that because someone is a counselor he is free from temptation. Question advice that is contrary to Scripture. And get additional advice if you are being treated unprofessionally.

If you do not need professional counseling, take advantage of support groups that can offer comfort when pain is fresh. Many churches have such groups for widows, divorcées, or people with codependent behaviors.

Another option to consider is a home Bible study group that provides fellowship and adult friendships. If the misfortunes of life have left your soul battered and hungry, turn that hunger toward God. As Jesus told His listeners, "Blessed are those who mourn, for they shall be comforted. . . . Blessed are those who hunger and thirst for righteousness, for they shall be filled" (Matt. 5:4, 6). Pain may not completely disappear, but you will not be alone to fight the battle against it.

RELEASE THE GHOSTS OF THE PAST

In the process of moving toward healing, the past must be released. I talked with several women who said they just wanted their pasts to be different. That cannot happen. The past happened, but it is *past*.

With time and the help of counseling, individuals can reach a point of being able to look ahead with hope and give up continually looking back with regret. We do not ever completely forget the past, but we need to move on without carrying the burden of wishing it were different.

Paul stated, "But one thing I do, forgetting those things which are behind and reaching forward to those things which are ahead, I press toward the goal for the prize of the upward call of God in Christ Jesus" (Phil. 3:13–14). In other words, we are to view the past as over and settled. If there was sin, it is forgiven if we turn from it and confess it. If there was abuse, it is over if we are now out of the abusive relationship, and we do not have to be bound by the effects of that abuse again. If there was continual unhappiness, it is past, and new joy is available in the process of healing.

Many women had dreams of a wonderful family life with a loving husband. Divorce or death may have painfully ended those dreams. Living in this fallen world requires letting go of those shattered dreams.

Clinging to the past is unhealthy. We do not need to forget it or become pessimists about the future because the past did not work out the way we wanted. But we do need to release those cherished, idealistic dreams of happiness.

Once they are laid to rest, there is room in the broken heart of the dreamer for the Great Physician to come in and begin His healing: "The LORD is close to the brokenhearted and saves those who are crushed in spirit" (Ps. 34:18 NIV).

DON'T REMAIN A VICTIM

Nora was crossing a busy intersection one afternoon at lunchtime. Suddenly, a car sped through a red light and struck her. Knocked unconscious, she was rushed to the hospital.

Nora was a victim. She was simply crossing the street. The laws of the land and her expectations dictated that it should have been safe for her to cross, but she was hurt as a result of another person's actions.

After several weeks in the hospital recovering from a broken leg and some other injuries, Nora went home. She was told to rest and gradually get back into her normal routine. Her leg healed, and the cast was removed.

Nora's doctor told her she could return to work. But Nora didn't really feel well. She decided to take some additional sick leave. As the days passed, Nora continued to feel sorry for herself and for what she had innocently suffered. She slept a lot and still didn't feel much better. The doctor assured her that she was fine—she just needed to get out a little at a time and regain her strength. But she was unwilling to change her convalescent routine. She remained a victim.

After a death or divorce, a single mother is recovering from a severe blow. She is the victim of very painful circumstances. Even if she is partially responsible for her divorce, she will probably feel that she has been brutalized.

Victims need time and help to recover from their pain. They need to accept assistance on their road to recovery. They may become uncomfortable remaining in the care of others. But it may not be healthy.

There is no predetermined time when victims move from needing help to helping themselves. But somewhere in the healing process, they need to make that move.

People usually feel sorry for victims, and this natural reaction provides victims with attention and support that they may not have had for a long time. Pity may also short-circuit becoming healthy. The tragedy is that people who remain victims miss the joy of living responsibly again. Their self-esteem is low, and they find little fulfillment in life. Because other people meet their needs, they do not experience the satisfaction of being all they are meant to be.

If you see yourself in this trap, determine to change your behavior. It may be true that you have been badly and unjustly damaged. The pain of that damage may still be present, and you may find yourself in an adverse situation.

But you will not grow and enjoy life if you do not do what you can despite those conditions. I have talked with women in really distressing circumstances:

- A divorced woman raising three children alone whose husband abused her and then left her for another woman.
- A divorced woman who remarried and suffered as her new husband sexually abused her daughter.

- A single woman who had a child by her married, Christian coworker, but he deserted her emotionally and financially when he found out she was pregnant.
- A woman in her mid-thirties who has never married but has been sexually abused by her father, brother, and neighbor and assaulted in a parking lot, yet she works hard to support herself and—with the help of counseling—has a godly perspective on life.

These women have had plenty of opportunities to gripe about how life isn't fair. They have all been victimized, and all could be angry at life and the world twenty-four hours a day if they wanted to. But instead these women lead very contented lives because they have progressed from being victims to taking responsibility for themselves.

I spoke with one divorced mother of four who makes very little money. She works full-time and lives very modestly. Her teenage children work to help pay the bills. She almost never buys clothes or any luxuries. But she is fulfilled. She is involved with her children, she is active in her church, and she never complains. She has the gift of encouragement when she talks to people who are hurting. She is a joy to be around, and her view of life is one of gratitude.

On the other hand, I've met some other women in less extreme circumstances who do nothing but complain. They never seem to have any fun or any friends. They are down on everything. And they wait for other people to feel sorry for them and coddle them.

It would be easy for any single mother to feel this way. She has no man beside her to share her burdens, and she lives in a society that has not successfully helped her meet her needs. But it is not healthy to remain stuck in a rut of self-pity. After a time of recovery, a single mother needs to look up and see what she can do, because she can do a lot.

YOU CAN MAKE CHOICES

A woman once approached me to ask my opinion of her difficult situation. I listened to her and readily admitted that she was in a tight spot. Divorced with two children, she was terribly lonely. She could not seem to recover from the fact that her husband had left her two years ago for another woman. She was missing workdays because she just didn't feel that it was fair that she had to work.

I felt truly sorry for her and the pain she was going through. But I also heard a lot of woe-is-me in her voice. She admitted that she was in good health, had a fairly good job, and had wonderful children, but she just couldn't shake the feeling that life was unfair.

I had only a few minutes to talk with this woman so I tried to think of something helpful to tell her that would make a difference in her life. The word that kept coming to my mind was *choice*. She had a choice. She could continue to be immobilized by the fact that life is unfair, or she could choose to take steps to go on with life.

She said that she felt she had no choice, that she was just too hurt to do anything. She may have felt that she had no choice, but she did. We all do. We do not get to choose what happens to us, but we do get to choose how we respond to what happens.

Even when we are terribly hurt, we can choose to make wise decisions and move toward healing and responsible lives. A woman who has been hurt by divorce may not be able to choose to have her husband back, but she can choose not to feel sorry for herself.

The good news is that when we make the right choices—those that God would have us make, and those that ultimately promote our growth and health—we usually feel better about ourselves, even if we don't feel better about our circumstances.

START TODAY

It's exciting to make new beginnings. They are not always easy, but they help motivate us. If you have been dragging your feet in the process of healing, make a step. Determine to begin to work through the steps mentioned in this chapter:

- Be present for your children, even if you can't do any more.
- Release the need for the past to be different.
- Don't remain a victim; take responsibility for yourself and your children.
- Recognize that you have choices and begin to make wise ones.
- And finally, start today.

Chapter 20

Life Without Father

*A*s parents, we are all so eager to teach. But James has another suggestion: "Let every man be swift to hear, slow to speak, slow to wrath" (James 1:19).

Yet some parents' ability to hear—and help—their children is impaired because their own unmet needs, whether emotional, physical, or spiritual, scream so loudly at them. For other parents, the opposite is true. They may be so tuned in to their children that they ignore their own weaknesses. Either way, the result is the same: hearing will be defective. It is necessary to maintain balance between taking care of oneself and taking care of one's children.

Listening may involve hearing what is not said as well as what is said. A daughter who becomes withdrawn but insists that she is fine may not be fine at all. Another daughter may become involved in activities that continually keep her busy in a futile attempt to hide from her pain.

GOD GRANTS WISDOM

Parents may feel completely lost in the ability to figure out where their children really are. We are told that if we ask for wisdom, we will receive it: "If any of you lacks wisdom, let him ask of God, who gives to all liberally and without reproach, and it will be given to him. But let him ask in faith, with no doubting, for he who doubts is like a wave of the sea driven and tossed by the wind" (James 1:5–6).

The rub here comes with the condition of belief. How do you believe that God will give wisdom in a situation when you have already performed a series of complicated mental gymnastics trying to figure out a wise course of action?

Wisdom may be knocking at the door but may be denied entrance because the mother doesn't think that it is wisdom. For example, a mother may feel that it is wise to watch closely to make sure a daughter maintains good grades. In reality, the daughter might need just the opposite. Maybe she needs the freedom to let down a little. She might benefit more from her mother coming to school at lunchtime to take her out for a special afternoon than from a sermon on the value of academic achievement.

Each child is unique. Wisdom begins with knowing Christ and permeates all our lives as we learn more of Him. It becomes practical in our relationships as we learn more about ourselves and our children. Godly results are produced when we can discern our children's distinctive qualities and apply biblical principles to help them live out their lives.

FEELINGS AND BEHAVIOR

How children feel may be masked by how they behave. After a death or divorce, children often have trouble understanding their feelings. How can they communicate to others what they don't know themselves?

Sometimes Christian parents, in trying to be reassuring, say things that compound their children's confusion. If a daughter says that she doesn't think God loves her because He took her father away, her mother, meaning well, may say that she shouldn't feel that way because, of course, God loves her.

The problem with the mother's response isn't theological. God does love her daughter, and the daughter should know that. But the mother may be adding heavier burdens by telling her daughter she shouldn't feel the way she feels. People need to know that their feelings are valid—that they count. Particularly when people are hurting, they need to know that whether they are experiencing good feelings or bad feelings, they are real feelings and will be respected as such.

Suppose you had a toothache and the dentist treated you by telling you that you shouldn't have a toothache. Instead, he patted you on the head and sent you on your way. How would you feel? Or more accurately, how would your tooth feel? It would still ache. Treatment for something that is real is not worthwhile if it simply says that "it"—the feeling, the toothache—shouldn't exist.

When a daughter expresses a feeling, acknowledge that she has it. A mother can say she is sorry that a daughter feels God doesn't love her. She can say that even though the daughter feels unloved, she is still loved. Then she can ask why she feels unloved, how that makes her think, what she feels like doing as a result of that feeling. They can work through the daughter's concerns by beginning to explore why she feels a certain way and how that affects her thoughts.

In the preceding chapter we looked at people who allow themselves to remain victims by giving up to their moods and despair. That's not what we're talking about here. Feelings need to be experienced first. Then, and only then, can we talk about how to move to the next step of healing.

STRESS: THE COMMON CULPRIT

Webster's Dictionary defines *stress* as a "mental or physical tension or strain; pressure." Stress doesn't have to be big, bad, and heavy. In fact, it is a daily occurrence. Even normal changes in life can cause stress. Moving, beginning the first day of school, getting a new hairstyle, going to a new church— all are rather normal events that touch most people. But they can produce stress to one degree or another.

The stress of a change such as death or divorce can be intense. A person's whole life is turned upside down. Every area of life is changed. And at least most of the time, these changes are permanent and irrevocable. Adjustments are made, but life will never be quite the same as before the trauma.

Studying the effects of stress is big business today. Corporations do exhaustive studies and hire experts to help them relieve the stress of their employees. Many amateur and professional athletes have special consultants to work with them on mental exercises to reduce stress.

Children are no different; stress takes its toll on them, too. Researchers at the University of Wisconsin provided evidence of this in their experiments with monkeys whose physiology is very similar to that of children:

> Short, stressful events in early childhood may have long-lasting health consequences. When researchers isolated six-month-old monkeys—equivalent to human toddlers—for 24 hours, they found that the regulation of a white blood cell called the macrophage went awry for at least a month after infant and mother were reunited. The stress had increased the macrophage cells' production of suproxide, which provides short-term protection from bacteria.
>
> Some studies of the effects of equivalent separations on people have linked this kind of stress to diseases such as asthma, arthritis and leukemia.[1]

Stress was an accomplice to a bizarre murder in March 1989. An article, with the subtitle "baby-sitting pressures blamed," described the case of an eleven-year-old girl charged with the murder of her two-year-old brother and the attempted murder of her one-year-old sister. According to the case's chief investigator: "She was an 11 year old who had too much responsibility placed on her. She came home from school and she didn't go out to play. She had to take care of these kids."[2]

Many children in single-parent homes, especially girls, assume the responsibility of caring for younger siblings when mom goes back to work. Although few of these situations result in murder, single mothers need to be aware of the stress that may be caused by adding new responsibilities to a young daughter already facing a stressful situation.

HELPING DAUGHTERS COPE

Mothers can help daughters cope with stress by discovering the elements in their daughters' lives causing the discomfort. Most of the girls I interviewed were hesitant to complain about anything. They felt they needed to be responsible and strong for the benefit of their mothers. Mothers, therefore, have to look beneath the surface of what their daughters say and evaluate what they really mean and feel.

If a particular aspect of a family's new life is stressful—baby-sitting, helping with finances, caring for mom when she is sick—there are ways to relieve the child and still have the needs met. Other people may be willing to lend a hand if they are aware of the specific need.

Stability is one element of family life that reduces or prevents stress. When a father leaves, stability is interrupted. Many changes occur—financial, logistical, emotional, and more—that contribute to instability. After the dust settles, a new routine can begin to develop. Although stability as it was before is not possible, a single mother can create a secure environment.

A working mother can make sure her children always know how to reach her by phone. If she has to leave that number, she can leave a new number where she can be reached. She can have detailed notes at home, call her children soon after they arrive home, leave work early and come home when they really need her, have neighbors on alert as emergency sources of help, and have reliable baby-sitters with her children.

Stability can be enhanced, too, by doing what used to be normal. A mother can plan a special night in the week for a game night at home or a routine time when she and her children can discuss things that they want to see happen at home.

Divorced fathers can help, too. They can provide information so that children know how to reach them in emergencies. They can call at specific times just to talk to the children. When they are out of town, they can call and touch base with the children.

The Overburdened Child

Childhood is supposed to be a time of innocence and hope. But today's children occupy a world of stress and instability. In her book, *Children After Divorce*, Judith S. Wallerstein makes a plea for "a distinct psychological syndrome" she calls the "overburdened child": "It is more than a caretaking role. This phenomenon merits our careful attention, for it affected 15 percent of the children in our study, which means many youngsters in our society."[3]

Wallerstein goes on to describe an account of a little girl whose parents divorced when she was six years old. Her mother began drinking, leaving the daughter virtually without either parent. She took care of her mother, skipped school to be with her, allowed her mother to take out her anger on her. The daughter was attempting to rescue a troubled parent.

The results of Wallerstein's work show the importance of parents addressing their own needs in healthy ways, not at the expense of neglecting their children. It is possible, though, to participate actively in the adjustment of children after death or divorce and, at the same time, to intentionally care for your own needs.

Anger Becomes Rebellion

Unaddressed anger and bitterness will surface sooner or later. Often in the Christian community, we do not encourage the expression of anger. Children may become adept at hiding their true feelings—particularly if they are shunned feelings, such as anger or hostility. In time, this stuffed anger can lead to a root of bitterness.

Childhood rebellion can range from something like dressing in a nonconservative way to abusing drugs. The definition of rebellion in the Christian community may be very broad. I talked with one mother who was extremely distressed about the way her daughter dressed. It was less than the conservative way her mother perceived as appropriate; it was not, however, outlandish. The daughter seemed to be screaming for acceptance and approval of herself as a person, not based on the way she dressed.

Christians are admonished in Scripture to look at the inside of a person. Yet we continue to emphasize outward appearance to youth, especially our own children. There is nothing wrong with nonoffensive dress codes. But a narrow view of some youthful expressions of identity can cause more stress rather than nurture understanding.

Daughters who have experienced a significant loss don't need narrow rules of conduct forced on them. They need structure in the context of loving acceptance.

More serious rebellion may require counseling. True healing cannot occur until anger is dealt with. And that long and complex process could be aided by a professional counselor.

Anger Becomes Apathy

Some kids act as if they don't care about anything. They drag around and shuffle through daily schedules with their heads down.

A single mother wrote *Parents* magazine to ask for advice about her six-year-old son. He was doing poorly in school, and the teacher attributed it to his laziness. The magazine's counselor-writer responded,

> In many years of work in schools, I have never met a lazy child. If a child is so characterized you may be sure that other things are interfering with his success and motivation and that he would do anything he could to be more successful. But if he is not helped, his rejection at school will probably continue. Moreover, children in the midst of a parental separation commonly suffer a decline in self-esteem, possibly feeling that they have been rejected by one or the other parent or that somehow they contributed to the breakup."[4]

Because of physical problems, a child may appear to be lazy. But if a parent is certain that her child is getting enough sleep and the proper food and is in good physical health, emotional stress may be causing the apathetic attitude.

Again, professional help may be needed. Probing questions about how children really feel may produce uncomfortable feelings for parents and children; therefore they are avoided. It is better to venture into the deep water of uncomfortable communication than to attempt to glide serenely on the surface of life. For only then can mothers and daughters determine ways to help daughters regain normal childhood enthusiasm.

Seeking Love in All the Wrong Places

Abuse of drugs and alcohol and sexual promiscuousness are all too common responses to a young person's stress. The best medicine in any of these scenarios is preventive medicine.

In the throes of divorce or the immediate aftermath of death, the underlying emotional needs of children may be overlooked. If parents are unable to meet their needs because of their own stress, another person close to the family should keep an eye out for symptoms of harmful behavior in children.

If a daughter gets involved with drugs or alcohol, the parent should seek professional help immediately. If she is in unhealthy relationships with boys, help may be needed there, also. But a concerned and loving parent may be able to supply support to help the daughter transfer her dependence on boys to a healthy dependence on her parent(s) and, ultimately, on God.

Harmful behavior may also indicate that sexual abuse is occurring. Don't jump to conclusions, but if you are close to the daughter, ask her about her relationship with her father. If you show love and concern, the daughter may feel free to tell about the abuse she is suffering.

Parents must pay attention, follow hunches sensitively, and realize that their previously stable daughter may be headed for trouble as a result of the traumatic changes in her life and theirs.

Living a Fantasy

In interviewing girls whose fathers had died, I noticed an interesting phenomenon. Many of them didn't tell new people in their lives that their fathers had died. Some of the college girls told me that they didn't tell their roommates at school about their fathers. When I asked them why, they couldn't pinpoint an answer. They said that they were just uncomfortable discussing their fathers.

I asked Dr. Dan Allender, a counselor with the Institute of Biblical Counseling about this phenomenon, and he attributed it to shame, a subject he has researched extensively. According to Allender, a woman or girl who has lost her father has a "closet" in her mind where her father lives. She knows that he is really not alive, but she tends to keep him alive in her mind. Consequently, she doesn't let any of her friends into this mental closet.

The popular Broadway musical *Les Miserables* has a poignantly beautiful song, "On My Own," that expresses the mental closets and relationships people have. In the play Eponine, a young Frenchwoman, is secretly in love with a young man, Marius. He, however, is unaware of her affection for him, and he is in love with the beautiful Cosette. Eponine walks the streets of Paris at night and pretends that she and Marius are together.

In the play, Eponine never tells anyone of her love for Marius or of her fantasy about him. She has no love relationship with him, so she is ashamed to even speak to him.

For a daughter without a dad, the expression of shame enters in because the daughter doesn't want other people to know how she still thinks about her deceased father. The daughter realizes that people are growing in their understanding of divorce, but death continues to be an uncomfortable mystery.

Dr. Allender went on to describe this closeted mental state as a continual struggle with idealization. The daughter idealizes the father to the extent that he becomes, in her mind, the embodiment of the perfect man. Sometimes her feelings become uncomfortable, and she realizes that this idealized father means too much to her. She feels shame and, therefore, does not expose what she is thinking to anyone.

This idealization of her father can interfere with a girl's relationship with God. She doesn't need God because she has her father in a place of potential worship. She worships God through the icon of her father. If her father was a Christian, she may be a Christian—or think she is a Christian—because she wants to please her father.

The best prevention for the unhealthy growth of this kind of fantasy world is inherent in the job of parenting. Parents must be realistic with their children. Parents who survive the death of the other parent must be cautious about presenting the deceased parent as a god.

Women who have lost their fathers can live more realistically by thinking of their fathers in more human ways. Accepting him as a fallen man is not a threat to the daughter's respect for him or her love of him. Understanding that he was not perfect and didn't need to be perfect to be loved can free the daughter who has him on a mental pedestal. She can be free to have healthy relationships with men—all of whom will also be far from perfect—and free to accept her father for who he really was.

MOVING ON

Regardless of where a daughter without a dad is now, it is never too late for her to make positive changes. The next few chapters deal with some of these changes. It is possible to live well with loss, to have an abundant life in the middle of a complex network of people, and to have hope about the future.

Chapter 21

Living with Losses

*C*all it human nature, but we wish for what we have had and lost, and we wish for what we have never had and want. Wishes are required to be about something we don't have. The objects desired are usually just out of our reach, or they would turn from wishes to realities.

It's good to have wishes, and it's healthy to dream. In interviewing daughters without dads, I asked them what they would wish for if they could have anything at all. Their answers were directly related to their losses. The greatest loss to them appeared to be what they wished they had. Here are some of the responses:

> *"To have my past out of my life, and to be normal."*
> *"To have a successful career, husband, kids."*
> *"For my family and stepfamily to grow together OK."*
> *"To bring my dad back."*
> *"To be a happy family."*
> *"For my family to do well and be prosperous."*
> *"To go back and correct all my mistakes."*
> *"To take care of myself financially."*

Part of living with losses means living without something important that we can never have again. Most of the above wishes are related to happy and secure relationships in the family, such as having dad back or having fun family times again. Most teenagers I talked to who had experienced a happy family, the loving presence of a father, and the security all this provides would probably wish for more material things—cars, trips, or tuition for a good college. But in light of their losses, daughters without dads wish for the restoration of a relationship that is gone.

Wishes are good unless they impair growth and health. Growth means maturing as a responsible person in a right relationship with the Lord and with other people. Health means the ability to function in the way God intended an individual to function.

Obviously, a wish like having "my past out of my life" is unobtainable. If a person longs for such unattainable, unrealistic wishes, growth and health are impossible. If these things are desired so intensely that a person somehow tries to manipulate her thinking to eliminate her past, growth and health are impaired. True health requires that we dream and wish simultaneously as we look reality straight in its unblinking eye.

Of course, God can restore a person to wholeness in spite of terrible damage done to her in the past. He does not, however, erase the past as if it never happened. The past will almost always leave marks of one kind or another, showing us where its waves washed into our lives.

The same is true for the girl who wanted to go back and correct all her mistakes. God can forgive all her mistakes and heal the damage done by them. But God won't wave a magic wand to make the past disappear entirely. She will not be a perfect person, and she will make mistakes again. It would be far healthier for her to learn from mistakes and grow toward maturity in decision making. Then she won't make the same mistakes again, and her new mistakes continue to help with growth.

EXCHANGING WISHES
FOR GODLY REALITIES

"I wish I weren't so tall," the high-school girl moaned. "All the boys in my class are shorter than I am."

"But you look wonderful in clothes," her mother would always reply. "You could be a model."

The teenager would have gladly swapped being a model for having more dates. But she could do nothing about her height.

The same is true for a daughter without a dad. She can do nothing about her family situation. If her father is dead, she probably realizes this with much more finality than the daughter who has lost her father to divorce. But either way, she can't change how things are.

She can change how she views things and how she behaves. She can exchange her wishes for an accurate picture of what really is, and she can respond to that more realistic picture. If she is in a relationship with God through Jesus Christ, "what really is" is pretty good. It is not painless, rose-colored, or easy. But she is loved and accepted by God, under His care and protection, headed for eternal peace and joy in heaven, and able to withstand abuses because of the power of the Holy Spirit in her life.

When my first husband was killed in a hot-air balloon accident, I witnessed his death and the deaths of the three people with him. Their balloon hit power lines and caught on fire. All four occupants jumped from the burning basket to the ground below.

As I was kneeling by the body of my husband's friend, I knew that all four were dead. But the overriding reality was that they were entering heaven at that very moment. It was a dramatically positive experience for me. Later, people would say to me that I was in shock and didn't realize my husband and his friends had been killed. That was partially true, but not entirely. I was in shock, but I was aware of the reality of what had just happened and of the reality of death. I had my hand on the body of one man and the body of the balloon pilot was just a few feet away. Death was very real. But the greater reality was the reality of heaven.

Our lives can be like that every day. When calamity strikes, we can run to God, our Protector. And when we suffer great loss, we can seek fulfillment from the Creator and Sustainer of all life.

GAINS IN SPITE OF LOSSES

A daughter without a dad can have the same kind of reality in her life. She can be aware of her loss. She can experience pain from the consequences of that loss. But at the same time she can receive the grace of God in the form of spiritual realities. Security about life can coexist with terribly uncertain circumstances.

Life for the Christian is a continual tension between the effects of sin and the effects of grace. Death is a result of sin; heaven is a result of grace. We will not get completely away from that tension this side of heaven, but beautiful music can still be produced in the life of a suffering saint.

Listen to a Beethoven symphony or a Brahms quartet. The music seems to be flowing so effortlessly, but those beautiful notes are the culmination of a long, complicated process. Stringed instruments do not produce such music if the strings are without tension. Relaxed strings don't allow for any lovely notes to be played.

No one chooses to suffer loss. But if loss does enter a life, there is still hope for joy and fulfillment through the grace God administers to the willing recipient.

LOSS CAN PRODUCE FEAR

When someone suffers loss, a natural reaction is for her to nurse her emotional and psychological wounds. Living without her dad creates fears in a young girl that, unless faced and handled, will adversely affect all her future relationships.

I asked daughters without dads about their fears. Here are some of their comments:

"Fear that something will happen to Mom."
"Fear of relationships with men."
"Fear of having a bad marriage."
"Fear of not being loved."

"Fear of not having friends. I seem to need everyone to like me."
"Fear of being deceived."
"Fear of being overpowered by men."

Many of these fears are associated with relationships with men. Girls who have seen their mothers suffer in an unhappy marriage naturally have that poor interaction as their model of a relationship between a man and a woman. If not explored, such fears may prevent a girl from experiencing healthy relationships later in life.

People who have been hurt and are fearful of a recurrence of that hurt protect themselves. Protection assumes many forms, such as being too busy to be involved, being extremely critical of men, having unrealistic expectations that no man can meet, and having surface relationships that end as they move toward any kind of intimacy. Girls I interviewed who were afraid of relationships with men did not have any experience with healthy male-female relationships. The ones who were in their teens did not date much, if at all. The older ones had not married, or they were divorced and fairly committed to not being hurt again.

Some of the women I talked with are currently married, but their fears prohibit a deeply intimate union. They were hurt as children by the absence of their fathers and never dealt with their fears. They admitted that they expect their husbands to leave. They don't feel adequate as loving wives. They have low self-esteem and anticipate rejection.

No one can totally control life. No one can predict or arrange what will happen to her personally. Even a woman committed to iron-clad protection from pain can be hurt. If in no other way, she is hurt by the lack of intimate involvement with other people.

People who live in fear are trapped. Protection isn't guaranteed to work, but dropping the barriers of protection looks so risky that they cannot bring themselves to do it.

Losses that daughters experience due to the absence of loving, caring fathers produce some fears, but they do not change the reality of who the daughters are. Regardless of how they have been treated by their fathers, daughters without dads are loved and accepted children of God. And they are protected by their heavenly Father.

Women may spend years planning the activity of their lives around protection for themselves and their children. But regardless of how they have lost and suffered in the past, women need to lay down protection from future losses in order to live well. If daughters who had poor relationships with divorced fathers refuse to risk loving men again, they forfeit potential healthy, meaningful, and redemptive relationships. They will live in the shadow of their past losses instead of growing into the joy of new relationships.

THE COURAGE TO LIVE DESPITE LOSSES

Identity is important. When people go through traumatic losses, their identities are challenged, and they ask themselves, Who am I? And how did I get into such a fix?

One hidden blessing of these traumas is that they can help women see that an essential part of their identities is based on who they are in Christ. This is in direct contradiction to the values of the world; there, evaluations of people are based on superficial qualities—looks, possessions, position—that ultimately prove to be unsatisfying anyway.

If women compare themselves to other women, they may become self-centered. They may become competitive instead of accepting of themselves and others. Daughters without dads may try hard to compensate for their losses by achieving according to standards of the world. They may become successful in the world's terms, but discontented with who they are.

With Christ, women can learn of their incredible worth based on how God loves them—not on what they do or do not have. No matter what their circumstances, if they have a personal relationship with Jesus Christ, they are loved. They are heirs with Christ, and they have eternal life as a reward. As Scripture tells us,

> That he would grant you, according to the riches of His glory, to be strengthened with might through His Spirit of the inner man, that Christ may dwell in your hearts through faith; that you, being rooted and grounded in love, may be able to comprehend with all the saints what is the width and length and depth and height—to know the love of Christ which passes knowledge; that you may be filled with all the fullness of God (Eph. 3:16–19).

> Strengthened with all might, according to His glorious power, for all patience and longsuffering with joy; giving thanks to the Father who has qualified us to be partakers of the inheritance of the saints in the light (Col. 1:11–12).

> Blessed is the man who endures temptation; for when he has been approved, he will receive the crown of life which the Lord has promised to those who love Him (James 1:12).

The love of God is so enormous it is difficult for us to grasp its reality. It is even more difficult when a girl has suffered the loss of her earthly father or if she has a father but has not felt the unconditional, consistent love from him that a father should provide. But even that kind of love-starved upbringing does not change reality. She *is* loved by the Creator of the universe.

God is a father with riches. His kingdom is unlike any known on earth. And His daughter inherits that kingdom. She may not have much to show for it during her troubled life on this earth, but wait until she gets to heaven!

Not all of God's riches need wait until heaven for their enjoyment. God has riches available here, too. They are not like the ones the world dangles in front of her. His riches include joy in the midst of suffering, hope in the midst of pain, and a future that is promised but is not seen now.

If she perseveres under trial—maintains her faith in her heavenly Father—she will receive that inheritance. To persevere under trial doesn't mean that she has to be a supersaint. She doesn't have to get good grades in the school of life. She needs to accept the gift of eternal life through a relationship with Jesus Christ and love Him. If she continues to love Him and seeks to serve Him, even though imperfectly, she receives great reward.

A daughter without a dad is in reality hurt, but she is also in reality loved. She does not have to tell herself what she has suffered has been insignificant. She can admit and understand she has been badly abused, but the abuse does not have to prevent her from moving toward fullness of life in Christ.

LEARNING TO LIVE WITH LOSSES

In previous chapters we have described steps in the process of grieving, which include denial, anger, guilt, and acceptance. For the person who does not have a relationship with Christ, the process may stop there. She accepts where she is and lives with it. This life is all she has, so she seeks fulfillment here in spite of her losses.

For the Christian, the steps don't stop here. The believer can take more steps, and they involve seeing a little differently from the way the world sees and receiving healing unavailable to those who don't know the Great Physician.

After a believer goes through the usual steps of grief over death or loss, she has a tremendous resource for healing available to her: she has the presence of the living God in her life. As she moves toward health, her view of Him is significant.

Health, for the Christian, is rightly perceiving who God is, relating to Him through His Son, and living responsibly according to His will for her life. The world's definition of health differs markedly. The world may consider someone healed who is able to function again in a responsible way, to be successful at what she does, and to live happily.

For the Christian, however, healing goes further. It includes an understanding that all our needs are met in Christ:

"And my God shall supply all your needs according to His riches in glory by Christ Jesus" (Phil. 4:19).

That does not mean we get everything we desire. It means we have all we need to live as Christ wants us to through our relationship with Him. If He wants us to live responsibly for Him without the benefit of an earthly father, He provides what we need to do that.

The opposite of loss is gain. We are told in Scripture that "godliness with contentment is great gain" (1 Tim. 6:6).

We need to seek to be godly, which will produce contentment and great gain. To see our lives as God wants us to see them, we have to translate life from the way it is defined in the world. The world might define *contentment* as having wealth, health, and happiness. God may prescribe trials and sufferings to produce authentic contentment, which cannot be taken away by other people or by circumstances. True wisdom does not fit the world's definition of wisdom: "Because the foolishness of God is wiser than men, and the weakness of God is stronger than men" (1 Cor. 1:25). Through knowing God, we can receive the strength that passes human understanding and fills us much more deeply than worldly satisfaction ever could.

ACCEPTING OUR SITUATION

The act of accepting where we are is the final step in the traditional description of the grieving process. But for the daughter without a dad, acceptance is an ongoing requirement for healing.

After believing that God is the loving, caring Father that He says He is, we look at our situation again and are able to accept it in a new way. Part of acceptance before may have included accepting something that we felt resembled a slap in the face. With a right view of God, we look at our situation and accept it as having passed through the filter of His love. It may not be a situation He was pleased with. It may not even be a situation He wished us to endure. But it was not one that caught Him unaware, and it is not one He can't help us through.

We are not told why all things happen as they do. But we *are* told God loves us and is in control of our lives. That means He can use even painful situations to enhance who we are. Paul was probably not humanly happy about being in jail, yet he could write, "I have learned in whatever state I am, to be content: I know how to be abased, and I know how to abound. Everywhere and in all things I have learned both to be full and to be hungry, both to abound and to suffer need" (Phil. 4:12).

And what was Paul's secret? He tells us, "I also count all things loss for the excellence of the knowledge of Christ Jesus my Lord, for whom I have suffered the loss of all things" (Phil. 3:8).

Paul had such an incredible relationship with Jesus that all other things in life were insignificant to him. We do not often experience that level of deep intimacy with the Lord. But the more we seek Him and know Him, the more we can be content with loss upon loss. Despite the pain, we can be content because the one thing that matters most is always present in our lives.

ACCEPTANCE OF SELF

The same man who penned those words about his relationship with Jesus Christ called himself chief among sinners. Paul, who once killed Christians, became a well-known preacher and the writer of much of the New Testament.

God graciously allows us to see ourselves and accept who we are. We are fallen, sinful people. We have made mistakes and will continue to do so. But we are also made in the image of God.

A daughter without a dad may have denied who she is for years. She may have been unable to accept that she is someone who is without something others have. And she may have held herself responsible for her father's disappearance from her life. But she can begin to experience healing by having a right view of a loving God, by accepting her situation, and by accepting who she is.

THE NECESSITY—AND AVAILABILITY—OF FORGIVENESS

No matter how long a person may have felt anger, bitterness, resentment, or other negative feelings, she has never felt those things for so long that God does not welcome her back into His presence with open arms. Following Christ is not a matter of never having sinned. We sin constantly, but we must constantly turn that sin over to Christ: "If we say that we have no sin, we deceive ourselves, and the truth is not in us. If we confess our sins, He is faithful and just to forgive us our sins and to cleanse us from all unrighteousness" (1 John 1:8-9).

A daughter who has lost a father may have been discouraged from expressing anger, so she denied her feelings about her loss. Or she may feel resentment toward God for allowing a particular sorrow in her life, but she is so uncomfortable with the thought that she has insisted she is not upset with God.

Often, this kind of inverted thinking happens in the Christian community when, as Dr. Larry Crabb, psychologist and author, says, people live from the outside in—letting their lives be ruled by appearances and looking good rather than living from the inside out and letting real feelings work themselves out in their lives. Many Christians believe that they need to control their feelings and act in a particular manner to be a Christian. But as we have already discussed, feelings are not right or wrong. They are just feelings. What we do with them can be right or wrong. It's unhealthy for us to deny feelings of anger, bitterness, or resentment. It's right to admit they exist, ask God to forgive, and allow Him to heal the hurt that caused them.

It is necessary, too, to forgive people we are angry with.

As Jesus told His followers at the end of the passage we call the Lord's Prayer: "Forgive us our debts, as we forgive our debtors" (Matt. 6:12).

Perhaps a daughter of a divorce is angry with her father for leaving her mother. She needs to forgive him, even if his actions were wrong and hurtful. She need not necessarily accept his behavior, but she needs to accept him as a person and forgive him for the hurt she has suffered.

You will require supernatural assistance to forgive a man who has hurt you and your mother. But it took the same assistance for Christ to forgive the people who crucified Him. Seek God's forgiveness, and as His grace flows through your life, you can show forgiveness to others.

Forgiveness is a continual process. People who hurt you may very well continue to hurt you. You may need to change some behavior to protect yourself from some of the inappropriate hurt, but you need to continually go before the Lord and seek forgiveness from Him and then forgive the person hurting you.

EVEN A BROKEN HEART CAN LOVE

One of the most damaging results of the loss of a father is an impaired ability to love. Because the loss and the pain are so great, the daughter erects walls of protection to prevent more hurt.

A certain amount of protection is wise and healthy. For example, a sexually abused child should not willingly choose to go back into the situation where she has been victimized for any reason. But most protection takes other forms, with the result that the self-protective daughter can become emotionally distant.

A fatherless daughter often assumes that any relationship she enters into will be ended by the other person. Therefore, if she does not allow herself to love too much, she will not be as hurt when the person leaves her.

Only God can heal her heart. He can give her a new way of seeing other people. He can allow her to move toward others with Christlike sacrificial love, and thereby receive love in return.

She can learn to risk again. Sure, she may get hurt again. There is no promise that loving will not produce pain. But she has a Comforter to be with her when pain occurs. She also has the opportunity to experience deep and meaningful relationships she was made to enjoy. The risk is there, but it is the only way to the reward.

EVEN A PAIN-SCARRED MIND CAN THINK NEW THOUGHTS

A girl who has been hurt needs healing in her heart, but she also needs renewing in her mind. She needs to change the way she thinks about some things. As we are told in Romans: "Do not be conformed to this world, but be transformed by the renewing of your mind" (Rom. 12:2).

If a daughter has felt the rejection of her father, she may see herself as a person worthy of rejection. Her mind may tell her, "Of course, my father left me—I am worthless."

A child of divorce almost always blames herself for her parents' divorce. That child might say, "I am no good—I cause trouble—if I were different maybe Mom and Dad would be together."

Psychologists call these things our minds constantly tell us "self-talk." Self-talk is a kind of program that plays over and over in the mind, conditioning all we see and experience. Self-talk can be exchanged for God-talk. A daughter without a father is priceless in the eyes of her heavenly Father; she is uniquely special to Him. He says that He is the Father of the fatherless (Ps. 68:5). God is, of course, Father to all His children, but He is more deeply appreciated as the heavenly Father to the daughter whose earthly father is absent.

God-talk doesn't mean telling yourself something that isn't true. It doesn't mean saying, "This doesn't hurt," when you are dying inside. It doesn't mean, "I don't feel this, because I'm going to heaven someday." Rather, God-talk means you honestly face the horror of your present situation at the same time you seek God's healing grace.

A fatherless daughter who practices God-talk can learn to approach things in this way: "This hurts, but I am of value to God and He is with me."

Reprogramming how we think takes time and diligence. But it has to happen in order to heal. If we think incorrectly, we will never be free to experience the goodness of God fully.

KEEPING HOPE ALIVE

Some people suffer repeatedly. How are they to hang on? Our greatest example of hope in the midst of continual trial is found in Hebrews. It is the famous Hall of Fame—God's list of those who lived by faith no matter what the cost. How could they do that?

> These . . . confessed that they were strangers and pil-grims on the earth. For those who say such things declare plainly that they seek a homeland. And truly if they had called to mind that country from which they had come out, they would have had opportunity to return. But now they desire a better, that is, a heavenly country. Therefore God is not ashamed to be called their God, for He has prepared a city for them (Heb. 11:13-16).

The people described in this passage could endure hard-ship because they had hope in what was to come. This world was not all there was for them. It is the same kind of hope that allowed Paul to say: "We are hard pressed on every side, yet not crushed; we are perplexed, but not in despair; persecuted, but not forsaken; struck down, but not de-stroyed" (2 Cor. 4:8-9).

Daughters may suffer unpleasant consequences all their lives because of the absence of their fathers. But they can still live whole lives because of their hope, and the object of their hope has to be Christ, not perfect lives. Their faith has to be in Him, not in the hope that they will never experience more pain. Their vision has to go beyond this world.

When the road of life is bumpy, full of potholes, and surrounded by unknown enemies who want to bring us woe, we need to claim a godly perspective on it. The following passage from John's Revelation does that for us:

> Now I saw a new heaven and a new earth, for the first heaven and the first earth had passed away. Also there was no more sea. Then I, John, saw the holy city, New Jerusalem, coming down out of heaven from God, prepared as a bride adorned for her husband. And I heard a loud voice from heaven saying, "Behold, the tabernacle of God is with men, and He will dwell with them, and they shall be His people. God Himself will be with them and be their God. And God will wipe away every tear from their eyes; there shall be no more death, nor sorrow, nor crying. There shall be no more pain, for the former things have passed away (Rev. 21:1–4).

Hope has to include heaven. An important part of healing from loss is to get a taste for heaven. It is not a preoccupation with the future, but an anticipation that perfect happiness is attainable and is a reward for those who persevere in their faith.

THE WOUNDED HEALER

While daughters without dads suffer, there is hope for recovery and growth. But God's plan doesn't stop there. He wants us to go further by reaching out to others who suffer as we did.

God is with suffering women, but perhaps He wants to speak to them through you. What qualifications do you have? You have been through loss and have survived. And by sharing your techniques for coping and overcoming with others who are suffering, you can help them grow.

It's a system that God recognizes, as described in Paul's

second letter to the Corinthians: "Blessed be the God and Father of our Lord Jesus Christ, the Father of mercies and God of all comfort, who comforts us in all our tribulation, that we may be able to comfort those who are in any trouble, with the comfort with which we ourselves are comforted by God" (2 Cor. 1:3–4).

God may not have called you to a large counseling ministry, but perhaps He has called you to minister His grace and love to one young girl or woman struggling with the consequences of her loss.

God may not have called you to preach the gospel of health and recovery to women throughout the land, but perhaps He has called you to start a home group or church class discussing these issues and exploring ways women can grow through the pain of loss.

He wants you to use the lessons you've learned in your pain to help other women through their pain. Seek God's will and keep your ears and eyes open, and He will show you how to comfort others with the comfort you have received in your pain.

Chapter 22

Finding Abundant Life

*P*atricia was an only child and the apple of her father's eye. She was an adored object of his affection until she was about nine years old. Then, unexplainably, he changed. He became distant, angry, and ambivalent toward her.

When Patricia was thirteen, she went to a church camp with a girlfriend. Around a campfire one chilly night, Patricia heard about Jesus, His love, His forgiveness, and His unchanging acceptance. She understood that Jesus offered her a lifetime of endless caring, and she prayed to accept Christ that night.

Patricia is now married with children of her own. Even though her longing for her father's consistent love has never been fulfilled, she nevertheless has been able to experience a joy and abundance of goodness in her life because of her campfire experience. The situation with her earthly father remains painful, but the love of her Heavenly Father comforts her.

Now, more than ever, children are without the support and nurture of their fathers. And many children are growing up in blended families where there can be a confusing mix of children and relatives, all from different marriages.

But into the complex context of today's families, Jesus speaks these words: "I have come that they may have life, and that they may have it more abundantly" (John 10:10). Abundant life is there for us all, no matter how rough and twisted the threads in our family tapestries. Our circumstances may not be perfect, but God promises us life and peace.

Jesus is our Good Shepherd, and we are His sheep. He

will care for us, no matter what size, color, or type of sheep we are. We don't need to live in a picture-perfect family to be a part of the Savior's flock.

Daughters without dads who have accepted Christ as their personal Savior are His. He has laid down His life for them. They are completely accepted and loved by Him. Just like daughters who enjoy the love and benefits of earthly fathers, daughters without that earthly relationship have full access to a relationship with the Lord.

They have the promise of abundant life, but how do girls living in a complex network of relationships experience that abundance? How do they have abundant life when they have so many losses? How do their single mothers share in the abundance of life when they have so much responsibility and pressure? And how do divorced dads who truly want to have meaningful relationships with their daughters also have fullness when their families are fractured?

In this chapter, we'll consider ways to embrace the grace God gives to enable each of His children to live with joy.

Young daughters will need help in appropriating the following attitudes into their lives. Parents and adults in their network can contribute greatly to these little ones' understanding of the abundance available to them in a relationship with Christ.

SELF-ACCEPTANCE IN A NEW FLOCK

Melanie was three when her parents divorced and ten when her mother remarried. She inherited a stepfather and two stepsisters. At first, Melanie was excited about her new family. But soon she began to feel uneasy about herself. She was big for her age and sometimes was teased at school about being "as tall as the Statue of Liberty."

One of Melanie's new stepsisters was several years older than Melanie but had a smaller build. Melanie would look at her petite stepsister and retreat quickly to a private mirror. When she looked at herself, she saw only big hands, big feet, and big body. The petite stepsister's presence served to promote constant self-disapproval for Melanie.

We are all God's sheep, but daughters without dads often find themselves in an entirely new flock surrounded by new and confusing sheep. The transition to either a single-parent family or a new blended family can be a real ordeal for them.

The new family flock may contain some sheep that cause tensions. Perhaps the daughter now has a stepsibling who is a better student than she is. Will she feel pressure to achieve more academically? Or maybe her new stepmother has a prestigious, well-paying job. Will this make the daughter feel that she now needs to pursue a professional career? Or she may have inherited a stepsister who was the May Queen last year and was Miss Homecoming this year. How will this make the daughter feel about her fair-to-average looks?

Suddenly, the young woman who has lost her father to divorce has gained a whole stepfamily of achievers. How does she now have abundant life when she has lost all or most contact with her father and when it seems that his new family has so much more abundance than she does?

To begin with, she has to give up making comparisons. Easier said than done. But it is necessary. It may be true that some of the people in her new network have assets that she feels are lacking in her life. Her measure of worth is not in what other people have. It is in who she is before the Lord. If she is to realize this, she must go back to the total love and acceptance by God as her heavenly Father and Jesus as her Good Shepherd. It takes more than a change of flocks to destroy the Shepherd's love.

A daughter in a new and complicated web of relationships needs to remind herself that she is a unique individual in the eyes of God, no matter how messy her network of relatives and relationships may be and no matter who is in it. Her value as a person is not threatened by how pretty her stepsister is or how hardworking her stepmother is. She is a unique sheep loved for who she is.

ACCEPTING OTHERS IN THE NEW FAMILY NETWORK

The daughter must accept others, too. We do not have to approve of all the behavior of people to accept them. A daughter may have terrible pain because her family has been torn apart by divorce. Now she may have to relate to a woman who was part of that disruption—her new stepmother.

If this woman is now married to her father, the daughter must understand that she is not the one to judge them. If there has been anything unbiblical in the marriage, she does not need to approve of what they have done. But she needs to forgive them and live at peace with them as best she can.

Dawn's parents had an unpleasant divorce when she was six years old. Her father remarried, and Dawn divided her time between her mother and her father and his new wife. Dawn knew that the woman who legally lived with her father had contributed to the breakup of her parents' marriage, and she didn't like her. There was a lot of tension for a number of years. But as Dawn grew older and understood the forgiveness of God, she began to change her attitude. She still did not approve of what had happened with her father and stepmother, but she forgave them. The tension in both households began to subside. Sympathetic to her mother's loss and poor treatment, Dawn maintained a close and loving relationship with her mother yet allowed herself to accept her father and stepmother as part of her life.

A daughter does not need to compromise what she believes to be the truth of Scripture. She may feel that her father was wrong to divorce her mother and marry another woman. But it is also a truth of Scripture that we are to be forgiving and loving.

Through living in blended families, girls can learn valuable lessons about getting along with others. They can use this challenging situation to be better prepared for life and marriage than girls who have to deal only with their nuclear family.

ACCEPTANCE DOESN'T MEAN RESPONSIBILITY

Keeping everybody happy seems like a worthwhile pursuit, but it can destroy any hope of real joy. A daughter cannot be responsible for the other people in her new network of relationships. She can be responsible only for herself and her treatment of others and her responses.

Of course, very young children have to be taught how to treat others and how to respond. Parents are responsible for this guidance. And if a father is absent, the responsibility falls to the mother. If children do not have this guidance from a caring parent, they may grow up hampered in their ability to relate in a healthy way.

But a child makes a grave mistake when she takes it upon herself to play Ms. Fix It in her new family setting.

It is common, in the midst of tension, to do all possible to relieve the tension. A daughter in a tension-filled network will naturally try to keep people happy. She may try to please mom by helping her with household chores. She may try to please her divorced dad by getting good grades in school or pursuing a career he deems admirable. She may try to please a stepsibling by sharing her room or giving up time with her friends to be with her new relative.

Some of these expressions of concern are healthy reflections of genuine caring. But if they are done to smooth rough waters, they can produce codependency, a complex of emotional and psychological problems that may come back to haunt a woman later in life. The daughter who tries to smooth over all the rough edges in her family is exposing herself to even more tension than she experienced previously.

Ann was an accomplished musician and performed frequently during her high-school years. Her parents came faithfully to her performances and were a source of real encouragement to her to pursue her musical talent. When Ann was a junior, her parents went through a separation that led to a divorce. During their separation, both parents continued to come to her concerts—separately. Her mother would sit on one side of the auditorium, and her father would sit on the other side. Ann was torn.

She felt responsible for the comfort of both her parents. After she played a piece, she would slip out into the audience and sit by her father. Then she would go backstage to await the cue for her next piece. After she finished her second number, she would slip back into the audience to sit with her mother. Ann was in constant turmoil.

Her mother recognized Ann's behavior and resulting tension. They talked about why Ann was running back and forth during her concerts. Ann said she felt responsible for the happiness of her parents, that both of them needed to know that she cared about them. Her mother explained that Ann was *not* responsible for her parents. She could perform in her concerts and feel free to enjoy herself—without needing to fix the discomfort of her parents. Yes, the parents were uncomfortable, but that was their responsibility to work out. Her mother also assured her that she and her father knew that Ann cared for them.

God commands us to love others as ourselves, but nowhere does He tell us to take responsibility for the sins, trials, and problems of others. God first holds us responsible for ourselves. Becoming a caretaker will be exhausting and will ultimately end in frustration for all concerned.

INTIMACY IN A CROWD

Part of living the abundant life means being in meaningful relationships with other people. But what happens when a daughter's immediate family changes into a large and complex setup involving two homes, steprelatives, real parents who don't live together anymore, and competitive relationships with stepsiblings.

She can be deeply involved with only a small number of people. It's impossible to be intimate with a crowd. Likewise, there is a limit to the ability to relate deeply to people she really doesn't know and with whom she shares a wide range of mixed emotions.

Realizing those limits, a daughter can sift through the relationships within her new family setting and decide to invest in a few where she is comfortable to really be herself. She can let go of unhealthy and unrealistic expectations that she can relate to all people in her life with depth and vulnerability.

Although she will not have the simple structure of a nuclear family, she can develop a circle of intimate friends she wants to be close to. The members of the web of relationships should not get into competitive situations for the affections of others in the web.

There will be plenty of opportunities for hurt feelings and misunderstandings. But there will also be opportunities for very meaningful relationships in this new environment.

FILLING IN THE GAPS

Daughters without dads can benefit from the kindness of others as they enter their new web of relationships. Whether it's coping with new people—those related by birth or by the remarriage of one or both parents—or fewer people after a father's absence, it can be tough.

People within this network can be supportive of one another. That can be tricky sometimes because of the overlapping relationships. A daughter may have a great relationship with a stepfather that has to be tempered by her relationship with her natural father who now does not live at home.

Someone outside the network can relate to a daughter without a dad on a one-to-one basis. Since her relationships with those within her family network can be tense and complicated, a trusting relationship with a nonfamily member who can sit down with her and provide counsel and undivided attention can be reassuring.

Caring Christian people can influence the life of a daughter without a dad in a way that will affect the rest of her life. In particular, a godly man with integrity and character can be a friend, counselor, and role model for her, even though she doesn't see him often.

People in certain roles—teachers, coaches, pastors, and others—have built-in opportunities with children. Then there are people whose paths cross those of children in the normal course of a day—neighbors, parents of friends, or friends of parents. All can reach out to these daughters and give them a taste of caring, loving adult-child interaction.

I learned just this year not to underestimate the thoughtfulness of children's peers. We so often hear and experience just the opposite, but young people can fill in gaps in wonderful ways. After being widowed for over nine years, I became engaged to be married. At first my two daughters had a rough time with this change in our lives. My younger daughter, Lara, was sixteen at the time and still living at home. Her older sister, Lisa, was nineteen and away at college. I couldn't be with Lisa to help her work through her feelings, and even though Lara and I were in the same house, we had a few days of discomfort.

Lisa's boyfriend and her college roommates were the ones she had to lean on. Because I was not there, I could not see the day-to-day working out of those relationships. But she was supported and she did work through these major changes in her life.

The day after I became engaged I experienced terribly mixed feelings. I was thrilled about my upcoming marriage and distraught over Lara's unhappiness. The phone rang that afternoon and Lara's best friend, Nichole, was on the line. She began by congratulating me and then told me how she and the rest of Lara's friends were supportive of the marriage. Nichole told me that they all felt that Lara would be fine soon. Nichole just wanted me to know that they were talking to her in supportive ways about the change in her life.

I sobbed as this young girl told me of how she and others were caring for Lara in this difficult time. I was touched, also, by the discernment of one so young with regard to my feelings. Her call was a wonderful ray of light in a dark moment.

Within a few days, Lara decided to accept Steve and try to get to know him in a loving way. They now enjoy a close and caring relationship. Lisa has also adjusted and become warm and loving in her attitude.

I am grateful that my daughters' peers stepped in and were supportive of them and of me at the same time.

While it is true that God is the Father of the fatherless, He uses other people to express love and concern. Anyone who is around a daughter without a dad—or any child with a need—can learn to spot opportunities to reach out.

The fatherless girls who cry out for kindness need us. It's an opportunity to worry a little less about social decorum and pray a little more about our willingness to reach out and care.

One woman told me about an incident at church. Although it didn't involve a child, it's an excellent example of our hesitancy to move toward hurting people.

My friend went into the restroom to comb her hair. A few other ladies were already there. As she was standing at the mirror, the door flew open and a distressed young woman came in. She ran over to the sink and held on to it as she sobbed uncontrollably. My friend watched as all the other women in the room fled. As the young woman continued to cry, my friend went over to her and said, "I don't know you, and I know you don't know me, but can I help you in any way?" The hysterical woman managed to blurt out that she wanted to speak to the pastor's wife. My friend hugged her and said she would find the pastor's wife right away.

The gesture was simple and immensely helpful. All it took was a willingness to get involved and a sensitivity to others that makes it difficult to turn and walk away. So often, we need only provide a little help to mean a lot. But we are afraid that we will not know what to do, so we do nothing. People in pain seldom want to be as alone as we perceive that they do. God doesn't want them to be lonely, either.

Think of these statistics representing millions of similarly sad stories:

- "Nearly one-half of all marriages in the U.S. are remarriages."[1]
- "In 1987, there were 65 million single adults." (This includes all never-married, widowed, and divorced Americans over the age of eighteen.)[2]
- "Married couples with children now represent only 27% of all households."[3]

I recently asked my pastor, Rev. Pat Hartsock, what he thought the church should do about the rising number of single parents in the church. His response was that since the church is called to minister to the whole body, it must find ways to reach out to that increasingly significant part of the body consisting of single-parent homes.

Rev. Hartsock believes that one way the church can minister to all people is to help them learn to deal with what is going on inside themselves and not to be so focused on the externals. He talked of learning to live on the basis of faith instead of waiting for circumstances to turn out better.

Other pastors I spoke with agree that the issue of single-parent homes is no longer one that the church can ignore. There may be confusion as to the best ways to minister, but there is a growing awareness of the need to do so.

When I was interviewing girls and women for this book, every one of them said that they were happy to talk about this issue and relieved that someone would ask them about it. Often, all we need to do is ask some caring questions to reach out to a hurting daughter. It may take a few questions to get her to open up, but answering questions may be easier for her than letting someone know that she is hurting.

An article in the *National Single Adult Ministries Resources Directory 1989* provides suggestions offered by two single parents, William Black and Sandi Harding:

- Offer help immediately.
- Provide support based on specific needs.
- Specify the kind and amount of help you can give.
- Commit help for an extended period of time.

- Terminate help at the appropriate time.
- Educate Christians to the needs and concerns of single parents.
- Provide pastoral support and teaching.
- Make church functions affordable.
- Encourage people to "adopt" a single parent family.
- Meet needs through a "practical advisor's network."[4]

One good place to start is to invite blended families and single-parent families to discuss their needs. They will give you enough ministerial objectives to keep you busy for some time to come.

As a final note, I want to remind you that the church is us. If nobody in your church is doing anything, maybe you should stop grumbling and get to work!

NO MORE ISOLATION

Married couples can help daughters without dads and the new families in which they find themselves. While married couples in traditional families are not yet in the minority in the church, they are in the minority in the world. There may have been a feeling of safety for marrieds in years gone by, but now the isolation can't go on if the church is to effectively reach out to all its members.

The task looks overwhelming, but what better place to learn how God would have all of us work together for the good of the body than in the context of the church. In his article "Is the 'Traditional' Family Biblical?" Rodney Clapp suggests that the *first* family ought to be the church: "If the church were understood as the First Family, the single parent would more easily find assistance with childcare, household chores, and meal preparation. And the children of single parents would be provided, at least to a degree, with needed role models of both sexes."[5]

Is Clapp suggesting that married couples mix with singles and children, thus exposing spouses to needy single people of the opposite sex? Yes, he is.

Although the fears of the married couples may not be particularly scriptural, we can certainly understand them. Part of educating the church to the needs of single parents seems to include addressing these potentially unhealthy relationships in ways that would prevent problems and would promote sincere help for all parties concerned. Partners in strong marriages and singles committed to godly lifestyles would allow the healthy interaction so desperately needed to minister to this hurting part of the body.

We have friends who extend themselves to a wide range of people in such a loving, caring way that their house is almost always a haven for someone. Our family has been fortunate to receive large doses of this love over the years. These friends provide such a comfortable retreat that last year Lisa asked them if she and three of her college roommates could spend a week with them in Florida. That's right—four college-age girls for a week.

The only reason Lisa would even feel the liberty to make such a request is because she has experienced such acceptance from this family over the years. The McCanns said it would be fine for the college crew to come. All the girls had a wonderful week, and some of the best evenings were spent with their hosts at home around the dinner table. The girls loved being with this dear couple who so willingly reach out and share their home with others.

WHAT CAN THE CHRISTIAN SCHOOL DO?

Just as in the church, there are more children from single-parent and blended families in Christian schools. While paying tuition can be a burden on single parents, the benefits to children of a Christ-centered education are worth the cost.

School administrators are trying to find ways to assist these families. One principal said the greatest need was for families to *adopt* children from single-parent homes and include them in their family unit. This is what happened with my daughter,

Lara, and the family of her friend, Nichole. One of the results was the added benefit for Lara of a healthy male friendship with Nichole's father.

Christian schools also need to address the needs of the nontraditional family. Just as often happens in the church, the only family that is described as *godly* and *Christian* is the family that comes complete with mom, dad, brother and sister, and dog and cat. Schools and churches need to show how nonideal families can be Christian, too.

TRUE IDENTITY

A daughter in a complex web of families and relationships may forget who she really is. One minute she is a daughter. The next she is a stepdaughter. Then she is a stepsister or a sister or a stepgrandchild.

She must realize that her identity is not based on other people. It is based on who she is before the Lord. And before Him she is complete. A daughter may feel as if she is cut up in little pieces that get passed around from one person to another. Her heavenly Father can weave the pieces together into a meaningful whole.

She can be lovingly shown that God never changes. Her role in her network may change. The people in her network may change. But God never changes. As she comes into His presence, there are no shocks. She is totally who she is and He accepts her. She does not have a role to play out. Her identity is secure with Him. She is His beloved daughter.

Often we get hung up describing identity in terms of physical appearance and role: she is tall, thin, the second of four children. These identifications are more accurately visible addresses rather than true descriptions.

My house is located at a specific number designation on a specific street in a specific city in a specific state with a specific zip code. It is a two-story, brick and gray traditional house with three bedrooms, living room, dining room, kitchen, and so forth. That is the outward identity of the house where my family lives.

Our home, however, is described in terms of what happens inside. It is a warm, safe place of comfort. We who live there relate to one another openly and are accepted as we are. We attempt to treat anyone who comes into our home graciously and express the love of Christ to them. Hopefully, the character of our home—its true identity—is a reflection of godly love and concern for others.

Our home's inner character can be there even if the paint is chipped on the outside, the lawn dies, or the city changes the name of the house number or street—those are just externals. The real home is the unseen quality of life among the people who inhabit the house.

The same is true with a person. The outward identity is just that—outward. A person may be defined in physical terms and role. She is a five-foot, four-inch brunette with braces on her teeth; her parents are divorced; she has two stepsisters; she is the youngest in her blended family. The combined families have four dogs.

No matter how long the list of outward descriptions, the true person lies within this packaged definition. She has full opportunity to develop all the wonderful characteristics that the Lord has given her. Labels may continue to change, but they do not make her what she is.

Chapter 23

Healing Losses

*I*n the second section, we looked at some specific losses suffered by daughters without dads. Whether a young woman suffers the loss of the "little girl" inside her, the loss of the fatherly provider and protector, or other losses—each can be the source of profound pain and sorrow.

The issue we will address in this chapter is this: if Jesus came to give life, how does He do that for the daughter living with these losses? As we will see, He does it supernaturally. He doesn't change the circumstances to make a fatherless daughter feel good. He transforms her from the inside out with the presence of the Holy Spirit in her life. Let's examine the specific losses we discussed earlier, and see how life can flourish in their midst.

RESTORING THE "LITTLE GIRL"

All girls and women have a "little girl" within. The presence of that "little girl" allows a young girl to respond warmly to the love of a caring father, and it allows her to grow into a mature woman. When a caring father is not present in her life, the "little girl" inside may never grow up. While the adult woman may believe the consequences of this loss are behind her, she may walk through life with a screaming "little girl"—with all her adolescent needs and fears—locked inside.

When Christ enters her life, He comes to make all things new. He can take a hurt "little girl" and love her into a mature woman. It takes a lot of time, healing, and changed thinking, but it is possible.

The New Testament is full of vivid illustrations of Jesus perceiving women in ways other than the ways in which they saw themselves. The same remains true today. If a woman can see herself as Christ sees her, she can allow the "little girl" in her to grow up. She can lay down the need to have people and circumstances take care of her. She can move away from addictive or manipulative behaviors, accept the hurt she has experienced, and begin to be healed from it.

There is no four-step plan to make this change. It is a process that involves what she thinks, how she acts, and—ultimately—how she feels.

She begins by coming into the presence of Christ—in her room, in her car, anywhere at all. She develops the habit of turning to Christ regularly—daily, hourly, or perhaps every moment—and fully expressing the "little girl" in her to Him. She denies nothing. She talks to the Lord about how she feels, how hurt she has been, and how distrusting she is. She opens her heart that is full to bursting with years (or even decades) of pent-up pain and places it all at His feet.

She continues the process of her healing by being ready and willing to listen as God speaks to her through the Bible, through the counsel of close and trusted Christian friends and godly leaders, and through the warmth He pours out in her pained heart during times of prayer and meditation. Professional counseling with a Christian counselor or psychologist may also be of great value.

Rachel is a single woman in her late thirties who has had somewhat of a roller-coaster experience in her six years as a Christian. Like most believers she has had some good and victorious times with the Lord and also some uncertain lows. In the last few years, the lows had gotten lower. Rachel tried to change some of her behavior and be more devoted to such Christian disciplines as Bible reading and prayer, but she was disturbed about her unhappiness. She finally sought the advice of a counselor.

Rachel's father had divorced her mother when she was a "little girl"; her mother remarried, but Rachel never had a close relationship with her stepfather. Although he wasn't hostile to Rachel, he didn't warmly relate to her, either. All her life, Rachel had a tremendous ache that lived just beneath her cool and competent exterior. By talking with the counselor, she was able to identify the source of much of her pain and anger—the "little girl" in her had never grown up and had remained a hidden part of the adult woman. The "little girl" needs were robbing her of joy and fulfillment.

Rachel is just now beginning the process of healing, and she is growing. Eventually the hurt "little girl" in her can risk being a grown up. As the "little girl" in this woman begins to heal, the woman can begin to behave with more maturity. She can experience acceptance from Christ and let go of the need to be affirmed the way a child needs affirmation. She can begin to be responsible in an adult way.

Daughters still in their early years need other people to help them become mature—people to appropriately hug them and hold them and tell them they are special. If a "little girl" grows up with a total absence of this sensitive, touching kind of love, she may seek love and fulfillment in inappropriate ways. And she may have a more difficult time understanding and resting in the reality of the love of Christ in her life. Again, counseling may be of tremendous help.

In Rachel's case, counseling helped identify the source of anxiety and helped change her thinking about herself, others, and God. Rachel is beginning to experience love that is truly accepting and lasting from her heavenly Father.

But regardless of her age, God always accepts her. She may be a very mature woman who has learned to live well in spite of losses. And yet, she may have times of suffering and feeling like a child. She can take those childlike feelings to her heavenly Father and receive the warm embrace of His love.

God's love is mysterious. His embrace is supernatural, so she can't expect physical arms to appear and hug her. But supernatural love hugs the heart. It penetrates the soul where deep hurt intrudes. There, at the very core of her pain, the love of God through Christ and the presence of the Holy Spirit intercede, and true healing begins to take place.

The mature woman or the woman who still has a hurting

"little girl" inside can go before God, bask in the light of His love, and return to her world able to live well. She will not be without pain, and she will need to go back to Him again and again. But she can learn to appropriate the wonderful grace He has available for her.

Basking in the love of God manifests itself differently to different people. Some people need to go off to a beautiful spot and absorb the beauty of God's nature around them. Others may need to sit quietly in an impressive church with wooden pews and stained-glass windows.

I prefer retreating to the privacy of my bathroom and running a steaming hot tub full of bubbling water. The warmth makes me feel secure and protected, and the bathroom is one of the few places I am usually not disturbed by children or phone calls. I like to soak in the depths of the sweet-smelling water, close my eyes, and cry.

Sometimes I cry because of frustration or pains in my own past. What remains of a "little girl" in me wishes some things had been different. These things will not be different, but I can express the emotion of that disappointment in a safe place to my heavenly Father and experience freedom to do so. Sometimes the tears are just an expression of my awareness of the awesome love of God—I think of how much I love my children and how much He loves His Son—and the familiar words "He gave his only begotten son" take on new meaning. I could not give my children for another—but God gave His Son for me.

RECEIVING GOD'S PROTECTION AND PROVISION

God promises to protect and provide for the fatherless and widows. We take that promise in the terms of material provisions and protection from harm. It would be more accurate to understand that God is promising protection and provision in spiritual terms. He promises protection from evil and mortality, and He promises provision of the means to live forever.

Evil can cause us discomfort and struggle but it cannot overcome us. God's Word offers these assurances: "He who is in you is greater than he who is in the world" (1 John 4:4); and "In the world you will have tribulation; but be of good cheer, I have overcome the world" (John 16:33).

God's protection from evil promises us that our souls are safe. We are not promised that we will be protected from financial poverty, adverse circumstances, or pain. But we are promised that what really matters—our souls—is protected even against the gates of hell.

Those who have experienced poverty of the soul would undoubtedly attest that that kind of poverty is more gut wrenching than financial poverty. We can die from lack of food, but our souls live on forever. Mortality is not the verdict of the children of God. Oh, we have to pass through the valley of the shadow of death. But it's only a shadow.

For believers, the shadow of death is not the end. Living in the shadow is unsettling indeed. But God promises to accompany us on the journey and assures us there will be a place for us when the journey is done.

The provision of a way to live forever is through our acceptance of Christ as Lord and Savior. A woman may lack food and clothing and be well provided for in her soul. This is hard to believe in this day and age when materialism, one of our most popular contemporary gods, tells us just the opposite.

Lynn is a rich woman. She has little in the way of material possessions. After a painful divorce, she was left to care for her three children on her own. Her earning potential is limited by jobs that barely provide enough money to pay her bills—but she is rich. She has a freedom in her spirit that allows her to enjoy a materially simple life.

This freedom from a need to compete with the Joneses also gives her plenty of room to delight in her relationship with the Lord. Gratitude is the signature of her countenance; God has met her innermost needs. She has a radiant smile and a heart that is overflowing with love.

I don't mean to minimize the impact of poverty on single-parent families. Mothers and their children often suffer when the father is gone. And just as God promises to provide for the fatherless and the widows, He commands all believers to care for these people in material ways. Unfortunately, many Christians and churches don't fulfill this command.

But the reality of poverty doesn't negate the reality of God's protection and provision for their souls. Some might feel like arguing with God that it would be nice to have protection combined with provision for their physical lives on earth.

The Bible is an account of life gone amok. Sin is the reason. And just as we may feel that we did not contribute to that first sin, we also did not contribute to our salvation. Because of the sin of Adam, we all suffer. Because of the sacrifice of Christ, we who are His have eternal life.

I cannot answer why some people lack physical provision and protection and others have an abundance. But I do know that perfect provision and protection are the possessions of the children of God.

There is no pill to take to end up feeling the way Lynn feels. She does not follow a four-step program of how-to-feel-better-while-you-have-no-money. She simply lives on a higher level. That level is not a wishy-washy, fairy-tale place, but a solid reality that God is big enough to care for her in ways she cannot see.

ENCOUNTERING POSITIVE MALE ROLE MODELS

A daughter without a father grows up seeing only part of life. It's like viewing only one side of an old stereoscope or hearing only one track of a stereo recording.

God uses His people to meet the needs of others in the body. He provides male role models for a daughter without a dad through the godly men around her. Her human father may be gone, but the men at church, at school, and in the community may reflect the love of a father and become valuable examples for her.

I interviewed a family with three daughters who lost their father to cancer a number of years ago. Each of these young women spoke fondly of their father and expressed regret that they are growing up without him. Each of them also told me of a special man in their lives who has become a role model for them in the absence of their father. That male role model is a married neighbor who has several children of his own. When the girls' father died, the neighbor, a committed Christian leader in his own home, invited them to share in some of his family's activities. Sometimes the girls have dinner with this family and join in on conversations about the Lord. Other times they go with their neighbors on fun excursions and experience being accepted by a godly man and his family.

The three girls have been able to watch, firsthand, how a Christian father leads his family spiritually and how he relates as a father and a husband.

Christian men can be used by the Lord in the lives of others, including daughters without dads. And the mother's responsibility is to see that her fatherless daughter encounters positive male role models. This may require the mother to forgive men who may have hurt her and allow God's healing to happen in her own life.

REEXPERIENCING
CHILDHOOD ABANDON

A child in a single-parent home grows up fast. She has to take on responsibility at an early age. If she combines her responsibilities at home with a view of God as the Great Rule-Giver, she will experience guilt, anxiety, and worry, not childhood abandon.

If, however, she knows the love of Christ that allows for freedom, she can sing in her heart while she works hard. Unfortunately, much of the Christian community is still bound by legalism. Children think that the abundant Christian life means to live by a set of rules to avoid getting in trouble.

Paul said, "Stand fast therefore in the liberty by which Christ has made us free, and do not be entangled again with a yoke of bondage" (Gal. 5:1). We are not free to sin, but we are free to be ourselves before God.

A girl who can see herself as loved by her Creator can be free from having to keep rules to please an angry parent. She can be free to live obediently for Christ because she loves Him and wants to bring Him pleasure, not because He is so strict that all He wants to do is punish her. Although she may not have the time for hours of uninterrupted revelry and play, she can cultivate and build her ability to experience God's joy.

Many years ago, I had the opportunity to hear Corrie ten Boom speak at our church. This diminutive little woman spoke melodiously of her love relationship with her Father. She had been imprisoned in a Nazi concentration camp during World War II for hiding Jews in her home in Amsterdam. She told about the trying living conditions she encountered in the camp.

One of the least life threatening, but most frustrating, conditions was the proliferation of fleas. These almost invisible pests plagued the residents of the women's barracks mercilessly. Corrie had learned through her life to give thanks in all things. She had learned to experience the joy of Christ no matter what the circumstances. So while scratching her fleabitten skin, she thanked God for all things—even the fleas.

Each night, Corrie and her cellmates would clandestinely study the Word of God. They would hover together in their barracks and whisper portions of Scripture and talk of the Lord. All this activity was undetected by their guards. The guards didn't like fleas any more than Corrie and her friends did, and since the guards knew the barracks were flea infested, they stayed away. God turned something painful and frustrating into something good. The women renewed their spiritual strength every night, not in spite of the fleas but because of the fleas.

For the daughter in a seemingly unbearable situation— hang in there. The "fleas" in your life may turn out to be

God's way of sending a blessing. Circumstances may rob a daughter of the experience of childhood abandon, yet joy and freedom may fill her heart as she realizes how much God loves her.

CREATING NEW MEMORIES IN DADDY'S ABSENCE

When a daughter loses a father, she cannot create any more good times with him—for now. But as we noted earlier, she will be with him forever in heaven, so she doesn't need to try to hold on to being with him in this world. If her father wasn't a believer, she should not judge the condition of his soul but look forward to heaven as a perfect place—whether he is there or not.

Jesus promised, "I will never leave you nor forsake you" (Heb. 13:5). Human fathers may leave. Jesus will not. Sometimes He may not seem to be present, but He is. It requires faith to believe that He is present when we are hurting and suffering.

Believing that God is with a daughter who suffers loss, and the effect of that loss all her life, may be a lifelong struggle. The struggle cannot be won on the ground where we walk daily. It has to be won on a spiritual level:

"Therefore we do not lose heart. Even though our outward man is perishing, yet the inward man is being renewed day by day. For our light affliction, which is but for a moment, is working for us a far more exceeding and eternal weight of glory, while we do not look at the things which are seen, but at the things which are not seen. For the things which are seen are temporary, but the things which are not seen are eternal (2 Cor. 4:16–18).

How do people who are wasting away experience renewal? If they continually look at what this world has to offer—success, money, relief from pain, baubles to play with, power, ease—they will be happy or sad based on the portions of these things they have. When circumstances are going well—lots of recognition, money, material things, and so on—they feel that God is blessing them. When things aren't going well, they feel that God has forsaken them.

For the people who focus on what is unseen—God, His kingdom, His peace, His power—they can experience abundance while having great earthly loss. Focusing on God may seem extremely difficult on planet earth in the 1990s, but I imagine if we could have interviewed a local resident of Rome or Corinth in the first century he would have felt the same way. Trials and tribulations have always been around and always will be. For the person who places hope in Christ, adversities hold little threat.

Focusing on the unseen is not easy. The worldly reality of this life is that happiness is measured on a vertical ladder— each rung representing another step up toward a nebulous goal called "success." Even though our values are supposed to be based on a horizontal plane of unseen qualities such as honesty, integrity, selflessness, and godliness, our measure of success in this world is still determined by a financial, social, and achievement-oriented yardstick.

But don't lose heart. It helps simply to be aware that many people around you don't view life the same way as you do. It helps to know that God gives unseen kinds of happiness to those who seek Him. Building beautiful memories with your father may be over, but creating new experiences of the heart is still available. It isn't easy, but it's possible.

Mothers can work to create events in their daughters' lives that can be fondly remembered. These will never replace the memories of an absent father, but they can provide needed comfort as well as an assurance that life still holds much worth living for.

RECOVERING FROM A WORKAHOLIC FATHER

The daughter who misses her father because he is overcommitted at work needs the grace of her heavenly Father to enable her to be a plus to her earthly father. Clearly, the many fathers who abandon their loved ones for their jobs are guilty of misplaced priorities. Our prayer must be that they regain a proper perspective on their priorities, but many never do.

The daughter should not assume responsibility for her father, but she may need to show understanding for his situation. She can go into God's presence and ask for wisdom in relating to her sometimes-absent father. God may even use her to reveal to her father ways that he can be home more regularly.

The heavenly Father had the biggest job of them all—creating the universe. Yet, He still found time to enjoy His creations. He even took the entire seventh day off! Seeking comfort in God's love may help the daughter who is near fatherless. But again, her healing depends not on her circumstance but on the Lord.

One young woman I talked with had a workaholic father. She said she tried to enjoy him while he was around rather than punish him by her attitude. She remained unhappy all her growing-up years because he wasn't home much, but she tried to accept him as he was and be pleasant when he was home. She admits that she missed much, but at least she had some positive moments with him.

A few years ago, it was popular to say that "quality" of time and not "quantity" of time was what mattered. There seems to be some disagreement on that issue today. Some psychologists and leaders are now saying that the amount of time spent with children matters a lot. Children benefit from the presence of the parent in the home—even if a lot of interaction isn't always happening. Spending time at home and being available conveys to children that they are important—important enough to be around.

HEALING OLD HURTS

A girl or woman who has lost her father may have worked through many aspects of that loss but may still experience a disturbing anxiousness about her life. She may have made great progress in relationships and may feel that the pain of the past is behind her. Yet something seems wrong.

Unless she experiences inner healing, there will be a recurring sting whose pain cuts deeply into the very fiber of her soul. Pain resulting from her loss remains a part of her life. It is like a wound that heals completely and leaves a scar—a reminder of what has happened, but not a repeatedly opened sore. Lack of inner healing, however, can result in old hurts causing new pain.

A daughter who has lost her father and has not experienced inner healing may add to her suffering with each new circumstance of her life. She may not be able to feel peace because she dwells on the past. Perhaps her divorced father remarries. Because she has never overcome the divorce of her parents, his new marriage becomes a source of ongoing pain. Inner healing does not mean that she has to agree with the actions of her father, but she can accept him and her circumstances. Pain will still remain over the loss, but it will not produce the bitter, unresolved frustration that occupies the soul when inner healing is absent.

GOD PROVIDES HEALING

The only source of inner healing is God. He can renew and restore the pain-ridden soul to true health. He doesn't use a prescription drug to accomplish this healing; He uses the power of the Holy Spirit and the working of the body of Christ.

A daughter can begin by being aware that inner healing is something she needs. Abundant life will elude her if she does not allow God to touch the deep pockets of pain within her.

After acknowledging her need for inner healing, she should enlist the prayers of some committed believers on her behalf. This supernatural work requires supernatural ingredients. Members of the body of Christ are meant to bear one another's burdens, and mature believers will welcome the opportunity to participate in the intercessory work of praying for another believer in pain. Inviting others into her pain will provide strength that will enable her to face her hurt and go on. Without the love and prayers of others, it is a lonely, rough road toward wholeness.

It takes time to heal. The damaged person needs to hang on to the hope that she is on the way toward a healthier life. And people who have an understanding of her pain will be a great source of comfort to her.

Some women require professional counseling to assist them in dealing with their losses. Others may move through this process by relying on friends. The important thing is for the wounded individual to apply the balm of the healing power of Christ to her damaged life.

There is no pat formula for inner healing. After becoming aware of the need of healing's restorative work and allowing others to walk with her, she needs to look at unresolved areas in her life. Perhaps she still has anger toward her father or toward God. Or she may be unable to move from feeling sorry for herself to accepting her situation. She may harbor bitterness and resentment toward others who seem to have what she wants and cannot have.

These unresolved issues must be confronted in order to complete healing. We have talked about many of these issues throughout this book. Many other fine books are written on particular areas, such as bitterness, forgiveness, and anger. Many churches offer programs or workshops designed specifically to address these subjects.

Our church recently offered Communion in a way that promoted healing for many of the participants. The elders positioned themselves at six different locations around the sanctuary. Two elders were at each station and had a cup of juice and a loaf of bread. People in the congregation were invited to go to one of the six stations, take a piece of the loaf of bread, dip it in the juice and take Communion. They were then invited to ask the elders to pray for them specifically. If they did not want to ask for specific prayer, the elders would pray for them in more general terms. As they prayed, the elders laid hands on each person individually.

There was an obvious sense of the Holy Spirit in the sanctuary as, one by one, people partook of Communion and of the healing care of others in the body of Christ. Some cried quietly and were comforted by the embraces of others around them.

LAYING DOWN YOUR LOSSES

After working through these painful aspects of coping with loss, the woman without a father finally has to lay down any remaining demands that her life be different. She needs to come humbly before her heavenly Father and accept from Him the grace He offers to live in her circumstances.

It is so easy and understandable to beg God to make things different. And sometimes He does give exactly what we ask. Sometimes, though, He does not. Sometimes a father leaves home; sometimes a father stays emotionally distant all his life; sometimes a father dies in spite of endless prayers for his recovery from a terminal illness.

Inner healing will not be complete until a daughter gives up the need to control her life. Faith will not be operative until she really trusts God and believes in His healing love. As a daughter places the painful package of her life at the foot of the cross, she has the room in her being to allow the Great Physician to come in and care for her.

BEGINNING THE PROCESS

You may be saying to yourself, *So, how do I begin to do all this?* Begin by going before the Lord and pouring out your heart to Him. Don't hold anything back. Tell Him of your anger or weariness or whatever has you bound to the past. Ask Him to touch that very deep and protected part of yourself that you have hidden from others and tried to hide from Him.

Imagine that you have a neatly wrapped package tied with a bow that contains the entreaty of your painful situation. Hand it to Him; don't carry that package anymore. Give up the need to make its contents different. Ask Him for direction to the people you should talk to and pray with. And then trust a few godly friends enough to tell them what you feel your needs are.

Don't be surprised when you dash back to the cross and pick up the package of your life and run away with it. It takes time and practice to really release control to the Lord. When you realize that you are holding tightly to the need to change your circumstances, just go back to the Lord and lay it all down before Him again. He is continually available, accessible, and willing to receive what you will give Him.

Once you have acknowledged your need and are praying about it, don't worry about the next step. Relax. Do what the routine of life requires, but remind yourself of your responsibility to place yourself before the Lord and ask Him to move you along the path to wholeness. This does not mean that you will sit with your hands folded while watching soap operas. He will give you the push you need to move in the right direction.

One of the most wonderful results of true inner healing is a sense of freedom—freedom from having to have life work a certain way, from needing to fit an image of the presumed ideal picture of Christian life, from making decisions based on pleasing a complicated network of people, from being fearful that your destiny is in your own hands.

Inner healing is a painful, lengthy process, but the results are worth the journey.

Chapter 24

Helps and Reminders

The subject of daughters without dads is an emotional one. The loss of fathers has a lifelong impact on their daughters and on others in their network of relationships. It is easy to get bogged down with the complexity of these situations. And emotions cloud the ability to see things clearly.

This chapter will help you review some of the key points, and it includes some brief reminders.

FOR THE MOTHER WHO HAS LOST A HUSBAND

- Evaluate where you are in the process of healing from your own loss.
- Be there for your children. Even if you can't give much emotionally, let your children know that you are on their side, that you are in the struggle with them.
- Seek and accept help from friends and church support systems with the care of your children until you are strong enough to move back into areas of responsibility.
- Seek professional counseling if you are unable to handle your responsibilities within a reasonable amount of time. There is no set time, but if you see that you are in the same spot month after month, you may need some help in moving forward toward health.
- Do not remain a victim. Take the initiative to help yourself and your family be restored to completeness. Even if your family is fractured by divorce, death, or desertion, you do not need to remain a victim.

- Recognize that you have choices. Start to exercise some of your options.
- Take care of yourself physically, emotionally, and spiritually.
- Do not accept feeling guilty if you aren't supermom.
- Bring some fun into your children's disrupted lives. The fun need not be elaborate—it can be a hike or a picnic or popcorn in front of the TV.
- Try to relieve extreme fatigue. Learn to say no to those things that you do not have to do and are exhausting.
- Maintain contact with some healthy families so your children can see good role models. If you are not invited out with families, take the initiative and ask them over. It may be just for dessert and coffee and some conversation. Chances are, they will respond with invitations for your family to join them too. If not, you can still make attempts to be with families and not wait for them to come to you.
- Let your children know that what is important to them matters to you. Children's issues may get lost in the emotional shuffle of death or divorce. But when they want to talk about a school function or a friendship, listen and be involved.
- Encourage your children with hope in spite of a painful situation.
- Feed your faith by consistent godly input—Bible, sermons, tapes, support groups—even if you don't feel that they are doing anything positive.
- Be on the lookout for Satan. He will try to discourage you at every turn. Pray specifically that he will be bound.
- Be accountable to some adult friends. You are in a vulnerable situation and need the objective opinions of godly friends who can see if you are slipping into an unhealthy situation. Often, women who are still in the throes of being hurt by death or divorce get into unhealthy relationships with men because they do not see their own vulnerability. Friends can be invaluable.
- Don't rationalize disobedience to God because of your pain.
- Accept your pain and get help in dealing with it.
- Take time to relax.

- Don't be overly hard on yourself.
- Remember that your greatest resource is the Lord. Go to Him with everything, no matter how trivial or how enormous.
- Accept His forgiveness, love, and acceptance.
- Look ahead with hope.
- And remember that God loves you.

FOR THE FATHER A DAUGHTER IS WITHOUT

- Attempt to have as healthy a relationship with your daughter as possible despite the situation.
- Accept your responsibility to her regardless of the fact that you are not now living with her.
- Communicate that you still love her.
- Endeavor to have a peaceful relationship with her mother for the sake of your daughter.
- Try to develop consistent value systems with her mother so that your daughter will not be confused about the behavior expected of her.
- Seek counseling to restore the relationship with your daughter.
- Do not live a double standard. If you want your daughter to respect you, don't ask her to behave in ways that you aren't willing to adhere to yourself. You need not have the same rules—she may have an earlier curfew—but be consistent with the principles you ask her to live by and the ones you live by. If you expect her to live a pure and godly life, you need to do the same.
- Take care of yourself physically, emotionally, and spiritually.
- Restore your relationship with the Lord.

FOR A DAUGHTER WITHOUT A DAD

- Seek to know God as your Father. Get help from your pastor, a counselor, support groups at your church, trusted friends, and/or your mother.

- Accept your situation and don't dwell on wishing it were different.
- Accept yourself in your situation. You are still a special, loved child of God.
- Forgive people who have hurt you and continue to hurt you.
- Ask God to help you love the people in your network of relationships.
- Begin to see life from God's perspective by the renewing of your mind.
- Keep hope alive. You have choices and can participate in your own healing. Although it may seem that life is over, try to look ahead and believe that the Lord will get you through this situation and will be with you always.
- As you gain strength, reach out to others.

FOR A FRIEND, AN ASSOCIATE, OR A PASTOR OF A DAUGHTER WITHOUT A DAD

- Talk to her. Don't avoid her because you don't know what to say. Just ask her how she is, what she is doing in school—any nonthreatening question to break the ice and communicate that you care about her.
- Invite her over for dinner with your family.
- Invite her and her mother to join you when you have some other families over. Don't feel that you have to have even numbers of people around your dinner table. If you are having some couples over for dinner, invite her mother to come too. You need not feel you have to supply a male dinner partner for her. She will appreciate the company of adults without the pressure of a dating situation.
- If you are a communicator (pastor, teacher, coach, etc.), don't always talk about kids having both parents at home. Acknowledge that you know there are families with only one parent. If there is a father-daughter event, offer to have the daughter without a father be involved with another family.

• Think about ways that the church and the Christian community can help single mothers earn better incomes. The financial pressure is great on these women, and they seldom have anyone to share the burden.

• Don't tell a single mother that you are praying for her to find a husband. Encourage her to be all she can be as a woman on her own. If God brings a man into her life, that's fine. But don't imply that the only answer to her problems is another husband.

• Don't feel that you have to meet enormous needs. It is good to reach out even if it is only in some small way.

• Pray for creative ways to help single parents and their children feel a significant part of the body of Christ.

Notes

CHAPTER 2

1. Carol Tavris, "A Remedy But Not a Cure," *New York Times Book Review*, February 26, 1989, p. 13.
2. Ibid.
3. Ibid., p. 14.
4. Candace M. Turtle, "A Father's Homecoming," *Reader's Digest*, February 1989, pp. 57–59.

CHAPTER 3

1. Fran C. Sciacca, taken from syllabus notes on seminar, "Understanding This Generation," June 1989, used by permission, p. 4.
2. "More Children Live With Only One Parent," in People Patterns in *Wall Street Journal*, March 3, 1989, p. B1.
3. Ibid.
4. "24% of U.S. Children Live With Just One Parent," *New York Times*, January 28, 1988, p. C8.
5. Merrill McLoughlin with Jeannye Thornton, Pamela Ellis-Simons, Lynn Adkins, and Tracy L. Shryer, "The Children's Hour," *U.S. News and World Report*, November 7, 1988, p. 40.
6. Anthony M. Casale with Philip Lerman, *USA Today: Tracking Tomorrow's Trends* (Kansas City, Mo.: Andrews, McMeel & Parker, 1986), p. 49.
7. Ibid., p. 56.
8. "Study Casts Doubt on Decline in Divorces," *Gazette Telegraph* (Colorado Springs), March 13, 1989, p. A1.
9. Arthur H. Matthews, "Study Says Two Marriages of Three Will Fall Apart," *World*, March 25, 1989, p. 4.
10. Lisa Schwarzbaum, "Television Makes Room for Daddy," *Us*, June 27, 1988, p. 48.
11. Harry F. Waters and Janet Huck, "Networking Women," *Newsweek*, March 13, 1989, p. 48.
12. "Milestones," *Life*, March 1989, p. 105.

13. Virginia Culver, "Pope Praises U.S., Calls Nation 'Playground of God,'" *Denver Post*, March 12, 1989, p. A1.

14. Gregory Jaynes, "Key to the Future," *Life*, February 1989, p. 53.

15. James R. Schiffman, "Teen-agers End Up in Psychiatric Hospitals in Alarming Numbers," *Wall Street Journal*, February 3, 1989, p. A1.

CHAPTER 4

1. Jeff Lilley, "Evil in the Land," *Moody Monthly*, March 1989, p. 16.

2. Jack R. Taylor, *The Hallelujah Factor* (Nashville, Tenn.: Broadman Press, 1983), pp. 50–54.

CHAPTER 7

1. Elizabeth Fishel, *The Men in Our Lives* (New York: William Morrow, 1985), pp. 50–51.

2. Signe Hammer, *Passionate Attachments* (New York: Rawson Associates, 1982), p. 13.

CHAPTER 8

1. Sheila Weller, "One Woman's Family: The Plight of Single Mothers," *McCall's*, February 1989, pp. 75–76.

2. Irwin Garfinkel and Sara S. McLanahan, "Single Mothers and Their Children" (Washington, D.C.: Urban Institute Press, 1986), pp. 11, 22–26.

3. Marcey Deacon and Chris Neelon, "Women and Careers," Social Science Term Paper, the University of Denver (1988), used with permission.

CHAPTER 10

1. Mary Mintzer, "Orphans of a Storm," *Health*, February 1987, p. 26.

2. Margo Kaufman, "Hers," *New York Times*, March 3, 1988, p. C2.

CHAPTER 11

1. Harry Verploegh, ed., *Oswald Chambers: The Best From All His Books* (Nashville, Tenn.: Oliver-Nelson, 1987), p. 75.

2. Loudon Wainwright, "Some Last Words," *Life*, February 1989, p. 20.

CHAPTER 13

1. Joshua Fischman, "Stepfamilies," *Health & Fitness News Service.*

CHAPTER 14

1. Nancy Hathaway, "Working Mothers . . . does your child need you now?" *Harper's Bazaar,* July 1988, p. 108.
2. Ibid.
3. "Women Who Work for Themselves," *Good Housekeeping,* February 1989, p. 48.
4. Maxine Abrams, "For Mothers and Daughters Only," *Good Housekeeping,* May 1988, pp. 142, 144.
5. Caryl S. Avery, "Jackie, A Mother's Journey," *Ladies' Home Journal,* March 1989, p. 198.

CHAPTER 15

1. John Rosemond, "When Children Grieve," *Better Homes and Gardens,* August 1988, p. 26.

CHAPTER 16

1. Lawrence Kutner, "Parent & Child," *New York Times,* October 27, 1988.
2. Ibid.
3. Ibid.
4. Ibid.
5. Lawrence Kutner, "Parent & Child," *New York Times,* June 30, 1988.
6. Joshua Fischman, "Stepfamilies," *Health & Fitness News Service.*
7. Jane Marks, "We Have a Problem," *Parents,* January 1988, pp. 52–56.
8. Kutner, "Parent & Child," June 30, 1988.
9. Ibid.
10. Ibid.
11. Ibid.

CHAPTER 18

1. Mona Charen, "Let's Look at Two-Track Career Plan for Women," *Gazette Telegraph* (Colorado Springs), March 20, 1989, p. B9.

CHAPTER 20

1. "Long Effects of Early Stress," *American Health,* March 1988, p. 48.
2. "11-Year-Old Charged in Stepbrother's Death," *Gazette Telegraph* (Colorado Springs), March 18, 1989, p. A5.
3. Judith S. Wallerstein, "Children After Divorce," *New York Times Magazine,* January 22, 1989, p. 41.
4. Francis Roberts, "Parental Separation and School Problems," *Parents,* December 1987, p. 51.

CHAPTER 22

1. Jerry D. Jones, ed., *National Single Adult Ministries Resources Directory 1989* (Colorado Springs, Colo.: Single Adult Ministries Journal, 1989), p. 9.
2. Ibid., p. 6.
3. Ibid., p. 7.
4. Ibid., pp. 34–36.
5. Rodney Clapp, "Is the 'Traditional' Family Biblical?" *Christianity Today,* September 16, 1988, p. 28.

About the Author

Lois Mowday Rabey had to raise two young daughters without their father after he was killed in a hot air balloon accident. Rabey played herself in *Fire in the Sky*, a film that documents the accident. She is a frequent speaker and the author of *The Snare*. She currently resides in Colorado Springs, Colorado.